EDWARD CLARK LIBRARY CATALOGUE

CATALOGUE

OF THE

EDWARD CLARK LIBRARY

With typographical notes by
HARRY CARTER
and an essay on the Printing of Illustrations by
FRANK P. RESTALL

General Editor
P. J. W. Kilpatrick

VOLUME II

Privately Printed for
Napier College of Commerce & Technology
Lothian Regional Council
1976

SBN 902703 12 9

Printed in Great Britain by
R. & R. Clark Ltd., Edinburgh

CONTENTS

v

LIST OF ILLUSTRATIONS

Volume I

Edward Clark 1864–1926   xvii

vii

VOLUME II

LIST OF ABBREVIATIONS

Fol.	Folio
4to	Quarto
8vo	Octavo
12mo	Twelve-mo
16mo	Sixteen-mo
32mo	Thirty-two-mo
*	used in the Catalogue number indicates that only one leaf, or a few leaves are in the Library
JOH.	used at the end of an entry, indicates that the book came from the collection of the late A. F. Johnston
Anon.	Anonymous
c.	circa = about
cf.	compare
C.U.P.	Cambridge University Press
(D)	Didot
1498/9	Old Style and New Style dates
1498-9	two different dates
ed.	edition
3rd ed.	Third edition
edn.	edition
e.g.	for example
et al.	and others
et seq.	and the following
ff.	and the following pages
imp.	imperial
MS	Manuscript
M. & R.	Miller & Richard
n.d.	no date
N.T.	New Testament
Obl.	Oblong
O.U.P.	Oxford University Press

p.   page
pp.   pages
pt.   point or part
S. & B.   Stephenson, Blake & Co. Ltd.
ser.   series
St.   Saint
Vol.   Volume

[ ] square brackets. The wording inside the brackets is inferred, not stated.

( ) round brackets. The wording inside the brackets is parenthetical.

REFERENCE BOOKS
Arranged in
CATEGORIES

I

G. *Books, Book-Making, Book-Binding*

G1

Adams, John. *The House of Kitcat: a story of bookbinding, 1798–1948*. Printing House of Lloyd's Register of Shipping: London, for G. & J. Kitcat, Ltd., 1948. 8vo.

G2

Aldis, Harry G. *The Printed book*. Cambridge University Press. 1916. 8vo.

G3

—— 2nd edition, revised and brought up to date by John Carter and E. A. Crutchley. Cambridge University Press. 1941. 8vo.

G4

—— 3rd edition, revised and brought up to date by John Carter and Brooke Crutchley. Cambridge University Press. 1951. 8vo.

G5

Besterman, Theodore. *The Beginnings of systematic bibliography*. Oxford University Press for Humphrey Milford. 2nd ed., revised. London, 1936. 8vo.

G6–8

Bibliographica. Papers on books, their history and art. Vols. 1–3. T. and A. Constable, Edinburgh, for Kegan Paul, Trench, Trübner: London, 1895–7. 8vo.

G8A

Bibliophile, The, a magazine and review for the collector, student and general reader. Vol. 3, No. 14, April, 1909. 8vo. Bibliophile Publishing Co.: London, 1909. JOH.

G9

Birrell, Augustine. *Three essays.* 1. Book-buying; 2. Book-binding; 3. The Office of literature. Village Press, Marlborough-on-Hudson, N.Y. for the Grolier Club: New York, 1924. 4to. No. 6 of the 'Printers' Series'.

G10–2

Bookbinder, The. Vols. 1–3. William Clowes and Sons: London, 1888–9. 4to.

G13–24

Book-Collector's Quarterly. Edited by Desmond Flower and A. J. A. Symons. Nos. I–XII. Curwen Press, Plaistow, for Cassell and Co.: London, 1930–33.

G25

Book Craftsman. No. 2. Edited by James Guthrie. Pear Tree Press: Bognor Regis, 1935. 8vo.

G26

Bouchot, Henri. *The Book: its printers, illustrators, and binders . . . with a treatise on the art of collecting and describing early printed books . . .* Edited by H. Grevel. Hazell, Watson and Viney, for H. Grevel & Co.: London, 1890. 8vo.

G27–30

British Bookmaker, The. Vols. 4–7. Raithby, Lawrence & Co.: London, 1890–4. 4to.

G31

Carter, John. *A B C for book-collectors.* Hazell, Watson and Viney Ltd., Aylesbury, for Rupert Hart-Davis: London, 1952. 8vo.

G32

Cockerell, Douglas. *Some notes on bookbinding*. Oxford University Press, for Humphrey Milford: London, 1929. 8vo. Line drawings by Doris Meyer.

G33

—— Another edition 1948. 8vo.

G34–7

Colophon, The. A Book collector's quarterly. Parts 5–8. Pynson Printers: New York, *et al.*, 1931. 4to. The New Colophon.

G38–46

Colophon, The New. Vols. 1–3. Anthoensen Press, Portland, Maine, for Duschnes Crawford, Inc.: New York, 1948. 9 parts. 4to.

G47

Davenport, C. J H. *English embroidered bookbindings*. T. & A. Constable, Edinburgh, for Kegan Paul, Trench, Trübner & Co.: London, 1899. 4to. (The English bookman's library).

G48

—— *Royal English bookbindings*. Seeley and Co. London, 1896. 8vo. Back title: 'English and French bookbindings'. Bound with G59A.

G49–52

Dibdin, Thomas Frognall. *Typographical antiquities; or, The History of printing in England, Scotland, and Ireland; containing Memoirs of our ancient printers, and a register of the books printed by them. Begun by Joseph Ames, considerably augmented by William Herbert and now greatly enlarged.* 4 volumes. 4to. Vol. 1, William Savage, for William Miller: London, 1809. Vol. 2, W. Bulmer and Co., for William Miller: London, 1812. Vol. 3, W. Bulmer and Co., for John Murray: London, 1816. Vol. 4, W. Bulmer and Co., for Longman, Hurst, Rees, Orme and Brown: London, 1819.

G53–4

Dolphin, The. A Journal of the making of books. Nos. 2–3. Yale University Press, New Haven, Conn., for the Limited Editions Club: New York, 1935–38. 8vo. No. 3: 'A History of the Printed Book'.

G55

Dore, J. R. *Old Bibles: an account of the early versions of the English Bible*; 2nd ed. Eyre and Spottiswoode: London, 1888. 8vo.

G56

Duff, Edward Gordon. *A Century of the English book trade . . . from . . . 1457 to . . . 1557*. Blades, East & Blades, for the Bibliographical Society: London, 1905. 4to.

G57

Early printed books. T. and A. Constable, Edinburgh, for Kegan Paul, Trench, Trübner & Co.: London, 1893. 8vo.

G58

Ede, Charles, edited by. *The art of the book, some record of work carried out in Europe and the U.S.A., 1939–1950*. Folio Society, for The Studio: London, 1951. 4to.

G59

Edinburgh Bibliographical Society. *Transactions*. Vol. 3, part. 1 (Session 1948–9). R. & R. Clark Ltd.: Edinburgh, 1952. 8vo.

The Edinburgh Bibliographical Society was founded in 1890 and is therefore the oldest Bibliographical Society in the world. The Bibliographical Society in London was founded in 1892.

G59A

Fletcher, William Younger. *Bookbinding in France*. Seeley and Co.: London, 1894. 8vo. Bound with Davenport's *Royal English Bookbindings*, G48.

G60

Fletcher, William Younger. *Bookbinding in France*. Richard Clay for Seeley and Co.: London, 1895. 8vo.

G61

—— *Foreign bookbindings in the British Museum*. Illustrations . . . with introduction and descriptions by W. Y. Fletcher. T. & A. Constable, for Kegan Paul, Trench, Trübner & Co.: London, 1896. Fol. Plates chromo-lithographed by W. Griggs.

G61A

Flower, Desmond. *The paper-back, its past, present and future.* Northumberland Press for L. Arborfield. 1959. 8vo.

G62

Fournier, Pierre Simon, LE JEUNE. *Dissertation sur l'origine et les progrès de l'art de graver en bois. De l'origine et des productions de l'imprimerie primitive en taille de bois. . . . Observations sur un Ouvrage intitulé 'Vindiciæ Typographicæ . . .' Remarques sur un ouvrage intitule 'Lettre sur l'origine de l'imprimerie . .'* 4 volumes in 1. J. J. Barbou.: Paris, 1758–61. 8vo.

G63

Goldschmidt, E. P. *The Printed Book of the Renaissance*. Three lectures on type, illustration, ornamentation. Cambridge University Press. 1950. 4to.

G64

Greenhood, David, and Gentry, Helen. *Chronology of books and printing.* Revised edition. Stratford Press, Inc., for the Macmillan Co.: New York, 1936. 8vo.

G65

Harrison, Frederick. *A Book about books.* Butler & Tanner Ltd. Frome, for John Murray: London, 1943. 8vo.

G66

Harvey, William. *Scottish chapbook literature*. Alexander Gardner: Paisley, 1905. 8vo.

G67

Hitchcock, Frederick Hills. *The Building of a book*. A series of practical articles, written by experts in the various departments of book-making and distributing. Edited by F. H. Hitchcock. T. Werner Laurie: London [1907]. 8vo.

G68

Horne, Herbert P. *The Binding of books: an essay in the history of gold-tooled bindings*. T. & A. Constable, Edinburgh, for Kegan Paul, Trench, Trübner: London, 1894. 8vo.

G68A

Imprint, The. Nos. 6 and 8. Also Vol. 1, 1913. Westminster Press for The Imprint Publishing Co. Ltd.: London, 1913.

Contains articles on 'Decoration and its uses' by Edward Johnston.

G69–70

Jackson, Holbrook. *The Anatomy of bibliomania*. 2 volumes. Curwen Press, Plaistow, for the Soncino Press: London, 1930. 8vo.

G71

Jacobi, Charles Thomas. *On the making and issuing of books*. Chiswick Press, for Elkin Mathews: London, 1891. 8vo.

G71A

Jacobi, Charles T. *Some notes on books and printing, a guide for authors, publishers & others*. Chiswick Press: London, 1903. 8vo.

JOH.

G72

Johnson, William H., and Newkirk, Louis V. *The Graphic arts*. For the Macmillan Co.: New York, 1942. 4to.

G73

Kepes, György, and others. *Graphic forms, the arts as related to the book*. Harvard University Press: Cambridge (Mass.), 1949. 8vo.

G73A

Library Association. Book Production Committee. Interim report. Chiswick Press for the Library Association: London, 1913. 8vo.   JOH.

G74

Macintosh, Charles A. *Popular outlines of the press, ancient and modern; or, A Brief sketch of the origin and progress of printing, with a notice of the newspaper press.* Alex. Macintosh, for Werthein, Macintosh and Hunt: London, 1859. 8vo.

G75

McMurtrie, Douglas C. *The Book: the story of printing and book-making* J. J. Little and Ives Company, New York, for Pitman: London, 1938. 8vo.

G76

—— *The Golden book: the story of fine books and bookmaking;* 2nd ed. [Douglas McMurtrie, New York, for] Pascal Covici: Chicago, 1927. 8vo.

G77

Mason, John. *A Practical course in bookcrafts and bookbinding.* C. H. Gee and Co.: Leicester, 1935. 8vo.

G78

Matthews, Brander. *Bookbindings, old and new.* George Bell & Sons: London, 1896. 8vo.

G79

Matthews, William. *Modern bookbinding practically considered: a lecture.* De Vinne Press, for the Grolier Club: New York, 1889. 4to.

G80

Meerman, Gerard. *Origines typographicae.* 2 volumes in 1. Jacob A. Karnebeek: Haarlem, 1765. 4to.

G81

Meynell, Sir Francis. *English printed books.* Sun Engraving Co. Ltd., for William Collins: London, 1946. 8vo.

G82

Muir, Percy. *English Children's Books, 1600 to 1900.* William Clowes and Sons, Ltd., for B. T. Batsford, Ltd: London, 1954. 8vo.

G83

Murray, David. *Bibliography: its scope and methods, with a view of the work of a local bibliographical society.* Robert MacLehose & Co., Ltd., for James MacLehose: Glasgow, 1917. 8vo.

G83A

Nash [Ray]. *Printing as an art.* Harvard University Press, Cambridge, Mass., for the Society of Printers: Boston, 1955. 8vo.

Written to commemorate the fiftieth anniversary of the Society of Printers and designed by Bruce Rogers.

G84

Newdigate, Bernard H. *The Art of the book.* Shakespeare Head Press, Oxford, for The Studio: London, 1938. 8vo.

G85

Oldham, J. Basil. *Shrewsbury School Library bindings: catalogue raisonné.* Oxford University Press. 1943. 4to.

G86

Orcutt, William Dana. *In quest of the perfect book: reminiscences and reflections of a bookman.* Plimpton Press, Norwood, Mass., for Little, Brown and Co.: Boston, 1926. 8vo.

G87

Orcutt, William Dana. *The Kingdom of Books.* Plimpton Press, Norwood, Mass., for Little, Brown and Co.: Boston, 1927. 8vo.

G88

Payne, Roger. *Extracts from the diary of Roger Payne.* Harbor Press: New York, 1928. 8vo.

G89

Philobiblon. Zeitschrift für Bücherliebhaber. (Odd numbers.) Jahoda & Siegel, for Herbert Reichner: Vienna, 1934–38. 8vo. The 1938 number published by Rudolf M. Rohrer, at Brünn.

G90

Pollard, Alfred William. *Fine books.* William Brendon & Son, Plymouth, for Methuen and Co.: London, 1912. 8vo. One of 'The Connoisseur's Library'.

G91

Poortenaar, Jan. *The Art of the book and its illustration.* Drukkerij Buys & Zoon, Amsterdam, for George G. Harrap: London, 1935. 4to.

G92

Powell, G. H. *Excursions in Libraria: being retrospective reviews and bibliographical notes.* Richard Clay & Sons, for Lawrence and Bullen: London, 1895. 8vo.

G93

Prideaux, S. T. *An Historical sketch of bookbinding;* chapter on early stamped bindings by E. Gordon Duff. Richard Clay & Sons for Lawrence & Bullen: London, 1893. 8vo.

G94

Putnam, George Haven. *Authors and their public in ancient times: a sketch of literary conditions and of the relations with the public of literary producers, from earliest time to the invention of printing.*

Knickerbocker Press, for G. P. Putnam's Sons: New York, 1894. 8vo.

G95

Rodenberg, Julius. *Die Druckkunst als Spiegel der Kultur in fünf Jahrhunderten*. Druckgewerblicher Verlag der Preussischen Verlags- und Druckerei GmbH.: Berlin, 1942. 8vo.

G96–7

Sanderson, T. J. Cobden-. *Ecce Mundus: industrial ideals and the book beautiful*. Chiswick Press, for the Hammersmith Publishing Society: London, 1902. 4to.

Two issues in different bindings.

G98

Sarre, F. *Islamic bookbindings*. Dr Selle & Co., Berlin, for Kegan Paul, Trench, Trübner & Co.: London, 1923?. Fol.

G99

Simpson, Percy. *Proof-reading in the sixteenth, seventeenth and eighteenth centuries*. Oxford University Press, for Humphrey Milford: London, 1935. 4to.

G100

Tuer, Andrew W. *History of the horn-book*. Leadenhall Press, Ltd., for Simpkin, Marshall, Hamilton, Kent & Co.: London, 1897. 4to.

II

H. *Booksellers and Publishers*

H1

Black, Adam. *Memoirs*; edited by Alexander Nicolson. 2nd ed.
R. & R. Clark, for A. & C. Black: Edinburgh, 1885. 8vo.

H2

Blagden, Cyprian. *Fire more than water, notes for the story of a ship.*
Spottiswoode, Ballantyne & Co., London, for Longmans,
Green: 1949. 8vo.

Pamphlet issued to mark the 225th anniversary of the firm of Longmans,
Green & Co.

H3

Blaikie, Walter Biggar, 1847 1928. Privately printed by T. & A.
Constable: Edinburgh, 1929. 8vo.

H4

Bolitho, Hector, edited by. *A Batsford centenary, 1843–1943.*
B. T. Batsford: London, 1943. 8vo.

H5

Burton, John Hill. *The Book-hunter.* William Blackwood &
Sons: Edinburgh, 1882. 8vo.

H6

Cadell and Davies. *The Publishing firm of Cadell & Davies: select
correspondence and accounts, 1793–1836*; edited . . . by Theodore
Besterman. Oxford University Press, for Humphrey Milford:
London, 1938. 4to.

H7

Castle, Egerton. *English book-plates: an illustrated handbook for students of ex libris*. Chiswick Press for George Bell: London, 1892. 8vo.

H8

Couper, W. J. *The Millers of Haddington, Dunbar and Dunfermline: a record of Scottish bookselling*. Unwin Bros. Ltd. (The Gresham Press), for T. Fisher Unwin: London, 1914. 8vo.

H9

Elton, Charles I., and Mary A. *The Great book-collectors*. T. & A. Constable, Edinburgh, for Kegan Paul, Trench, Trübner: London, 1893. 8vo.

H10

Fabes, Gilbert H. *The Romance of a bookshop, 1904–1929* (i.e. Foyle's). Privately printed [London], 1929. 8vo.

H11

Hardy, W. J. *Book-plates*. T. & A. Constable, Edinburgh, for Kegan Paul, Trench, Trübner: London 1893. 8vo.

H11A

Hornung, Clarence P. *Bookplates by Harold Nelson*. Caxton Press: N.Y. 1929. 4to.

H12

Hughes, Thomas. *Memoir of Daniel Macmillan*. R. Clay, Sons, and Taylor, for Macmillan and Co.: London, 1882. 8vo.

H13

Lang, Andrew. *The Library*; with a chapter on modern illustrated books by Austin Dobson. R. & R. Clark, Edinburgh, for Macmillan & Co.: London, 1881. 8vo.

H13A

Limited Editions Club. *Quarto-millenary: the first 250 publications and the first 25 years, 1929–1954, a critique, a conspectus, a biblio-graphy, indexes.* Clarke & Way: New York, 1959. 4to.

H14

Terry, Charles Sanford. *A Catalogue of the publications of Scottish historical and kindred clubs and societies and of the volumes relative to Scottish history issued by H.M.S.O., 1780–1908.* Robert Mac-Lehose & Son, for James MacLehose & Sons: Glasgow, 1909. 8vo.

H15

[Wyman. Charles W. H.] *B.Q.* [i.e. Bernard Quaritch]. *A Biographical and bibliographical fragment.* 1880. 16mo.

One of an edition of 25 copies, with a portrait and newspaper cuttings inserted.

III

I. *Calligraphy, Writing and Lettering*

I1

Astle, Thomas. *The Origin and progress of writing, as well hiero-glyphic as elementary.* London, second edition 1808.   JOH.

I1A

Another copy. New edition 1876.

I1B

Benson, J. H. *Elements of lettering.*   JOH.

I2

British Institute of Industrial Art. *The Art of lettering and its use in divers crafts and trades.* London, 1931.

I2A

Cappelli, A., compiled by. *Dizionario di abbreviature.*   JOH.

I2B

Day, L. F. *Alphabets old and new.* 1898.   JOH.

I2C

—— *Lettering in ornament.* 1902.   JOH.

I3

Degering, Hermann, edited by. *Lettering: a series of 240 plates illustrating modes of writing in western Europe from antiquity to the end of the 18th century.* Berlin, 1929.

I4

Degering, Hermann. *Die Schrift. Atlas der Schriftformen des Abendlandes, etc.* Berlin, 1929.

I5

Delitsch, Hermann. *Umgang mit Buchstaben. Lehrbuch des künstlerischen Schreibens.* Berlin, 1933.

I6

Dürer, Albrecht. *Of the just shaping of letters, from The Applied geometry of Albrecht Dürer, book III.* New York, 1917.

I7

—— *Underweysung der messung . . . in truck gebracht im jar MDXXV.* Strasburg, 1531.

I7A

Ehmcke, F. H. *Ziele des Schriftunterrichts.* 1911. JOH.

I8

Hager, Joseph. *An Explanation of the elementary characters of the Chinese; with an analysis of their ancient symbols and hieroglyphics.* London, 1801.

I8A

Hasbuck, P. N. edited by. *How to write signs, tickets and posters.* JOH.

I9

Hewitt, Graily. *Handwriting: everyman's craft.* London, 1938.

I9A

Jacobi, C. T. *A few suggestions on plain letterings.* JOH.

I10

Jessen, Peter. *Meister der Schreibkunst aus drei Jahrhunderten*; Zweite Auflage: Stuttgart, 1936.

110A

Johnston, E. *Hand und Inschrift-Alphabete*. 1912.   JOH.

110B

—— *Schreibschrift*. 1910.   JOH.

110C

—— [Paste up of sheets].   JOH.

110D

Journal of the Society of Arts. Vol. 53, Feb. 17, 1905.   JOH.

110E

Klingspor (Gebr.). *Eine Unziale nach Zeichnung*. 4to.   JOH.

110F

Knuttel, Dr Gerard. *The Letter as a Work of Art*. Amsterdam, 1951.

111

Koch, Rudolf. *Das Schreibbüchlein. Eine Anleitung zum Schreiben*. Kassel, 1930.

111A

Larden, W. *Inscriptions from French chalets*. 1913.   JOH.

112

Lettering of to-day. The Studio, London, 1937.

113

Mallon, Jean, and others, compiled by. *L'Écriture latine de la capitale romaine à la minuscule; 54 planches reproduisant 85 documents originaux*. Paris, 1939.

113A

Manuscript writing and lettering. 1918.   JOH.

114

Palatino, Giovanni Battista. *Libro nelqual s' insegna a scriver ogni sorte lettera, Antica, & Moderna, di qualunque natione.* Rome, 1561.

115

—— *Libro nuovo d' imparare a scrivere tutte sorte lettere . . . antiche et moderne di tutte nationi.* Rome, 1540.

115A

Paleography.   JOH.

116

Reinhardt, Charles W. *Lettering for draftsmen, engineers and students*; 14th ed. New York, 1920.

117

Rogers, Bruce. *Champ rose, wherein may be discovered the Roman letters that were made by Geofroy Tory and printed by him at Paris in his book called 'Champ fleury'.* New York, 1933.

118

Roland. *Le Grand Art d'Ecriver Necessaire a ceux qui veulent se perfectionner dans cette science . . . dedié Aux Enfans de France par Roland.* Paris, 1758.

119

[Scrap-book containing collection of ornamental initials, head- and tail-pieces and printers' ornaments.]

120

Simons, Anna. *Titel und Initialen für die Bremer Presse.* Munich, 1926.

120A

Smith, Percy J. Delf. *Lettering and writing.* Fol.   JOH.

121

—— *Civic and memorial lettering.* London, 1946.

122

Smith, Percy J. Delf. Lettering. *A Handbook of modern alphabets.* London, 1936.

123

Stone, A. Reynolds. *A Book of lettering.* London, 1935.

123A

Strange, E. F. *Alphabets,* 1895.   JOH.

124

Swedlund, R., and Svenonius, O. *Svenska skriftprov 1464–1828, texter och tolkingar.* Uppsala, 1948.

125

Tagliente, Giovanni Antonio. *Lo presente libro insegna la vera arte de lo excellente scrivere.* Venice, 1524.

126

—— Another edition. Antwerp, 1545.

127

Thompson, Sir Edward Maunde. *Handbook of Greek and Latin palaeography;* 2nd ed. London, 1894.

128

—— *An Introduction to Greek and Latin palaeography.* Oxford, 1912.

129

Verini, Giovanni Battista de. *Incipit liber primus elementorum litterarum.* Florence, [1526].

130

Wright, A. *Court-hand restored.* 1879.   JOH.

131-2

Zeitgemässe Schrift. *Studienhefte . . .* 1935-6.   JOH.

IV

J. *Decoration, Illustration*

J1

Abbey, J. R., compiled by. *Scenery of Great Britain and Ireland in aquatint and lithography, 1770–1860, from the library of J. R. Abbey: a bibliographical catalogue.* Plaistow, 1952.

J2

Arabesque and other ornaments in typographical use at Zurich in MDLIX. London, 1868.

J3

Austin, Stanley. *The History of engraving from its inception to the time of Thomas Bewick.* London, n.d.

J4

Balston, Thomas. *English wood-engraving, 1900–1950.* London, 1951.

J5

—— *The Wood-engravings of Robert Gibbings.* London, 1949.

J6

Craig, Edward Gordon. *Woodcuts and some words, with an introduction by Campbell Dodgson.* London, 1924.

J7

Crane, Walter. *Of the decorative illustration of books, old and new.* London, 1896.

J8

Guillot, E. *Ornementation des manuscrits.* XIIe siècle.   JOH.

J8A

Guillot, E. *Ornementation des manuscrits. XIVe siècle.*   JOH.

J8B

—— *Ornementation des manuscrits. XVe siècle.*   JOH.

J8C

—— *Eléments d'ornementation pour l'enluminure.*   JOH.

J9

Hambourg, Daria. *Richard Doyle, his life and work.* London, 1948.

J10

Hamill, Alfred E. *The Decorative work of T. M. Cleland: a record and review.* New York, 1929.

J11

Harling, Robert. *Edward Bawden.* London, 1950.

J12

(Headpieces, vignettes, initials, mainly French, of the eighteenth century, mounted on cards.) (In box.)

J13

Hind, Arthur M., edited by. *Albrecht Dürer, his engravings and woodcuts.* London, 1911.

J13A

Hope, W. H. St. John. *Heraldry for craftsmen.*   JOH.

J14

Hubbard, Hesketh, edited by. *How to distinguish prints, written and illustrated by members of the Print Society.* London, 1926.

J15

Jackson, Mason. *The Pictorial Press: its origin and progress.* London, 1885.

J16–6A

Johnson, A. F. *Decorative initial letters*; collected and arranged with an introduction by A. F. Johnson. London, 1931. 2 copies.

J17

Jombert, Charles-Antoine. *Catalogue de l'œuvre de Ch. Nic. Cochin fils.* Paris, 1770.

J18

Kilian, Lucas. *Lucas Kilians Neues ABC Büchlein, Augsburg, 1627; Herausg. für den Freundeskreis der Bibliothek des Kunstgewerbemuseum.* Berlin, 1922.

J19

Kristeller, Paul. *Kupferstich und Holzschnitt in vier Jahrhunderten.* Berlin, 1921.

J20

Krüger, Otto. *Die Illustrations-Verfahren . . . ; Zweite Ausgabe.* Leipzig, 1929.

J21

Langridge, Irene. *William Blake: a study of his life and art work.* London, 1904.

J22

Lewis, C. T. Courtney. *The Picture Printer Price List.* Supplement to 'George Baxter the Picture Printer'. London, 1924.

J23

McKerrow, R. B., and Ferguson, F. S. *Title-page borders used in England and Scotland, 1485–1640.* London, 1932.

J24

Mayne, Jonathan. *Barnett Freedman.* London, 1948.

J24A

Morison, Stanley. *Richard Austin, engraver to the printing trade between the years 1788 and 1830.* Cambridge University Press. 1937.

J25

Ottley, William Young. *An Inquiry into the origin and early history of engraving upon copper and in wood* . . . London, 1816.

J26

Pennell, Joseph. *Pen drawing and pen draughtsmen, their work and their methods: a study of the art to-day with technical suggestions.* London, 1894.

J27

Piper, Myfanwy. *Reynolds Stone.* London, 1951.

J28

Das Plakat in Beispielen neuzeitlicher Formgestaltung. Berlin, n.d.

J29

Plomer, Henry R. *English printers' ornaments.* London, 1924.

J30

Pollard, Alfred W. *Early illustrated books: a history of the decoration and illustration of books in the 15th and 16th centuries.* London, 1893.

J31

Reiner, Imré. *Grafika, modern design for advertising and printing.* Switzerland, 1947.

J32

Reitlinger, Henry. *From Hogarth to Keene.* London, 1958.

J33

Reynolds, Graham. *Thomas Bewick, a résumé of his life and work.* London, 1949.

J34

Salomons, Vera. *Choffard.* London, 1912.

J35

Schreiber, W. L. *Der Buchholzschnitt im 15. Jahrhundert in Original-Beispielen: 55 Inkunabelproben.* Munich, 1929.

J36

Shaw, Henry. *The Art of illumination as practised during the middle ages, with a description of the metals, pigments, and processes employed by the artists at different periods.* London, 1870.

J37

Smith, Janet Adam. *Children's illustrated books.* London, 1948.

J37A

Sullivan, E. J. *Art of illustration.* 1921.   JOH.

J38

Trattner, Johann Thomas. *Röslein und Zierrathen*, Vienna, 1760. Vienna, 1927.

J39

Tymms, W. R. *The Art of illuminating as practised in Europe; with an essay and instructions by M. D. Wyatt.* London, 1860.

J40

Whistler, Laurence. *Rex Whistler, 1905–1944, his life and his drawings.* London, 1948.

J41

White, Gleeson. *English illustration, 'the sixties': 1855–70.* London, 1906.

J41A

Whitehard, P. *Illuminating and missal painting.* 1909.   JOH.

J42–2C

Woodcut, The: an annual. Nos. 1–4. London, 1927–30.

J43

Woodcuts from books of the 16th century: from German/Swiss/ Dutch/French/Spanish and Italian presses; with an introduction by Max Geisberg. Olten, 1937.

V

K. *Materials*

K1

Churchill, W. A. *Watermarks in paper, in Holland, England, France, etc., in the XVII and XVIII centuries, and their inter-connection.* Amsterdam, 1935.

K2

Clapperton, R. H. *Paper: an historical account of its making by hand, etc.* Oxford, 1934.

K3

Craig, Robert, and Sons, Ltd. *A Century of papermaking, 1820–1920.* Edinburgh, 1920.

K4

Hunter, Dard. *A Papermaking pilgrimage to Japan, Korea and China.* New York, 1936.

K5

Labarre, E. J. *A Dictionary of paper and paper-making terms.* Amsterdam, 1937.

K6

Lamb, M. C. *Leather dressing, including dyeing, staining and finishing*; 2nd ed. London, 1909.

K7

Renker, Armin. *Das Buch vom Papier.* Wiesbaden, 1950.

K8

Wheelwright, William Bond. *Printing papers.* Chicago, 1936.

K9

Wiborg, Frank B. *Printing ink: a history with a treatise on modern methods of manufacture and use.* New York, 1926.

VI

L. *Presses and Printers*

L1

Aldis, Harry G. *A List of books printed in Scotland before 1700, including those printed furth of the realm for Scottish booksellers, with brief notes on the printers and stationers.* 1904. See also U1.

L2

American Institute of Graphic Arts and the Grolier Club. *The Work of Bruce Rogers, jack of all trades: master of one, a catalogue of an exhibition; with an introduction by D. B. Updike, a letter from John T. McCutcheon and an address by M. Rogers.* New York, 1939.

L3

Ballantyne Press and its founders, 1796–1908. Edinburgh, 1909.

L4–4A

Blades, William. *The Life and typography of William Caxton . . . with evidence of his typographical connection with Colard Mansion.* 2 volumes. London, 1861–63.

L5

—— 2nd edition. London, 1882.

L6

Bushnell, George H. *The Life and work of Edward Raban, St. Andrews' most famous printer.* 1928.

L7

Cartier, Alfred. *Bibliographie des éditions des de Tournes, imprimeurs lyonnais; mise en ordre par Marius Audin et un notice biographique par E. Vial.* Vol. 2. Paris, 1938.

L8

Cary, Melbert B. *A Bibliography of the Village Press.* New York, 1938.

L9

Chalmers, George. *The Life of Thomas Ruddiman, A.M., the keeper, for almost fifty years, of the Library belonging to the Faculty of Advocates at Edinburgh, to which are subjoined new anecdotes of Buchanan.* Edinburgh, 1794.

L9A

Constable, T. & A., Ltd., Brief Notes on the Origins of [1760–1936]. Edinburgh, 1937.

L10

Daniel Press, The. *Memorials of C. H. O. Daniel, with a bibliography of the Press, 1845–1919.* Oxford, 1921.

L11

Davenport, Cyril. *Roger Payne, English bookbinder of the eighteenth century.* Chicago, 1929.

L12

Davies, David W. *The World of the Elseviers, 1580–1712.* The Hague, 1954.

L13

De Vinne, Theo. L. *Christopher Plantin and the Plantin-Moretus Museum at Antwerp.* New York, 1888.

L14

Dickson, Robert. *Introduction of the art of printing into Scotland.* Aberdeen, 1885.

L15

Dickson, Robert. *Who was Scotland's first printer?* London, 1881.

L16

Dickson, Robert, and Edmond, John Philip. *Annals of Scottish printing from 1507 to the beginning of the seventeenth century.* Cambridge, 1890.

L17

Dobson, William T. *History of the Bassandyne Bible, the first printed in Scotland, with notices of the early printers of Edinburgh.* Edinburgh, 1887.

L18

Catalogue raisonné of Books Printed & Published at the Doves Press, 1890–1911; 2nd ed. Hammersmith, 1911.

L18A

Crutchley, Brooke. *A Printer's Christmas Books.* Privately printed at the University Printing House, 1974.

Although the book on Emery Walker, L23A, had been thought to be the last of the Cambridge Christmas Books, this final book was issued at Christmas 1974 by the present Printer to the University and by his predecessor. This book describes the series which was began in 1930.

L19

Dupont, Paul. *Une Imprimerie en 1867.* Paris, 1867.

L20

Edmond, J. P. *The Aberdeen printers—Edward Raban to James Nicol, 1620–1736.* 4 parts. Aberdeen, 1884–86.

L21

Elliott, R. C. *Early Scottish printers: a brief history.* London, 1927.

L22

Fairley, John A. *Agnes Campbell, Lady Roseburn, relict of Andrew Anderson, the King's printer: a contribution to the history of printing in Scotland.* 1925.

L23

Forman, H. B. *Books of Wm. Morris described.* 1897.   JOH.

L23A

Franklin, Colin. *Emery Walker. Some light on his theories of printing and on his relations with William Morris and Cobden-Sanderson.* Privately printed for the University Printer at the University Press, Cambridge, 1973.

Each Christmas for the previous 25 years the University Printer at Cambridge had produced, for his friends, a publication. This is the last of the series. The subjects have been associated either with printing or with Cambridge.

L24

Gallatin, A. E. *Modern fine printing in America: an essay.* New York, 1921.

L25

Gent, Thomas. *The Life of Mr. Thomas Gent, printer, of York*; written by himself. London, 1832.

L26

Glasgow Bibliographical Society. *Book of the Foulis Exhibition*; comprising catalogue, President's opening address and descriptive account. 1913.

L27

Golden Cockerel Press. *Chanticleer: a bibliography of the Golden Cockerel Press, April 1921–1936 August.* London, 1936.

L27A

—— *Pertelote: a sequel to Chanticleer: being a bibliography of the Golden Cockerel Press, October 1936–1943 April.* London, 1943.

L28–8A

Greswell, E., edited by. *A View of the Early Parisian Greek Press.* 2 volumes. Oxford, 1833.

L29–9A

Greswell, William Parr. *Annals of Parisian Typography*. London, 1818. 2 copies.

L30

Haas, Irvin. *Bibliography of modern American presses*. Chicago, 1935.

L31

Hessels, J. H. *Gutenberg: was he the inventor of printing? an historical investigation, embodying a criticism on Dr van der Linde's 'Gutenberg'*. London, 1882.

L32

Hornby, C. H. St John. *A Descriptive bibliography of the books printed at the Ashendene Press, MDCCCXCV–MCMXXV*. Chelsea, 1935.

L33

Jansson, Theodore. *De Vitis Stephanorum, celebrium typographorum, dissertatio epistolica*. Apud Janssonio-Waasbergios. Amstelaedami, 1683.

L34

Johnson, A. F. *The First century of printing at Basle*. London, 1926.

L35

—— *French sixteenth century printing*. London, 1928.

L36

—— *The Italian sixteenth century*. London, 1926.

L37

Johnson, John, and Gibson, Strickland. *Print and Privilege at Oxford to the year 1700*. London, 1946.

L38–8A

Johnstone, James F. K., and Robertson, Alex. W. *Bibliographia Aberdonensis: being an account of books relating to or printed in the shires of Aberdeen, Banff, Kincardine . . . 1472–1700.* 2 volumes 1929–30.

L39

[Kelmscott Press, List of publications.] Hammersmith, 1895.

L40

Kent, Rockwell. *Rockwellkentiana: Few words and many pictures by R.K., and, by Carl Zigrosser, a bibliography and list of prints.* New York, 1933.

L41

Lejard, André, edited by. *The Art of the French book from early manuscripts to the present time.* London, 1947.

L42–2A

Mackail, J. W. *The Life of William Morris.* 2 volumes. London, 1899.

L43

McKerrow, R. B. *A Dictionary of printers and booksellers in England, Scotland and Ireland, and of foreign printers of English books, 1557–1640.* London, 1910.

L44

McMurtrie, Douglas C. *The Beginnings of printing in Virginia.* Lexington, Va., 1935.

L45

—— *The Gutenberg documents, with translations of the texts into English, based with authority on the compilation by Dr. Karl Schorbach.* New York, 1941.

L46–6A

Mayer, Anton. *Wiens Buchdrucker-Geschichte, 1482–1882.* 2 Parts. Vienna, 1883–87.

L47

Moore, Thomas Sturge. *A Brief account of the origin of the Eragny Press and a note on the relation of the printed book as a work of art to life.* London, 1903.

L48

Morison, Stanley. *John Bell, 1745–1831. Bookseller, printer, publisher, typefounder, journalist, etc.* 1930.

L49

(Morris, William.) *Catalogue of an exhibition in celebration of the centenary of William Morris, held at the Victoria and Albert Museum.* Plaistow, 1934.

L50

Nonesuch Century, The. *An Appraisal, a personal note and a bibliography . . . 1923–1934.* London, 1936.

L51

Officina Bodoni, The. *The Operation of a hand-press during the first six years of its work.* Paris, 1929.

L52

Orton, Vrest. *Goudy, master of letters.* Chicago, 1939.

L53

Oxford University Press. *Some account of the Oxford University Press, 1468–1921.* 1922.

L54

Pillans, H. & J., and Wilson. *A Printing house of old and new Edinburgh, 1775–1925.* Edinburgh, [1925].

L55

Plomer, Henry R. *A Dictionary of the booksellers and printers who were at work in England, Scotland and Ireland from 1641 to 1667.* London, 1907.

L56

—— *William Caxton (1424–1491).* Newcastle upon Tyne, 1924.

L57

—— *Wynkyn de Worde and his contemporaries . . . to 1535. A chapter in English printing.* London, 1925.

L58

Pollard, Alfred William. *Cobden-Sanderson and the Doves Press.* San Francisco, 1929.

L59

[Royen, J. F. van.] *Over Boekkunst en de Zilverdistel door J. F. Royen and P. N. van Eyck.* 1916.

L60–60A

Sanderson, Thomas James Cobden-. *The Journals, 1879–1922.* 2 volumes. London, 1926.

L61

Schwenke, Paul. *Die Turkenbulle Pabst Calixtus III. Ein deutscher Druck von 1456 in der ersten Gutenbergtype.* Berlin, 1911.

L62

Scott, John. *The Arithmetica of Jordanus Nemorarius, Paris 1496; is it the first book with the printing of which a Scotsman was connected?* Edinburgh, privately printed, 1892.

L63

Simon, Oliver. *The Curwen Press Miscellany.* London, 1931.

L64

Skeen, William. *Early typography.* Colombo, 1872.

L65

Straus, Ralph, and Dent, Robert K. *John Baskerville: a memoir.* London, 1907.

L66

[Strawberry Hill.] *Journal of the printing-office at Strawberry Hill: with notes by Paget Toynbee.* London, 1923.

L67

Thomas, Henry. *Spanish sixteenth-century printing.* London, 1926.

L68

Thorp, Joseph. *B. H. Newdigate, scholar-printer, 1869–1944.* Oxford, 1950.

L69

Timperley, Charles H. *A Dictionary of printers and printing.* London, 1839.

L70

Tomkinson, G. S. *A Select bibliography of the principal modern presses, public and private, in Great Britain and Ireland.* London, 1928.

L71

[Vale Press.] Ricketts, Charles. *A Bibliography of the books issued by Hacon & Ricketts.* London, 1904.

L72

—— *List of books issued by Messrs. Hacon & Ricketts, at the Sign of the Dial, 52, Warwick Street . . . London.* London, 1898.

L73

Vindel, Francisco. *El arte tipográfico en España durante el siglo XV: Cataluña.* Talleres tipográficos de Góngora. Madrid, 1945.

L74

Warren, Arthur. *The Charles Whittinghams Printers.* New York, 1896.

L75

[Watson, James.] *History of the art of printing . . . its invention and progress in Europe, with the names of the famous printers, the places of their birth, and the works printed by them.* Edinburgh, 1713.

L76

[Weiss, E. R.] *E. R. Weiss zum fünfzigsten Geburtstage, 12 Oktober 1925.* Frankfurt-am-Main, 1925.

L77

Winship, George Parker. *The Merrymount Press of Boston. An account of the work of Daniel Berkeley Updike.* Vienna, 1929.

L78

—— *William Caxton, a paper read at a meeting of the Club of Odd Volumes in Boston Massachusetts U.S.A. in January MDCCCCVIII.* Hammersmith, 1909.

L79

Wm. Morris Society. *Typographical adventure of Wm. Morris, an exhibition.* 1958.

VII

M. *Printing and Processes*

M1

Archiv für Buchgewerbe und Gebrauchsgraphik 4. Heft, 1932. Breitkopf und Härtel, for Deutschen Buchgewerbevereins. Leipzig, 1932.

M2–2E

Atkins, William. *The Art and practice of printing.* 6 volumes. London, 1934.

M3

Author's Printing and Publishing Assistant; 5th ed. London, 1840.

M4

Autotype Printing and Publishing Co. Ltd. *The Autotype process: being a practical manual of instruction in the art of printing in carbon, or other permanent pigment.* London, n.d.

M5

Beniowski, Bartolomiej. *Improvements in printing, invented and patented by Major Beniowski*.. London, 1864.

M6–6B

Bigmore, Edward Clements, and Wyman, C. W. H. *A Bibliography of printing.* 3 volumes. London, 1880.

M7

Bliss, Douglas Percy. *A History of wood-engraving.* London, 1928.

M8

Bodoni, Giambattista. *G. B. Bodoni's Preface to the Manuale tipografico of* 1818. London, 1925.

M9

[Bradbury, Henry.] *Autotypography; or, Art of nature-printing.* [London] 1860.

M10

British Federation of Master Printers. *Estimating for Printers.* London, 1926.

M11

Brown, Louise Norton. *Block printing and book illustration in Japan.* London, 1924.

M12

Carter, Thomas Francis. *The Invention of printing in China, and its spread westward.* New York, 1925.

M13

Curzon, Robert, Lord de la Zouche. *History of printing in China and Europe.* London, 1860–61.

M14

Cumming, David. *Handbook of lithography.* London, 1904.

M15

Earhart, John F. *The Color printer: a treatise on the use of colors in typographic printing.* 1892.

M16

Fielding, T. H. *The Art of engraving.* London, 1844.

M17

Fletcher, F. Morley. *Wood-block printing.* London [1916].

M18

Fournier, Simon Pierre. *Traités historiques et critiques, sur l'origine et les progrès de l'imprimerie.* Paris, 1758–63.

M19

Fuhrmann, Otto W. *The 500th anniversary of the invention of printing.* New York, 1937.

M20

Ged, William. *Biographical memoirs of William Ged; including a particular account of his progress in the art of block printing.* Newcastle, 1819.

M21

Gillespie, Sarah C. *A Hundred years of progress: the record of the Scottish Typographical Association, 1853 to 1952.* Glasgow, 1953.

M22

Griffits, Thomas E. *The Technique of colour printing by lithography: a concise manual of drawn lithography.* London, 1944.

M23

Hansard, Thomas Curson. *The Art of printing.* Edinburgh, 1851.

M24

—— *Typographia.* London, 1825.

M25

Hawkins, G. L. *Pigment printing: the bromoil process from the negative to the transfer.* London, 1933.

M26–6A

Hind, Arthur M. *An Introduction to a history of woodcut.* 2 volumes. London, 1935.

M27

Hodgson, Thomas. *An Essay on the origin and progress of*

stereotype printing, including a description of the various processes. Newcastle, 1820.

M28

Hoernle, Edward F. *Technical education: a portal to the palace of truth.* A lecture delivered before the Edinburgh Typographia, on the 9th of November 1903. Edinburgh, 1903.

M29

Howe, Ellic, edited by. *The London compositor: documents relating to wages, working conditions and customs of the London printing trade, 1785-1900.* London, 1947.

M30

—— *'The Trade': passages from the literature of the printing craft, 1550-1935.* 1943.

M31

Humphreys, H. Noel. *A History of the Art of Printing from its invention to its wide-spread development in the middle of the sixteenth century, preceded by a short account of the origin of the alphabet.* London, 1868.

M32

Jacobi, Charles Thomas. *Gesta Typographica; or, A Medley for printers and others.* London, 1897.

M33

—— *The Printers' vocabulary.* London, 1888.

M34-4c

Johnson, John. *Typographia; or, The Printers' Instructor.* 2 volumes. London, 1824. 2 issues.

M35

La Serna, Santander, Carlos Antonio de. *An Historical essay on the Origin of Printing.* Bound with Hodgson's *Essay on Stereotyping* and *Memoirs of William Ged.* Newcastle, 1819.

M36

La Serna, Santander. Another copy.

M37

Legros, Lucien A., and Grant, John C. *Typographical printing surfaces, the technology and mechanism of their production.* London, 1916.

M38

Linotype & Machinery Ltd. *List of some newspapers and other publications in Great Britain set by the Linotype composing machine.* 1901.

M39

Linton, W. J. *Wood-engraving: a manual of instruction.* London, 1884.

M40

Luckombe, Philip. *The History and art of printing.* London, 1771.

M41

MacMurtrie, Douglas C. *A History of printing in the United States.* Vol. II. *Middle and South Atlantic States.* New York, 1936.

M42

[Marchand, Prosper.] *Histoire de l'origine et des premiers progrès de l'imprimerie.* 2 parts bound together. The Hague, 1740.

M43

Meteyard, Eliza. *A Group of Englishmen (1795 to 1815); being records of the younger Wedgwoods and their friends, embracing the history of the discovery of photography and a facsimile of the first photograph.* London, 1871.

M44

Middleton, Conyers. *A Dissertation concerning the origin of printing in England.* Cambridge, 1735.

M45

Orme, Edward. *An Essay on transparent prints and on transparencies in general.* London, 1807.

M46

Oswald, John Clyde. *A History of printing: its development through five hundred years.* New York, 1928.

M47

Palmer, Samuel. *The General history of printing.* London, 1732.

M48

Pennell, Joseph. *The Illustration of books: a manual for the use of students, notes for a course of lectures at the Slade School, University College.* London, 1896.

M49

Pepler, Hilary Douglas C. *The Hand press: an essay.* Ditchling, 1934.

M50

Plomer, Henry R. *A Short history of English printing, 1476–1898.* Edinburgh, 1900.

M51

Printers' grammar, The. London, 1787.

M51A–H

Printing Historical Society. *Journal.* Nos. 1–8. London, 1965–1972.

M52

Raucourt, A. *A Manual of lithography, clearly explaining the whole art; to which is added selections from the work of M. Bregeaut;* 3rd ed. London, 1832.

M53

Ricketts, Charles. *Dell' arte della stampa.* Verona, 1926.

M54

Rudge, William Edwin. (Specimen sheet of photo-litho offset.) New York, n.d.

M55

Sampson, Thomas. *Electrotint; or, The Art of making paintings in such a manner that copper plates and 'blocks' can be taken from them by means of voltaic electricity.* London, 1842.

M55A

Moxon, Joseph. *Mechanick exercises on the Whole Art of Printing.* H. Davis and H. Carter, edited by. London, 1958.

M56

Savage, William. *A Dictionary of the art of printing.* London, 1841.

M57

—— *Practical hints on decorative printing with illustrations engraved on wood and printed in colours at the type press.* London, 1822.

M58

Sculptura historico-technica; or, The History and art of engraving. London, 1770.

M59

Simon, Herbert, and Carter, Harry. *Printing explained.* Leicester, 1931.

M60

Slater, John Rothwell. *Printing and the Renaissance.* New York, 1921.

M61

Smith, John. *The Printer's grammar.* For the Editor. London, 1755.

M62

Stower, Caleb. *The Printer's grammar; or, Introduction to the art of printing.* London, 1808.

M63

Sutton, Thomas. *The Calotype process: a hand book to photography on paper*. London, 1855.

M64

'Times, The'. *Printing in the twentieth century: a survey*. London, 1930.

M65

Timperley, Charles H. *The Printers' manual*. London, 1838. Bound with Timperley's *Dictionary of printers, etc.*

M66

Vinçard. *L'Art du typographe*. 2nd ed. Paris, 1823.

M67

Willett, Ralph. *A Memoir on the origin of printing*. Newcastle, 1820. Bound with La Serna, Santander's 'Historical essay'.

M68

—— Another edition 1819. Bound with La Serna, Santander's 'Historical essay'.

M69

Wilson, Frederick J. F. *Stereotyping and electrotyping: a guide for the production of plates*. 5th ed. London, 1922.

M70

Winship, Geoffrey Parker. *Gutenberg to Plantin: an outline of the early history of printing*. 1926.

M71*

Winsor & Newton, Ltd. Colouring No. 1. (3 leaves from sample colour book with notes.) Wealdstone, n.d.

M72

Wroth, Lawrence C. *The Colonial printer*; 2nd ed. Portland, Maine, 1938.

M73

Turnbull, A. *Scott Fitzgerald*. The Bodley Head. London, 1962.
Set in Linofilm Caledonia (photo-composition) by William Clowes & Sons, Beccles.

VIII
N. *Type Design, Typefounding*

N1
Aird & Coghill. *Specimens of music engraving and printing.* Glasgow, 1932.

N2
Aldus Manutius. *Alphabetum Hebraicum, Venedig c. 1510.* Munich, 1927.

N3
American Type Founders Co. *American line type book, borders, ornaments.* Jersey City, N.J., 1906.

N4
—— *Specimen book and catalogue, 1923.* Jersey City, N.J., 1923.

N5
Arrighi, Ludovico degli, called Vicentino. *The Calligraphic models of Ludovico degli Arrighi . . . a complete facsimile and introduction by Stanley Morison.* Paris, 1926.

N6
Austin Letter-Foundry. *The Specimen book of types cast at the Austin Letter-Foundry by Wood & Sharwood's.* London, 1839.

N7
Balston, Thomas. *The Cambridge University Press collection of private press types: Kelmscott, Ashendene, Éragny, Cranach.* Cambridge, 1951.

N8

Berry, W. Turner, and Johnson, A. F. *Catalogue of specimens of printing types by English and Scottish printers and founders, 1665–1830.* London, 1935.

N9

Biggs, John R. *An Approach to type.* London, 1949.

N10–10A

Bodoni, Giambattista. *Manuele tipografico del cavaliere Giambattista Bodoni.* 2 volumes. Parma, 1818.

N11

Boubers, J. L. de. *Épreuves des caractères de la fonderie de J. L. de Boubers.* Brussels, 1777.

N12

Caslon, William. *A Specimen by William Caslon: letter-founder, in Chiswell Street, London.* (London, 1738).

N13

—— Another ed. (1785).

N14

Country Press. *A Selection of types from the Country Press.* Bradford, 1927.

N15

Cowell, W. S., Ltd. *A Handbook of printing types, with notes on the style of composition and graphic processes used by Cowells.* Ipswich, 1947.

N16

Curwen Press. *A Specimen book of types and ornaments in use at the Curwen Press.* London, 1928.

N17

Didot, Pierre. *Spécimen des nouveaux caractères de la fonderie et de l'imprimerie de P. Didot.* Paris, 1819.

N18

Dürer, Albrecht. *The Construction of Roman letters.* Cambridge, 1924.

N19

(Dwiggins, W. A.) *WAD to BR, a letter about designing type.* Camb. (Mass.), 1940.

N20

Enschedé, Charles. *Fonderies de caractères et leur matériel dans les Pays-Bas du XVᵉ au XIXᵉ siècle. Notice historique principalement d'après les données de la collection typographique de Joh. Enschedé en Zonen à Haarlem.* Haarlem, 1908.

N21

Enschedé, J. (*Letterproef.*) Haarlem, 1768.

N21A

—— *A Selection of types from six centuries in use at the office of Joh. Enschedé en Zonen at Haarlem, Holland.* Haarlem, 1930.

N22

Ettenberg, Eugene M. *Type for books and advertising.* New York, 1947.

N23–4

Fell, John. *A Specimen of the several sorts of letter given to the University by Dr. John Fell, Oxford, 1693.* London, 1928. 2 copies.

N25–6

—— *Specimens of books printed at Oxford with the types given to the University by John Fell.* Oxford, 1925. 2 copies.

N27–8

Fournier, Simon Pierre, *le jeune. Manuel typographique utile aux gens de lettres, & à ceux qui exercent les différentes parties de l'art de l'imprimerie.* 2 volumes. Paris, 1764–6.

(Plate LI)

N29

Fournier, Simon Pierre. *Fournier on typefounding. The text of the Manuel Typographique . . . translated . . . by Harry Carter.* London, 1930.

N30

Fry, Edmund, and Co. *A Specimen of printing types, by Edmund Fry and Co., Letter-Founders to the Prince of Wales.* With *The Printer's grammar.* London, 1787.

N31

Fry, Joseph, and Sons. *A Specimen of printing types, by Joseph Fry and Sons.* London, 1785.

N32

Gardiner, Alan H. *Catalogue of the Egyptian hieroglyphic printing type, from matrices owned and controlled by Dr. A. H. Gardiner.*

N33

Gesellschaft für Typenkunde des XV. Jahrhunderts. *Veröffentlichungen.* Vol. 6. Fasc. III. 1912.

N34

—— *Veröffentlichungen.* Vol. 7. Fasc. I–III. 1913.

N35–6

Greek Printing Types, 1465–1927. Facsimiles . . . with an historical introduction by Victor Scholderer. London, 1927. 2 copies.

N37

Grotesque Alphabet of 1464 reproduced in facsimile from the original woodcuts in the British Museum. London, 1899.

N38

Goudy, Frederic William. *The Alphabet. Fifteen interpretative designs.* New York, 1918.

N39

Goudy, Frederic William. 2nd ed. 1922.

N40

—— *Typologia: studies in type design and type making.* Berkeley, U.S.A., 1940.

N41

Haddon, John, & Co. [*Catalogue.*] London, n.d.

N42

Hewitt, Graily. *The Pen and Type-design.* 1928.

N43

Humphreys, Henry Noel. *Masterpieces of the early printers and engravers.* A series of facsimiles. London, 1870.

N44

Isaac, Frank. *English and Scottish printing types, 1535–58, 1552–58. Collected and annotated by F. Isaac.* London, 1932.

N45

Jannon, Jean. *The 1621 specimen of Jean Jannon, Paris and Sedan, designer and engraver of the caractères de l'université . . . edited in facsimile with an introduction by Paul Beaujon.* London, 1927.

N46

Koch, Rudolf, and Wolpe, Berthold. *Das ABC-Büchlein.* Leipzig, 1934.

N47

Lamesle, Claude. *Épreuves générales des caractères qui se trouvent chez Claude Lamesle, fondeur de caractères d'imprimerie.* Paris, 1742.

N48

Lanston Monotype Company. *Italian Old Style: a new type designed by Frederic W. Goudy.* Philadelphia, 1924.

N49

Lanston Monotype Corporation Ltd. *Pastonchi: a specimen of a new letter for use on the 'Monotype'.* London, 1928.

N50

McMurtrie, Douglas C. *American type design in the twentieth century; with specimens of the outstanding types during this period.* Chicago, 1924.

N51

—— *The Pierre Cot type specimen of 1707 with a reproduction in facsimile of the original specimen.* Chicago, 1924.

N52

[McRae, John Findlay.] *Two centuries of typefounding, annals of the letter foundry established by William Caslon in Chiswell Street, London, in the year 1720.* London, 1920.

N53

Miller, William, and Co. *Specimen of printing types by William Miller & Co.* Edinburgh, 1841.

(Plate LII)

N54

Miller & Richard. *Specimens of modern, old style and ornamental type cast on point bodies.* Edinburgh and London, 1906.

N55

Mores, Edward Rowe. *A Dissertation upon English typographical founders and founderies.* New York, 1924.

N56

Morison, Stanley. *German Incunabula in the British Museum . . . Facsimile plates . . . in Gothic letter and derived founts.* London, 1928.

N57–7A

Morison, Stanley. *Type designs of the past and present*. London, 1926. 2 copies.

N58

Moyllus, Damianus. *A Newly discovered treatise on classic letter design, printed at Parma . . . circa 1480*. Paris, 1927.

N59

Neill and Company. *Neill and Company's Typographic guide. A series of specimen pages*. Edinburgh, n.d.

N60

[Proctor's Otter Greek type, Specimen of.] n.d.

N61

Shaw, Henry. *The Hand Book of mediaeval alphabets and devices*. London, 1856.

N62

Stephenson, Blake & Co. *Printing types*. Sheffield, 1924.

N63

Stephenson, Blake & Co., and Reed & Sons, Sir Charles. *Specimens of point line type, borders, brass rules, etc., material and machinery*. Sheffield and London, 1911.

N64

Taylor & Taylor. *Types, borders and miscellany of Taylor & Taylor*. San Francisco, 1939.

N65–5A

Updike, Daniel Berkeley. *Printing Types: Their History, Forms and Use*; 2nd ed. 2 volumes. Cambridge, Mass., 1937.

N66

Walker, Sir Emery. [Specimens of printing.]

N67

Wilson, Alexander, and Sons. *Selection from the Specimen book of Alex. Wilson & Sons, Glasgow Letter Foundry.* London, 1834.

N68–9

—— *A Specimen of printing types.* Glasgow, 1783. 2 copies.

N70

Wyse, Henry T. *Modern type display and the use of type ornament.* Edinburgh, 1911.

IX

o. *Typography*

O1–1A

Aldenham Institute, London. *Annual reports of the Aldenham Institute printing class, 1900–1901* and *1901–02*. 2 volumes. London, 1901-2.

O2

Bartlett, Edward Everett. *The Typographic treasures in Europe.* New York, 1925.

O3–3C

Carteret, Léopold. *Le Trésor du bibliophile, romantique et moderne, 1801–1875.* 4 tom. Paris, 1924–27.

O4

Cobden-Sanderson, T. J. *The Ideal book or book beautiful: a tract on calligraphy, printing and illustration, and on the book beautiful as a whole.* Hammersmith, 1900.

O5–5A

De Vinne, Theodore Low. *The Practice of typography. A treatise on the processes of type-making.* 2 volumes. New York, 1900-01.

O6

—— *Title-pages as seen by a printer; with . . . illustrations in facsimile.* New York, 1901.

391

O7

Dulau and Company. *A Catalogue for typophiles of books of typographical interest*. London (1932?).

O8

Ehrlich, Frederick. *The New typography and modern layouts*. London, 1934.

O9

Fleuron, The. A Journal of typography. Nos. 1–4 edited by Oliver Simon. London, 1923–25. 2 copies of No. 4.

O10

—— Nos. 5–7 edited by Stanley Morison. 1926–30.

O11

Gill, Eric. *An Essay on typography;* 2nd ed., London, 1936.

O12

Hall, S. Roland. *Writing an advertisement*. Boston and New York, 1915.

O13

Johnson, A. F. *One hundred title-pages, 1500–1800; selected and arranged with an introduction and notes by A. F. Johnson*. London, 1928.

O14

Johnson, John. *The Printer: His customers and His men*. London, 1933.

O15

Jones, Herbert. *Type in action*. London, 1938.

O16

Klingspor, Karl. *Über Schönheit von Schrift und Druck: Erfahrungen aus fünfzigjähriger Arbeit*. 1949.

O17

Linotype & Machinery Ltd. *Typographical lay-out and design;* 2nd ed. London, 1930.

O18–8C

Livre d'or du bibliophile. Première (–deuxième) année. Paris, 1925–27. 2 copies.

O19–20

Lock, H. F. *Basic typography.* London, 1940. 2 copies.

O21

Meynell, Francis. *The Typography of newspaper advertisements; with a display of English, American, French, Dutch and German typefaces.* London, 1929.

O22–3

Morison, Stanley. *The Art of printing.* London, 1937. 2 copies.

O24

—— *Four centuries of fine printing . . . examples of the work of presses established during the years 1500 to 1914; with introduction, text and indexes by Stanley Morison.* London, 1924.

O25

—— *Modern fine printing. An exhibit of printing issued . . . during the twentieth century.* London, 1925.

O26–6A

—— *On type faces. Examples of the use of type for the printing of books; with an introductory essay and notes.* London, 1923. 2 copies.

O27–7A

—— *A Review of recent typography in England, the United States France and Germany.* 1927. 2 copies.

O28

—— *The Typographic arts, past, present and future: a lecture delivered at the College of Art, Edinburgh, 17 February 1944.* Edinburgh, 1944.

O29

Reiner, Imré. *Modern and historical typography: an illustrated guide.* Switzerland, 1946.

O30

Rogers, Bruce. *Paragraphs on printing, elicited from Bruce Rogers in talks with James Hendrickson on the functions of the book designer.* New York, 1943.

O31

Royal Society of Arts. *Cantor lectures. Typography and mass production;* by Harold Curwen. *Typography and illustration;* by John Farleigh. *Modern typography on the continent;* by Bertram Evans. Rochester, 1940.

O32

Signature: a quadrimestrial of typography and graphic arts. 1948.

O33

Simon, Oliver, and Rodenburg, Julius. *Printing of to-day. An illustrated survey of post-war typography in Europe and the United States.* London, 1928.

O34

Tarr, John Charles. *How to plan print.* London, 1938.

O35

Trezise, F. F. *The Typography of advertisements.* Chicago, 1911.

O36

Typography. The written word and the printed word; some tests for types. London, 1923.

O37

Warde, Beatrice. *Typography in art education: a paper read at the Annual Conference, 1945, of the National Society for Art Education.* London, 1946.

X

P. *Catalogues, Bibliographies*

P1

Biblioteca Apostolica Vaticana. *Biblioteche ospiti della Vaticana nella seconda guerra mondiale, con catalogo dei cimeli esposti nel salone sistino.* Rome, 1945.

P2

Birmingham School of Printing. *Catalogue of books issued from the City of Birmingham School of Printing, a department of the Central School of Arts and Crafts, from March 1925 to July 1933.* [?1933]

P3

—— *Catalogue of books, six series issued by the Limited Editions Club of U.S.A.,* presented . . . by Sir Charles Hyde, Bart. from the library of George W. Jones. 1937.

P4

British Museum. *Catalogue of an exhibition of books illustrating British and foreign printing, 1919–1929.* 1929.

P5–5c

Darlow, T. H. and Moule, H. F. *Historical Catalogue of the Printed editions of Holy Scripture in the Library of the British and Foreign Bible Society.* London, 1903. 4 volumes.

P6

Heriot-Watt College, Edinburgh. *Catalogue of an exhibition of contemporary book-typography: the fifty best books of 1932 chosen by the First Edition Club, London, a selection of the publications of the Nonesuch Press, London, a selection from the work of the book printers of Edinburgh.* Edinburgh, 1933.

P7

Incunabuli, manoscritti, autografi, libri illustrati dal secolo XVI al XIX, vendita all' asta in Roma 27 Aprile. Milan 1933.

P8

Parrish, M. L. *Victorian lady novelists, George Eliot, Mrs Gaskell, the Bronte sisters: first editions in the library at Dormy House, Pine Valley, New Jersey, described with notes.* London, 1933.

P9

Pollard, A. W., and Redgrave, G. R., compiled by. *A Short-title catalogue of books printed in England, Scotland, and Ireland, and of English books printed abroad, 1475–1640.* London, 1926.

P10

Roscoe, (S.). *Thomas Bewick: a bibliography raisonné of editions of The General history of quadrupeds, The History of British birds and The Fables of Aesop issued in his lifetime.* 1953.

P10A

Manchester Public Libraries. *Reference library subject catalogue. Private press books.*

P11

Rosenbach Company. *Check list of English books, printed in England, Scotland and Ireland and on the continent, 1475–1640.* Portland, Maine, n.d.

P12–3

Sadleir, Michael. *XIX century fiction: a bibliographical record based on his own collection.* 1951. 2 volumes.

P14

Saint Bride Foundation, London. *Catalogue of the Technical reference library of works on printing and the allied arts.* 1919.

P15

Steele, Robert. *The Revival of printing: a bibliographical catalogue of works issued by the chief modern English presses; with an introduction by Robert Steele.* London, 1912.

P16

Thurston, Ada, and Buehler, Curt F. *Check list of Fifteenth-century printing in the Pierpont Morgan Library.* New York, 1939.

P17

Universidad de Barcelona. *Incunables de la Biblioteca Universitaria.* Barcelona, 1945.

XI

Q. *Manuscripts*

Q1*

Single leaf from a collection of Vitae Sanctorum, containing parts of the lives of SS. Ursula and Mary of Egypt. Late 13th–14th century.

Q2*

Bifolium containing a list of saints' lives, and two sermons: 'De sancta katherina' and 'De corpore Christi'. 14th century.

Q3*

Single leaf from a work on canon law. 14th century.

Q4*

Manuscript leaf on vellum from a lectionary for Divine Office, 15th century. It contains part of the ninth lesson for the feast of St Vincent Martyr, and the first seven lessons for the Conversion of St Paul.

Q5

Manuscript Book of Hours on vellum, 15th century, with Calendar and rubrics in Dutch.

The signature 'Anna Portebois' occurs on the verso of leaf 17 in a 16th- or 17th-century hand. French binding of the 19th century.

Q6*

Manuscript leaf on vellum from a Bible. Germany, 15th century. It contains Jeremiah X, v. 3–XII, v. 5. It has been mounted with the verso foremost.

Q7*

Manuscript leaf on vellum from the 'Eunuchus' of Terence, written in a round Italian humanist hand, second half of the 15th century.

Q8

Bible. The Holkham Bible picture book; introduction and commentary by W. O. Hassall. London, 1954.

Q9–9B

Book of Kells. 3 volumes. Vol. I, Reproduction of folios 1–182. Vol. II, Reproduction of folios 183–339 end. Vol. III, Introductory. Switzerland, 1950–51.

Q10

Borland, Catherine R. *A Descriptive catalogue of the western mediaeval manuscripts in Edinburgh University Library.* Edinburgh, 1916.

Q11–1C

British Museum. *Illuminated manuscripts in the British Museum: miniatures, borders, and initials reproduced in gold and colours; with descriptive text by George F. Warner.* London, 1899–1903. 4 portfolios.

Q12–2A

Chaucer, Geoffrey. *The Ellesmere Chaucer; reproduced in facsimile.* 1911. 2 volumes.

Q13

British Museum Quarterly. Vol. IV., No. 3. 1929.   JOH.

Q14

Carnaro, Giovanni. *Ioannes Cornelius Dei Gra. dux Venetiar. E.C. commettemo . . . Marin Pesaro diletto cittadin Procur. a Salo, et Capitanio della Riviera . . . 1624.*

Q15

Ferarianus, Jacobus Philippus Androphilus, Frater. *Sacre theologie . . . ? Ferrara, ?1504.*

Q16

Kenyon, Sir Frederic G., edited by. *Facsimiles of Biblical manuscripts in the British Museum.* 1900.

Q17

Lindisfarne Gospels, three plates in colour and thirty-six in monochrome . . . ; with introduction by Eric G. Millar. London, 1923.

Q18

Madan, Falconer. *Books in manuscript, a short introduction to their study and use, with a chapter on records.* London, 1893.

Q19

Pächt, Otto. *The Master of Mary of Burgundy.* London, 1948.

Q20–3

Schilling, Diebold. *Berner Chronik.* 4 volumes. Berne, 1943.

XII

R. *Geographical Books*

R1

1716. London. Gordon, Pat, edited by. *Geography anatomiz'd or, The Geographical grammar.*

R2

1777. London. Guthrie, William. *A New geographical, historical, and commercial grammar, and, Present state of the several kingdoms of the world.*

R3

1780. London. Guthrie, William. *A New system of modern geography; or, A Geographical, historical, and commercial grammar.*

R4

1796. London. Paterson, Daniel. *A New and accurate description of all the direct and principal cross roads in England and Wales*; 11th ed.

R5

1804. London. Guthrie, William. *An Atlas to Guthrie's Geographical grammar.*

R6

1808. London. Paterson, Daniel. *A New and accurate description of all the direct and principal cross roads in England and Wales, and part of the roads of Scotland with correct routes of the mail coaches*; 14th ed.

R7

c. 1812. Edinburgh. Lizars, Daniel. *A New and elegant general atlas of the world, comprehending all the empires, kingdoms and states in the old and new hemispheres* . . . ; beautifully engraved on 59 copper-plates.

R8

1827. Glasgow. Duncan. *Duncan's Itinerary of Scotland, embellished with a correct travelling map of Scotland* . . . ; 6th ed.

R9

c. 1831. London. Paterson, Daniel. *Paterson's Roads, being a* . . . *description of all the direct and principal cross roads in England and Wales with part of the roads of Scotland*; 18th ed. remodelled by Edward Mogg.

XIII

s. *Illustrated Books*

The Printing of Illustrations

As mentioned in the Preface, it was realised during the growth of this collection, that in acquiring books with the purpose of showing the main *typographic* developments of the printed book in western Europe, a number of books were being accumulated which were also of special interest from the point of view of *illustration*, and steps were subsequently taken in the College, over a brief period, to augment the books in this category.

Much of the work was done during the war of 1939–45 and the immediate post-war period, but inevitably came to a halt during the phase of intense development and rehabilitation which followed, since when additions have only infrequently been made. The books in this section therefore do not generally extend beyond the early 1950s, although certain books of interest from the aspect of illustration, issued during the subsequent years, will be found in the general library of the College. There are also naturally obvious gaps and inequalities in the sequence of a selection gathered together under such conditions, and some of the books added during the later war years show very clearly the material restrictions under which they were produced. The books in the collection representative of illustration during the 19th and 20th centuries, that is from the period following the Industrial Revolution, are largely of British origin.

Book illustration and decoration may be considered from many aspects, all of which are interrelated, but in making use of a collection of this kind for educational purposes it is inevitable that the sequence of technical development should play a dominant part, as this has always exerted a controlling influence in design. The principles of design do not change and the true designer has always been very conscious of the possibilities of every new technical resource as it is introduced, exploiting them to the utmost, but always within their respective limitations. The most satisfying books which have been produced, whether hand-written or printed, are those in which all the operations involved in their making have been successfully co-ordinated.

The call for the illustration or decoration of the printed book, as of the manuscript which preceded it, has varied with the requirements of the age and with those of the individuals or institutions who have sponsored it, and can only be fully understood when related to the social, economic, and historical background of the time.

The approach to the illustration of imaginative literature has often but not necessarily always been different from that to the illustration of books dealing with say scientific or historical fact, and in every age there have been those who have had little or no use for the illustration of books, either because they prefer to 'illuminate' them from their own minds or because they are more interested in words and ideas than in facts. Some books call for illustration and are enhanced by it, while others do not require it, and there are many phases in between.

The transition from the manuscript book of the Middle Ages to the printed book of the Renaissance, with the variety of influences which came to bear upon the content and design of the latter, is admirably summarised in the late E. P. Goldschmidt's *The Printed Book of the Renaissance* (G63 in the collection) from which the following paragraphs—up to the beginning of those dealing with the technical aspects (page 414) have for the most part been condensed. References to specially relevant books in the collection have been made in the later paragraphs.

The illustrated book, that is the book carrying *narrative* illustration, is largely a medieval conception. It was the Middle Ages which evolved the great masterpieces of calligraphy and illustration, the combined work of scribe, miniature painter, and illuminator, which were at their supremacy during the two hundred years preceding the invention of printing. Most of these books were devotional in character—bibles, psalters, and prayer books—and the script associated with them is usually some variety of the gothic hand. The earliest of the manuscript books of this period carrying illustrations of secular or worldly subjects are generally those associated with such subjects as medieval romances of chivalry or romanticised history.

But the scholars and 'literati' of the Renaissance rejected this medieval conception of the book, largely because they were interested in a different kind of literature, which was also inevitably associated in their minds with a different form of script.

Italian scholars of the late 14th and early 15th centuries, many of whom were also accomplished calligraphers, revived the study of classical Latin texts and copied them in the round, clear handwriting that they admired in the manuscripts of the 9th–12th centuries. Soon after 1400 they began making the capitals of their script approximate to Roman inscriptional models and so evolved the 'humanistic' handwriting on which the printers' Roman and Italic types are based. The new humanistic scripts, which were in contrast to the more tightly packed, monkish, 'gothic' hands generally practised in the ancient foundations of learning, were strictly confined to books containing the classics and are not associated with legal or ecclesiastical books of the period. After the capture of Constantinople by the Turks in 1453, Greek texts, previously forgotten in western Europe, were brought to Italy, and the study of them became an essential part of the New Learning which spread slowly over the whole of Europe.[1]

Latin was still the universal language of the educated in the 15th century and the Renaissance scholars were largely concerned with the language of their favourite classical authors in their original texts, for which illustration was quite superfluous. The early manuscripts from which they drew inspiration were not illustrated.

Neither illustration nor the gothic character is therefore

[1] For fuller detail see introduction to Typographical Notes, 15th-century.

normally associated with the Renaissance book devoted to the classics, and this differentiation between the humanist book and the legal, theoretical, and devotional book was observed for about a century, not only by the scribes but by their successors the printers. Illustration was regarded by the scholars of the Renaissance as for the 'unlearned', and it did in fact find an increasingly mnemonic application in educational books after the invention of printing.

The book travels, and has been a means of spreading knowledge, ideas, and art forms, especially when for the first time, as a result of the mass production made possible by printing, the book became very largely the property of the individual owner rather than that of the learned institution, to the desks or tables of which it was frequently chained.

Besides traditional romances, the Middle Ages did also possess some literature based on the Antique—stories about the siege of Troy and the wandering Trojan survivors, derived from Homer and Virgil—but in all the illustrations on these themes, no attempt is made to reproduce classical art-forms. Buildings, costumes, etc. appear as in Western Europe of the 15th-century, easily recognisable by the unlearned in a feudal age—as may be verified in some of the pages from 15th-century illustrated books (West-European incunabula) in the Schreiber box-portfolio, J35, referred to later.

Apart from illustrated classics intended for schoolboys, most early illustrated books were printed in the vernacular, as they were not intended for educated Latin scholars but for more popular appeal. It is for this reason that easily understood contemporary symbols are employed.

In 1499 there was printed by Aldus in Venice the *Hypnero-tomachia Poliphili* of Francesco Colonna, which was to become the most famous illustrated book of the Renaissance. It was the first book to bring a scholarly archaeological approach to illustration and was thus a book before its time. It was written by an eccentric cleric in a strange language which cannot be called Latin, and in spite of its magnificent woodcuts—whose designer is unknown—it was in its own day financially a failure.

But in time it did find an appreciative public, not for its unreadable text but through its *designs*, by which it ultimately became the leading source-book of Renaissance ornament.

The *Poliphilus* thus heralded a phase in the Renaissance book when the picture became more important than the text, which is really ancillary to it. The Renaissance was, as already indicated, largely responsible for the death of the 'illustrated' book, that is the book with narrative pictures illustrating an existing story, substituting the 'picture book' or volume of *designs* in its place, the artist taking precedence over the author. Throughout the history of printing there have been books produced on this principle. For instance, many of the publishers of the 'annuals', 'keepsakes', and other drawing-room books of the early 19th century employed eminent artists and engravers to provide pictures for which appropriate text was afterwards written literally as 'illustration',[1] and Walter de la Mare's *This year: next year* (F20 in the collection) was similarly written for Harold Jones's drawings.

Woodcuts by the great Albrecht Dürer (or imitations thereof) found their way all over Europe as separate prints, and his well-known large books on Biblical subjects, such as the *Life of the Virgin* (1511) are also essentially picture-books with ancillary text, rather than illustrated books in the original sense.[2]

Another notable artist whose name is connected with the printed book of the 16th century is Hans Holbein the younger, but as a decorator rather than as an illustrator. Even his well-known drawings for his *Dance of Death*, which somehow passed out of his hands, were made into woodcuts and published in 1538 in a book which makes no reference to his name.[3]

[1] See, for instance, S103 *Christmas tales*, 183–, preface; also S100, *Death's Doings*, 1827, in which the text is described as illustration to the plates.

[2] For monograph on Dürer see J13, A. M. Hind, edited by. *Albrecht Dürer. his engravings and woodcuts*, London, 1911. See also F564, *Albrecht Dürer. Kupferstiche*, Holbein-Verlag, München, 1914, a large folio with fine mounted photogravure reproductions of Dürer's copper-engravings.

[3] See fine small woodcut after Holbein on leaf from 1567 Cologne edition, sheet 39 in J43, box-portfolio, Geisberg, *Woodcuts from books of the 16th century*,

Nevertheless his illustrations (woodcut) to the Bible[1] are naturalistic and magnificent technically, both as designs and as accompaniments to the text.

But Holbein's title-borders set a pattern for book designers, and the title-border became an important factor in disseminating Renaissance art-forms throughout Europe, acquiring also an advertising value in that it became associated with the work of particular printers and publishers. It was pioneered by Ratdolt and Maler in 1476 and became current during the 16th-century. The Renaissance had revived an interest in classical architecture as a leading form of art, so that the most frequent conception for the title-page border is the Roman arch with its supporting columns—so aptly described by Goldschmidt as 'the semblance of a gateway leading into an antique temple'.

This form of title-border, particularly through the influence of Holbein, accumulated every variety of Renaissance motif, especially as it passed through the 'Fontainebleau' and later rococo phases.[2] The titles to books of the 16th-century became in fact a happy hunting ground for the designer in search of such motifs, including also those of Byzantine origin, and it may be noted that it was in the latter half of this century that typographic ornaments, fleurons, and 'arabesques' began to appear. It is significant also that the *Poliphilus* was re-issued in Venice and in Paris in the middle of the century.

Another element of antique art revived during the Renaissance was the medal, and Roman coins provided inspiration

---

and sheet 38 of the same, Zurich, 1543, which shows small woodcut Bible illustrations after Holbein. See also S21, a Frankfurt edition of *Dance of death*, 1649, with copper-engravings by Matthew Merian the Elder, and S48, *Dance of death* (*Todtentanz*). *Emblems of Mortality*, London, 1789, small 8vo, containing quite accomplished wood-engravings elaborated from Holbein's designs. This little volume is lettered on the spine '*Bewick's* Dance of Death' (ital. ours) but the justification of this ascription—either to Thomas or to John Bewick—is still the subject of doubt. For Geisberg see pp. 90–94 of this catalogue.

[1] Adam Petri's editions of Luther's *New Testament*, Basle, 1522 and 1523, Thomas Wolff's edition of the same work, 1523, and Petri's edition of Luther's Old Testament, 1523.

[2] See pp. 420–1.

for elements of design in architecture and in all the crafts.[1]

Pattern books showing all these classical motifs, revived from the Antique by Renaissance influence, began to appear at this time for the use of craftsmen, and extended to such fields as lace-books and embroidery-books.[2]

As the title-border developed something of the character of an advertising symbol, it often incorporated another feature of the 16th-century book, the printer's or publisher's device, generally more elaborate and decorative than the early printers'

[1] See, for examples, S4, Fulvius, A., *Illustrium imagines*, Rome, 1517, small 4to, portrait medallions of Roman emperors and their consorts, with historiated woodcut borders enclosing biographical notes in italic: the medallions, one at the head of each page, in white on black ground, perhaps metal cut; S9, Vico, E., *Le imagini delle Donne Auguste . . .*, Venice, 1557, 4to, copper-engravings of portrait medallions in elaborate or grotesque (generally architectural) Renaissance border frames or background, woodcut historiated initials, finely engraved title; S13, Agostin, A., *I discorsi del S. Don Antonio Agostini sopra le medaglie et altre anticaglie*, Rome, [1592], 4to, numerous attractively freely drawn etchings of coins, usually twelve to a page, preceding text section: wholly engraved title with portrait of author on verso, in elaborate border-frame including heraldic cartouche. See also the following plates from Geisberg, the box-portfolio abovementioned: Pl. 9, Strada, *Imperatorum Roman. imagines*, Zurich, 1559, Fol., vigorous large-scale woodcut portrait-medallions on verso, with architectural surround and border for inscription below: on recto, typically elaborate late-Renaissance border, surrounding text in roman, and six finely cut arabesque medallions; Pl. 44, Keller, *Bildtnussen der Rhömischen Keyseren*, Zurich, 1558, 8vo, two small cuts, obverse and reverse, on text-page, probably woodcut, but in 'metal-cut' style, white on black ground, the main portions of which appear to have been inked in by hand after printing; Pl. 60, Goltzius, H., *Imperatorum Romanorum imagines*, Antwerp, 1557, 4to, large portrait-medallion described as 'etching (chiaroscuro)', although this probably applies to the line printing only, as the tint-printings appear to be from woodblocks—the usual technique—see David Bland, *A History of Book Illustration*, London, Faber, 1958, p. 151 (in College General Library).

[2] Two characteristic examples of pages from lace-books are included in the Geisberg portfolio: plate 94, Cesare Vecellio, *Corona della nobili donne*, Venice, 1591, and plate 95, E. C. Parasole, *Pretiosa gemma delle virtuose donne*, Venice, 1600. Both are oblong 8vos, and the graceful patterns, cut into the block, print, appropriately to the subject, in white on black. See also G63, E. P. Goldschmidt, *The Printed Book of the Renaissance* CUP, 1950, pp. 77–8; and for further information on lace and embroidery books see E. F. Strange, *Early Pattern-books of Lace Embroidery and Needlework*, Bib. Soc. Transactions, vol. 7, London, 1904; Palliser, Mrs Bury, *History of Lace*, revised by M. Jourdain and Alice Dryden, London, 1902; and Lotz, A., *Bibliographie der Modelbücher*, Stuttgart, 1863—all in National Library of Scotland.

marks which, when printer and publisher were almost always the same person, were at first used largely as trade-marks, for the protection of the books against piracy. And so there developed the printer's or publisher's mark pure and simple, and it is specially interesting that Aldus, the supreme classical and scholarly printer of the period, was a pioneer in its introduction to the book of the Renaissance. But the significant point is that his device was not an 'illustration', nor a 'picture', but an *emblem*—a 'conceit'—and was thus acceptable to the literati; and the printers' (or publishers') marks which followed thenceforth freely introduced Renaissance motifs.[1]

We can thus trace a train of thought from 'illustration' to 'design', and from 'design' to 'emblem'; and emblem books came in with a flood in the 16th century, following the publication of Alciati's book in Augsburg in 1531.

But with the development of humanistic thought and empiricism, and the desire to enlarge the bounds of human knowledge, which stemmed from the Renaissance and was so greatly facilitated by the mass-production of books made possible by printing, the range of subject-matter for illustration became correspondingly enlarged, embracing such fields as science, mathematics, astronomy, anatomy, and medicine, as well as the arts and crafts; and the growth of lay patronage following the decline of the feudal system helped forward this development. For such work illustration ultimately became more factual and representational, as will be realised, for instance, in the study of the development of such books as herbals, in the earlier examples of which the illustration is stylised and conventional, with little attempt at verisimilitude. David Bland has pointed out that the invention of printing coincided with a movement towards naturalism in art.

Having very briefly brought the general subject of illustration to the point where it enters wider fields, it may now be

[1] For information, amply illustrated, concerning the various forms of printers' marks, see H. W. Davies, *Devices of the Early Printers, 1457-1560*, London, 1935; W. Roberts, *Printers' Marks*, London, 1893; and also Goldschmidt, *The Printed Book of the Renaissance*, pp. 78–83.

appropriate to consider some of the aspects of technical development, especially in their relationship to the development of design, on which, as already stated, they have always exerted some controlling influence.

From the foregoing it will be seen that the incursion of illustration into the printed book was a slow development, and the early printers naturally found themselves working in competition (or collaboration) with the scribe and the illuminator, who had held the field unchallenged for many centuries before the advent of printing. It was therefore to be expected that they should follow the design of the manuscript-books which they sought to replace, as may be seen by comparing the leaf from the 'Gutenberg' or Mazarin Bible (A1* in the collection) with the manuscript vellum leaf (Q6*) in identical format. Indeed there is little doubt that most of the pioneer printers wished their books to simulate the manuscript as far as possible, and in some cases tried to palm them off as such, but by many patrons of literature printing was regarded as a poor substitute for the manuscript, the art of which continued to flourish long after the invention of typography. One advantage which the illuminator had over the early printer was the production of coloured illustration.

The scribe, and in some cases the illuminator, did in fact add rubrication, initials, and sometimes decoration to many printed books for about half a century after the invention of printing— spaces and 'guide-letters' being left for these purposes by the printer[1]—but it was not logical to slow down mass-production by combining it with handwork. Moreover, paper, as a mass-produced material, could not by its nature provide a worthy and workable base for the work of the illuminator, as can be seen by comparing the large capital on leaf 2 of A13, *Vitas patrum*, Koberger, Nuremberg, 1483, with Q5, a 15th-century illuminated manuscript on vellum from the Low Countries. The printer therefore soon began to provide these accessories from his own resources, and details of these phases are fully recorded in Mr Carter's typographical notes on the individual books.

[1] As may be seen by examples in the collection.

415

Conversely, some early printers—as have others since—occasionally *printed* on vellum, and although it is not appropriate to employ such a valuable natural material for mass-production, and difficult to secure an even impression upon it owing to its varying thickness, yet in careful hands it could provide a print of intense black and great richness of tone, as may be convincingly seen by comparing the block on the vellum leaf of the original 1517 Nuremberg edition of *Theuerdanck* (leaf 22 in J43, the Geisberg box-folio abovementioned) with the same block on paper in the Augsburg edition of 1537 (B51), and also by examining the magnificent trial pages for an edition of Froissart printed on vellum by William Morris in 1897 (F310B*).

Before the invention of printing from movable type, the press and relief processes of printing were in operation in the production of playing cards, broadsides, and perhaps also 'block-books' (in which both text and illustration were cut in relief, sometimes on the same wood-block) although it is a provocative fact that none of the last-mentioned have come down to us with a date prior to that of the advent of typography, and it may even be that the invention of printing from movable type quickened the work of the makers of these earlier forms of relief printing.[1]

Much of the earlier block printing was produced *au frotton*, that is, independently of a press, simply by positioning the paper on the inked block, and rubbing the back of the paper by hand to give the impression. But, having a relief surface, the wood-block had the advantage that it could be assembled and printed with type, and evidence indicates that a number of the early craftsmen engaged in the production of wood-blocks were among the first illustrators of books printed from movable type. At Augsburg there existed a guild of craftsmen engaged in the production of wood-blocks before the invention of printing from movable type, and although Albrecht Pfister of Bamberg was the first to issue books with woodcuts in about 1461, it is at Augsburg about

---

[1] A photographic reproduction of a block-book may be seen in item S1, *Biblia pauperum,* and a line-block facsimile in S2, *Exercitium super Pater Noster.*

ten years later that the production of printed illustrated books may be said to commence, and a fine series of pages from 15th-century illustrated books printed at this centre from 1471 to the end of the century may be seen in the great Schreiber portfolio (J35 abovementioned), which also includes representative pages from other German towns. Many of these early wood-block illustrations are hand-coloured, a rough but sometimes effective substitute for illumination, and Goldschmidt states that most, if not all, the early wood-cutters appear to have been Germans.

The early wood-blocks were generally cut with a knife in the side-grain of soft woods such as pear-wood, but soft metal such as pewter was also sometimes used, giving a sharper finish and encouraging the development of stippled or *criblé* effects, the design being rendered in 'white-on-black', thus anticipating the 'white-line' technique developed by Bewick and other wood-engravers some three centuries later. After the end of the 15th-century the blocks were seldom engraved by the artist who provided the illustration.

The wood-block has a natural affinity with type, not only as a printing surface, already mentioned, but as an illustration or decoration to the printed page, and some of the early examples show a simplicity and consistency of line in close harmony with that of the type-face accompanying. But with the increasing skill of the block-cutter there were naturally developed more detailed and sophisticated techniques in the rendering of tone values, such as 'shading' or simple cross-hatching, until the woodcut was generally supplanted, as the main method of illustration, by copperplate engraving, at the end of the 16th century.

All these phases of the wood-block can be well studied, not only in the Schreiber portfolio abovementioned, containing 55 leaves from woodcut illustrated books of the 15th-century, and in the equally impressive Geisberg portfolio containing 100 leaves with woodcuts from the 16th-century, but also in individual books in the collection; for instance, two early English examples may be seen in B21, *Cronycle of Englonde,*

London, 1520, and B33, *Golden Legend*, London, 1527, both printed by de Worde. An earlier example, in the form of a single leaf only, may be seen in F641, Hart. J. D., *Sebastian Brant and his ship of fools*, San Francisco, 1938, which includes an original leaf from the first edition of the *Ship of Folys*, the English translation of this popular book printed by Richard Pynson in London in 1509; and it is interesting to compare this with the leaf from Bergmann de Olpe's Basle edition of 1497 (plate 24 in Schreiber)—from the original (1494) edition of which the blocks used by Pynson were copied—and with a leaf from the Strasburg edition, also of 1497 (plate 30 in Schreiber).

The Schreiber portfolio includes leaves from some famous incunabula, such as Koberger's *Schatzbehalter*, Nuremberg, 1491, and the German-text edition of the *Weltchronik* (the 'Nuremberg Chronicle', Nuremberg, 1493), which characteristically is in *Schwabacher* type as compared with the famous Latin-text edition in the customary *rotunda*, A18 in the collection.[1] Incidentally, a point of interest in this great volume is that the large cut of Nuremberg shows, in the foreground, the earliest representation in a printed book of a paper-mill. This is reproduced on Plate 15 of K7, *Das Buch vom Papier*, by Armin Renker, Wiesbaden, 1950, a beautifully produced book printed in Stuttgart (on handmade paper), with collotype reproductions, and published by Insel-Verlag.

In the Schreiber assemblage may also be traced the transition from the early and roughly-cut narrative illustration to the stylised Renaissance 'designs', of which an example may be seen on sheet 50, from a Venetian edition of the *Divina commedia* printed in 1497, where it will also be noted that Italian *rotunda* has now given way to Roman—a much more harmonious companion to the designs. Another characteristic feature, already referred to, which may be followed in this series, is the use of 15th-century costume and architecture in the illustration of classical themes.

The brief but unique flowering of woodcut illustration in

[1] See A. M. Hind, *An Introduction to the History of the Woodcut*, London, 1935, vol. I, p. 374 *et seq.* and index to the same, p. 810, in College General Library.

Florence from 1492 to 1506 is not represented by an *original* book in the collection, but the beautiful edition of *Æsop's Fables* designed by Bruce Rogers for the Limited Editions Club, N.Y., and issued in 1933 (F380 in the collection) reproduces some very representative examples of this period, showing their characteristic simple ornamented borders. Printed at the University Press, Oxford, on fine handmade paper to the accompaniment of Fell type for the text, the 48 line-blocks succeed in conveying much of the old woodcuts' original flavour, and Victor Scholderer in his introduction states that the originals go back at least to 1496.[1]

But among the most interesting specimens in the collection to study in connexion with the development of woodcut illustration are undoubtedly those of the various editions of Colonna's famous *Poliphilus*, already referred to. The Schreiber portfolio includes two leaves (plates 52 and 53) from the original edition of Aldus of 1499 with its woodcuts of elemental simplicity and grace, in a pure 'line' in perfect harmony with the text, and S3 is a line-block facsimile of this edition. S5 is a copy of the 1545 revised and corrected edition with the original illustrations, but text type with a different and much less satisfactory set of capitals, and plate 69 of Geisberg is from a Paris Edition of 1554, with woodcuts of great beauty but more elaborate and sophisticated than those of the original edition, and showing more general use of three-dimensional shading or 'tone'. A very fine folio volume with beautiful woodcuts or architectural subjects and woodcut initals is B23, Vitruvius, *De architectura*, Como, 1521—described in the Typographical Notes. The Geisberg portfolio also includes examples of illustration by such artists as Dürer, Holbein, Jost Amman, Tory, and Bernard Salomon.[2] Incidentally plate 60 is described as an example of the 'etching (chiaroscuro)' process.[3]

At the time of the advent of typography Paris was a stronghold of the manuscript trade and was notable for its *Horae* or

---

[1] See Goldschmidt, *The Printed Book of the Renaissance*, pp. 53–55.
[2] See also Holbein Society facsimiles, E123-5.
[3] See footnote, p. 413.

books of hours with illuminated borders made up of small pictures of appropriate subjects. The printers who ultimately succeeded in establishing themselves in this centre, outstanding of whom are Pigouchet, Vostre and Vérard, maintained this tradition in the design of those beautiful little books which are especially associated with the *manière criblé* in their wood- or metal-cut borders and also in the larger pictures, generally at the beginning of sections, which these borders sometimes surrounded. Vérard, himself a calligrapher and illuminator, printed certain copies on vellum in which painters added illumination and ornament. An example of the work of Pigouchet, from a book of hours printed for Vostre in 1499, may be seen in A71*, a single leaf from Haebler (WEI 39); and characteristic leaves from such devotional books printed in Paris, with metal-cut borders and illustration, may be seen in Geisberg plate 62, *Officium B.V.M.*, 1505, and plate 63, *Horae*, 1514—in each case the printer is unknown.

Reference has been made in the Typographical Notes, under the 16th-century, to Geoffroy Tory and the influence on French typography of his famous *Champ fleury*, printed in 1529. It is also shown that it was Tory who introduced Italian influence into his books of hours, with borders of classical ornament taking the place of medieval illustration, and 'antique' or Roman type replacing the Black Letter of Pigouchet and Vostre. This may be clearly seen in sheet 64 of Geisberg (*Horae*, Paris, 1524/5) and in the volume B45 (*Horae*, Paris, 1531); and a 20th-century edition of *Champ fleury*, in general facsimile, designed by Bruce Rogers, and set in Centaur type, with line-block reproductions from the original designs, printed by W. E. Rudge for the Grolier Club, N.Y., 1927 (F689 in the collection) shows clearly something of the original impact of this work.

France came under the influence of the Italian Renaissance when François I (1515–47) conducted wars with Italy, very evident in the decorations with which this monarch covered the walls of Fontainebleau, the great palace begun in 1528, which became the centre of French Renaissance. French illustration began to show this influence, becoming more dramatic and 'mannered', and displaying a more conscious grace in its attenuated figures, with classical themes and mythological subjects (such, for instance, as Ovid's *Metamorphoses*) becoming especially dominant. The pursuit of emblems and allegories became in fact almost an obsession among the fashionable dilettanti of the period.

In this connexion reference has already been made to the stream of emblem books which followed the issue of Alciati's original edition in Augsburg in 1531, and a good selection of these may be seen in the collection. The earliest example is sheet 66 of Geisberg from a Paris edition of 1536, showing a good woodcut, and the earliest volume is S6, a Lyons edition printed by Roville in 1551, with lively and well-executed illustrations in the manner of Bernard Salomon, some of which are almost drowned by noisy and grotesque ornamental borders surrounding the page. Other examples are S10, S11 (a rare Antwerp edition of 1565), S15 and S16.

Bernard Salomon, 'Le Petit Bernard', worked at Lyons for Jean de Tournes the Elder, and his spirited little designs, reproduced by well-executed woodcuts in which delicate shading and occasional cross-hatching are employed, are typical of the Franco-Italian school of Fontainebleau. Salomon's work is also excellently represented in the collection, his Bible illustrations in B76-77 and B79, and those for the *Metamorphoses*, with typical ornamental frames to each page, some from the workshop of Tory, in B88.[1] Further examples are plates 76 and 78 of Geisberg, and arabesque ornaments, attributable to Salomon, appear in B89-90, the Froissart volumes printed by de Tournes the Younger.

During the 16th-century woodcut borders were increasingly employed in printed books, especially around titles, and those in the collection have been recorded in the Typographical Notes, along with details of initial letters, which are frequently

[1] See T. M. MacRobert, 'Jean de Tournes' [the Elder], *Motif 2*, edited by Ruari McLean, London, Shenval Press, February 1959 (one of nine issues of this periodical presented to the College in 1969 by W. B. Hislop).

historiated. The cult of classicism, reflected in 'Roman-arch' title-borders, may be observed in many of these examples, and the influence of the *Poliphilus*, the Emblem books, and the work of Holbein may also be followed in the great variety of motifs employed.[1]

Woodcut illustration reached its highest degree of accomplishment during the 16th-century, particularly in France with such artists as Le Petit Bernard and Bernard Cousin, and the technique of wood-cutting was carried about as far as possible within its natural limitations, but in the latter part of the century the woodcut began to be supplanted, as the main method of illustration, by metal-engraving, which in turn held the field almost unchallenged for about 200 years.[2] In metal-engraving—an 'intaglio' process, the reverse from relief printing—the design is cut with a graver or 'burin' into the surface of a polished metal plate—usually copper—which is inked and wiped clean, leaving the inked design in the hollows of the plate, from which it is drawn by considerable pressure on a copperplate press or 'mangle'. Metal-engraved book illustration was begun in Florence in the last quarter of the 15th-century, but more than a century elapsed before it generally displaced the wood-block. The earlier examples were evidently produced by separate stamping by hand, as in the case of the early prints from wood-blocks, and the impression obtained with the ink used was pale or 'grey' in tone compared with that obtained by the early printers from wood-block and movable type.

Metal-engraving had the advantage over the woodcut in that it could give finer and more precise detail and a more subtle range of tone. It could also give a single black line by means of a single cut, which in wood-cutting normally required at least two. In addition various types of lettering and script could be produced easily and naturally by a skilled engraver—in some

---

[1] See also J23, McKerrow and Ferguson, *Title-page borders used in England and Scotland, 1485–1640*, Bibliographical Society Illustrated Monograph No. XXI, 1932, and O13 A. F. Johnson, *One hundred title-pages, 1500–1800*, London, 1928.

[2] See J25, W. Y. Ottley, . . . *Early history of engraving upon copper and in wood*, London, 1816.

cases almost as quickly as they could be written.[1] But despite all these advantages metal-engraving introduced a note of complexity into the printed book, since text and illustration could no longer be printed together in one operation, so that the book ceased to be technically or aesthetically a unit. It is for this reason that books with the best examples of woodcut illustration possess a quality which metal-engraving could never quite supplant. Moreover, the advent of the print-seller, who developed the use of metal-engraving for the reproduction of pictures, and who sold illustrations direct to publishers and booksellers, was another factor in increasing the separation of 'illustrations' from 'text'. A few printers undoubtedly maintained engravers on their staff, or dealt direct with them, as may be observed in the records and collection of plates of the Musée Plantin in Antwerp, some of the plates having been engraved after designs by Peter Paul Rubens and his pupils for Moretus, Plantin's son-in-law and successor, who was so influential in the development of copperplate illustration during the 17th century. Specific examples of books in the collection printed by Plantin and Moretus are referred to in a later paragraph.

With the almost complete eclipse of the woodcut, which could so readily be associated with type, and the general acceptance of metal-engraving—which could not—there is a marked reduction of pictorial illustration in the book of the 17th century. Popular engravers were concerned with its decoration rather than its illustration.[2] The woodcut title-border

[1] For comparison of wood-cutting with wood-*engraving* (to which some of the above observations do not necessarily apply) see later, under Bewick and the 19th century.

[2] Notable among these, working principally in England, were Renold Elstracke, perhaps a native of Belgium (whose engraved portraits include one of Mary Queen of Scots), the extraordinarily accomplished and diligent Wenceslaus Hollar, born in Prague in 1607 and especially notable as an etcher and architectural draughtsman, and William Faithorne the Elder, among whose works is a portrait of Milton, dated 1670. A carefully documented and excellently illustrated article on Hollar, by Margery Martin, will be found in *Motif* 4, 1960, but it does not directly convey the duress and adversity under which Hollar worked, as his life covers the period of the Civil War (in which he was involved) the Great Plague, and the Fire of London.

almost disappeared and was replaced in many cases by the engraved title-page which, especially through the influence of the Plantin office, sometimes became very elaborate; and the engraved frontispiece—usually a portrait of the author—followed as a logical sequence.[1] Decorative headbands, tailpieces, and initials, for which space had to be allowed, were also metal-engraved. A small proportion of woodcut work was maintained, convincingly shown, for instance, in S20, *Bibels tresoor*, Amsterdam, 1646, 4to, which contains 797 quite vigorous woodcut illustrations to the Bible and the Apocrypha, showing a varied range of tone values obtained by sensitively cut line-shading, without cross-hatching. Some are copied from Dürer, and again the costume and architecture are for the most part Dutch. But the principal phases in the design and decoration of the printed book during the 17th- and 18th-centuries are fully summarised in the introductions to the Typographical Notes.

Etching, as used by artists and first developed during the 16th century, has had its place in book illustration. It is also normally the basis for metal-engraving in indicating at least the first outlines of the design. In etching, a copper or sometimes steel plate is coated with a 'ground', consisting of a mixture of asphaltum, resin, and beeswax, into which the artist draws with a needle, thus clearing the ground and leaving his design in exposed copper to be bitten into the surface of the plate by subsequent etchings with acid. The ground is smoke-blackened to aid definition of the work. A few early books contain etchings, generally separately inserted as illustrations, or pasted in, and the free line that this process gives by the needle working into the wax, which offers little resistance, makes it a suitable process for spontaneous drawing and the quick recording of scenes or objects which may have originally been sketched on the spot, but in its earlier phases etched illustration seldom ties up happily with the printed page, being

[1] See the fully illustrated article on 'The Cartouche in English Engraving in the 16th and 17th centuries', by Margery Corbett, in *Motif 10*, Winter 1962–3, which shows something of the extraordinary complexity reached in the ornamental use of the volute or scroll, with its many associated emblems, in its development from the classical style of the early Renaissance to the most exuberant Baroque.

frequently on paper of a different quality and colour, and sometimes of a different size.

With etching should also be mentioned 'drypoint', which is engraving with a specially sharpened etching-needle, without the use of acid. Drawing is made direct upon the polished copper plate, which bears no ground, and in working the needle throws up a 'burr', which gives the characteristic 'double-line' in the print. Drypoint, which is the most spontaneous of all methods of engraving, is also found in some early books, sometimes along with etchings. It is also sometimes used in conjunction with bitten-in work—and with other forms of engraving—in which cases the 'burr' is removed with a scraper.

While etching is essentially a means of 'direct expression' by the artist (which accounts for its later especial popularity among cartoonists and illustrators of the 18th- and 19th-centuries) copper-engraving, with its hard, incised line and elaborate formal cross-hatching employed in the rendering of tone-values, is essentially a process of *reproduction,* even if the artist is working from his own design.

A more subtle form of metal-engraving, in use from the 16th century but notably developed during the 18th, is that of stipple-engraving, which, on account of its peculiar suitability in rendering the form and lineaments of the flesh and the texture of costume, found a wide usage in production of portrait prints—generally reproducing oil paintings—and for finely drawn portrait-frontispieces in bookwork. Stipple is also a useful and natural ancillary to other forms of engraving—especially 'line'. In stipple-engraving the result is achieved by carefully graded dots initially made with an etching needle and strengthened with the graver after etching. The graver used has its point turned downwards for pecking out the metal, as opposed to that used for line-engraving which has the point curved upward for removing the metal cleanly from the incised lines.

'Chalk-engraving', a form of stipple using a rather coarser dot, enjoyed a brief vogue in the latter half of the 18th century, especially in France, notably for the reproduction of chalk

425

drawings by old masters, until it was displaced by the newly-discovered lithography. The tendency for the over-use of red or red-brown inks for this work is noticeable in the popular prints, generally of the more sentimental subjects, which were characteristic of the period. Francesco Bartolozzi, the eminent Italian engraver, invited to London in 1764 by George III's librarian, did much to familiarise a wider public with the use of stipple- and chalk-engraving, and many books catering for the more elegant tastes of the 18th- and 19th-centuries are 'embellished' with this kind of illustration—see, for instance, D100, a large folio edition of Thomson's *Seasons*, London, 1797, referred to later.

The development of all the foregoing methods of metal-engraving may be clearly followed by study of books in the collection. For example, S13, Agostin, A., *I discorsi . . . sopra le medaglie*, Rome [1592], referred to in the footnote under Coin Books on p. 413, shows the characteristically free line of etching. S14, *Apologi creaturarum*, Plantin, Antwerp 1592, shows interesting etched illustrations on the paper of the text, not always well registered and one upside-down with amendment inserted. It will be seen that the grey tone and the technique of the etchings do not make for homogeneity in the page. This book has a line-engraved title-illustration with border-frame of architectural motifs. C38, *De veteribus Ægyptiorum ritibus*, Rome 1644–45, has good copperplates, but roughly executed etchings in text. The full-page illustrations to S28, *Honor and Armory*, London, 1673, are almost entirely etched, with etched title pasted in, in addition to typographic title. S35, Evelyn's *Architecture*, London, 1707, shows fine line-engraved illustrations in the body of the work, with supplementary illustrations at the end which are for the most part very sketchily drawn etchings or drypoints, perhaps made on the spot. It is interesting to compare the engraved illustrations in this book with those of similar subjects in S30, Amsterdam, 1694, and S34, London, 1700, which are etchings, and also with the earlier woodcut illustrations of architectural subjects in say B23, the great Vitruvius volume, Como, 1521, already referred to (p. 419).

The influence of Plantin and Moretus in the application of copper-engraving to the illustration and ornamentation of the printed book has already been referred to, and B118, the folio *Bible* (1583) printed by Plantin at Antwerp, is a notable early example of a book in which can be observed a slight overlap over the column-rules of some of the single-column illustrations, showing the difficulty in obtaining close register of the engraved illustration with the separately printed text. A fine example of the printing of Jean Moretus, with engraved illustration, is C3, Natalus, H., *Adnotationes et meditationes in Evangelia*, 1607, and an example of that of Balthasar Moretus (grandson of Christopher Plantin) is C16, *Les ordonnances de l'Ordre de la Toison d'or*, undated [1626], printed on vellum. C60, *Officium B. Mariae Virg.*, 1677, a 32mo devotional book printed by B. Moretus, is of interest in that it employs woodcuts at this period. S17, Radi, *Varie inventioni per depositi*, Rome, 1625, and S19, Passe, *Oficina Arcularia*, Amsterdam, 1642, two works bound together in one folio volume, show copper engravings of characteristic baroque architectural façades and features, in each case with engraved titles, and S25-7, *Les Travaux de Mars*, Amsterdam, 1672, are three octavo volumes containing numerous interesting full-page copper engravings of consistently high standard.

A magnificent example of a book of architectural illustration, engraved throughout, is S29, *Oxonia illustrata*, Oxford, 1675, in splendid binding with all the plates securely guarded in. The engraving is by David Loggan, 'calcographer' to the University, and the finely engraved letter of Royal Command facing the title grants to him the copyright of the plates for fifteen years. The binding, in black sheepskin, bears in stamped gilt the arms and crest of the Hon. Robert Spencer. Other 17th-century examples of copper-engraved illustration are in C52, C68, C69-70, and C74.

C66 and C77 have special interest in that they are examples of books *engraved throughout*, of which D10, *The Book of Common Prayer*, 8vo, printed by John Sturt, London, 1717, is a notable 18th-century example. With text in double-column, ruled in red, very delicate engravings at the head of each column, and a variety of engraved borders—and with the inclusion of a volvette for use in ascertaining the date of Easter—this book altogether represents a very remarkable sustained effort on the part of the engraver. For further particulars of this book and descriptions of those before enumerated, see Typographical Notes.

An outstanding example of early 18th-century English book production with engraved illustration is S36, the great folio edition of *Caesar's Commentaries*, with notes by Samuel Clarke, London, 1712, printed for Tonson, in which title, frontispiece, plates, headpieces, tailpieces, and historiated initials are all line-engraved. The title design occupies two facing pages and there is a fine frontispiece portrait of the Duke of Marlborough. The double-page engraving of a bison between pages 134 and 135 is a *tour de force*. C74, the folio edition of Pindar, Oxford, 1697, and S37, a folio edition of 'Cave's Lives', London, 1716, show copper-plate engravings by Michael Burghers, at one time engraver to the University of Oxford—see Typographical Notes, under C74.

One of the most famous and influential books in the history of printing is the *Médailles de Louis le Grand*, the celebrated folio printed at the Imprimerie Royale and issued in 1702 after over a decade of sustained planning and production. This book (which is fully described in the Typographical Notes) is notable for its successful juxtaposition of the finest copperplate engraving with a specially commissioned text-type which shows the influences of this form of engraving in its evolution.[1] The changing features of the King from infancy to old age are progressively revealed in the engravings of the medals as one turns the pages, and a sequence of superbly engraved borders is employed to enclose illustration and text. The copy in the

---

[1] In this connexion, O28, *The Typographic arts, past, present and future: a lecture delivered at the College of Art, Edinburgh, 17 February 1944*, by Stanley Morison, is of particular interest in providing reproductions of the copperplate pattern-alphabets, evolved as a result of the work by the special commission set up by the Académie des Sciences to determine the shaping of the new royal types.

College, D1, is in perfect condition and one of the most important books in the collection.

Notable examples of 18th-century books printed in Italy with metal engravings are S39, Tasso's *La Gerusalemme liberata*, 1745, a folio printed in Venice with fine plates, borders, head- and tail-pieces and historiated initials; D31-3, *Musei Capitolini*, Rome, 1748–55, in three large folio volumes; and *Descrizione delle feste . . .*, a large quarto printed by Bodoni in Parma in or after 1769, which also has engraved plates, title, head- and tail-pieces and initials D58. D63, the well-known folio Sallust, *La Conjuracion de Catilina y la Guerra de Jugurta*, 1772, printed in Madrid by Ibarra, Spain's most distinguished printer, is another noteworthy book in the collection, with engraved title, plates, and ornament.

One of the successfully designed books of the elegant pre-Revolutionary period in France is the edition of La Fontaine's *Contes et nouvelles*, sponsored by a group of amateur-financier bibliophiles known as *Les Fermiers généraux*, and issued in 1762 in octavo size with exquisitely engraved illustrations by Eisen and text-type and typographical ornament by Fournier, all brought together with unerring skill.[1] S42 is the 1777 edition of this book, in two volumes, employing Fournier's condensed type; there are also a few woodcut ornaments in the preliminaries. Woodcut ornament does in fact persist in a number of 17th- and 18th-century books, in many cases looking almost crudely uncomfortable in association with metal engraving. D82-5, the 4-volume octavo *Bible—Gospels—Latin and French*, Paris, 1793, with engraved frontispiece and plates after drawings by Moreau le jeune, shows something of the influence of the Didots at the end of the century.

S56 is a quarto Scottish edition of Thomson's *Seasons* printed with distinction by Morison of Perth and issued in 1793 with

---

[1] For apt comment on the subject-matter of these illustrations by Eisen, see David Bland, *The Illustration of Books*, London, Faber, 1951, p. 51; and for comment on French 18th-century illustration generally, see *A History of Book Illustration*, 1958, by the same author, pp. 210–12 *et seq.* (in Printing section of the College General Library).

engraved frontispiece and plates, and it is interesting to compare this with D100 (already mentioned under chalk-engraving), a London edition of the same work printed in large folio by Bensley and issued in 1797 with characteristic engravings by Bartolozzi after equally characteristic illustrations by Hamilton, all of which appear Italianate rather than English in character. Other examples of stipple-engraving of 1799 are the oval portraits in S60-1, Junius, *Letters*, the text of which was also printed by Bensley, with woodcut head- and tail-pieces and title-device. Each volume also includes a finely engraved title. Volume 1 of S138 *The scenery and antiquities of Ireland*, London, [1842], 2 volumes, carries a portrait-frontispiece, finely stipple-engraved by F. C. Lewis, engraver to the Queen.

Aquatint is an interesting and beautiful intaglio process associated with book illustration in the late 18th- and early 19th-centuries, especially with large volumes on topographical subjects—such as those issued by the publisher and bookseller Rudolph Ackermann from his Repository of Fine Arts in the Strand—and with the work of the great English artist-caricaturist Thomas Rowlandson. The interest of this process is that it is essentially 'etching in tone', from which present-day photogravure is a logical development. In aquatint a resinously grained copper plate is painted by hand with an acid-resisting varnish, and selectively etched to varying depths by successive paintings-out and etchings. It is normally combined with ordinary etching and engraving to provide the line-work, and it was generally hand-coloured. Excellent examples of all the phases of aquatint may be seen in the collection, including its first use in the 1780's—with a charming simplicity—in the small oval scenic pictures, with single-colour wash, in the Rev. William Gilpin's octavo guide-books—see S45-6, S50-1, and also S49, J. Hassell's *Tour of the Isle of Wight*, in the same format. The Rev. Gilpin was later 'guyed' in the well-known *Tours of Dr. Syntax*, published by Ackermann in about 1819 in three attractively designed volumes with characteristic care-free illustrations by Rowlandson, reproduced in aquatint and brightly hand-coloured—S85-7 in the collection.

Among Ackermann's contemporaries and friends was C. A. Pugin, an architectural draughtsman, and Ackermann conceived the idea of bringing together Pugin and Rowlandson for his *microcosm of London* (the first parts of which began to appear in 1808) and for similar descriptive illustrated books on Oxford, Cambridge, and other cities, Rowlandson to enliven Pugin's precise draughtsmanship by peopling his architectural interiors with characteristic figures of the period. For further details and reproductions see S311, *The microcosm of London*, in the King Penguin series; and examples of Pugin's work, together with that of other artists, may be seen in S73, *The . . . Abbey Church of St. Peter's Westminster . . .*, published by Ackermann in two large volumes in 1812. Ackermann did much to develop the process of aquatint during the early 19th-century, and observations concerning the hand-colouring of prints for book-illustration, which was frequently carried out by children, are given below in the paragraph devoted to Thomas Frognall Dibdin (pp. 442–3).[1]

In connexion with the earliest use of aquatint a volume worthy of examination is S47, Allan Ramsay's *The Gentle Shepherd*, published in Glasgow in 1788 and illustrated with aquatint engravings by David Allan, the Scottish historical painter, which show very clearly the characteristic grain. Of special interest is David Allan's comment in the Dedication in which he explains the advantages of aquatint as a means of book-illustration 'for one trained as a painter'. At this period may be observed an increased use of wove paper in bookwork, not only for separately printed plates in illustrated books, but for the text also, and it may be noted that whereas this edition of *The Gentle Shepherd* is printed on laid papers throughout, Dr Gilpin's little guide books use wove for the plates only—and S58-9 Maton, *Observations relative to the natural history . . . of the Western Counties of England*, 1797 (in similar style to Gilpin's books, but with aquatints slightly more 'accomplished') employs wove paper throughout.

[1] For a summary of the life and work of Ackermann, see 'Rudolph Ackermann', an illustrated monograph by P. M. Handover in *Motif 13*, 1967, pp. 81–9.

Other examples of aquatint illustration in the collection—almost without exception hand-coloured—are S66, Spilsbury, *Picturesque scenery in the Holy Land*, London, 1803, a typical large 'topographical' folio of the period, printed by Bulmer and 'published by Edward Orme, printseller to His Majesty'; S75-6, Porter, *Travelling Sketches in Russia*, London, 1813, two quarto volumes, in vol. 2 of which the illustration facing p. 179 shows particularly clearly the characteristic grain of early aquatint; S83, Latrobe, *Journal of a visit to South Africa*, London, 1818; and S90, Pierce Egan's well-known *Life in London*, London, 1821, dedicated to King George IV, and generously interspersed with the liveliest hand-coloured aquatint illustrations showing something of 'the high life of the Regency bucks and blades, typified by Jerry Hawthorn',[1] drawn and engraved by I. R. and G. Cruikshank. Although in this and other of his early work George Cruikshank used aquatint, he soon turned his hand to etching, and his great satirical contribution to book illustration is referred to later under the subject of etching and caricature. S136, *The Spirit of the Woods*, London, 1841, 8vo, shows fine aquatint illustration beautifully hand-coloured in detail.

Dr Gilpin's little guide books also contain a few examples, in the form of full-page separately inserted 'bled-off' illustrations, of 'soft-ground etching', a process which gives—often very attractively—all the effect of pencil or chalk drawing in a way which is very similar to that of chalk-drawn lithography, the process which displaced it early in the 19th-century. In soft-ground etching, tallow is added to the usual ground and after the plate has been 'grounded' and smoked in the usual manner a sheet of thin writing paper is stretched over it. Drawing is made on this paper with a medium-hard pencil, pressing more strongly where a darker line is required, and when the paper is carefully removed it takes away with it more or less of the ground according to the indentations of the paper, leaving the copper exposed for etching the design. For examples see S46

[1] See Philip James, *English Book Illustration: 1800–1900*, King Penguin Books, London, 1947, p. 29.

(drawings of cattle and sheep) and S51, both already listed above among the Gilpin books. Soft-ground etching is sometimes combined with aquatint.

Another intaglio process developed during the 18th-century was the mezzotint, which, introduced from the Continent in the latter half of the century, became a peculiarly English art, particularly in the making of fine prints of portrait subjects after leading artists of the period. In this process a copper or steel plate is uniformly roughened or 'burred' by the use of a number of special tools ('cradles', rockers, roulettes, etc.) so that it will yield an intense and even black when inked and printed. The lighter portions are obtained by smoothing the surface of the plate with a scraper or burin, and the finished result has a softness (which *can* descend into muzziness) all its own. Mezzotint found its way into bookwork, principally for fine portrait-frontispieces, in which it was almost always supported by other forms of engraving, such as line or stipple, but the short life of the plate limited its use. For examples of mezzotint see D92-4, the Boydell Milton, London, 1794-7, printed by Bulmer in three folio volumes, and for catalogue and photogravure reproductions of English mezzotint portraits see S263, London, 1926, 2 volumes. S54, Dallaway's *Heraldry*, Gloucester, 1793, is a fine volume of interest for the variety of intaglio processes employed, most of the full-size plates being hand-coloured.

All the principal methods of engraving are described, with well-chosen illustrations, in T. H. Fielding's *The Art of engraving*, (M16), London, 1844, a slender royal octavo volume, attractively printed and bound, which also includes very clear representations of the various engravers' tools. There is also a treatise on lithography, and interesting early articles on 'electrography' (electrotyping) and photography or 'photogenic drawing', with paragraphs on the work of Niepce and Daguerre. It may be noted that during the 18th century it became common to employ a number of engravers in reproducing the work of one artist, a procedure which tended to be reversed during the 19th-century, although many Victorian books employ a variety of both artists and engravers for their illustrations.

Mention must be made of William Blake (1757–1827), whose work occupies an isolated and unique position in book illustration, embracing both the principles of the block-book and the manuscript of the Middle Ages, but with a style all his own. He developed a method of engraving, etching, and printing metal blocks in relief, and of adding or transferring colour by hand, and as text, calligraphy, and illustration were all his own and closely 'inverwoven', the integration of the page was complete. S369 is a magnificent reproduction by Jacomet, in collotype and hand-stencil, issued in 1951, of Blake's great work, *Jerusalem*, completed in 1818.[1] See also S88.

The revival and re-introduction of the wood-block—now within the field of *engraving*—largely associated with Thomas Bewick (1753–1828) and his pupils at the close of the 18th century, and employing a very different technique from that of the earlier craftsmen, was a major influence in bringing the wood-block back into general use as a means of printing illustration with type, in one operation, in both bookwork and general printing during the 19th-century; and because of its selective capacity it continued in certain illustration work—especially technical illustration—even after the advent of photo-mechanical methods of engraving. Although by the end of the 16th-century the wood-block had been generally supplanted, as a means of book illustration, by metal-engraving, its use was nevertheless maintained in certain cheaper and more general forms of printing, such as chap-books, broadsides, etc., and it is of interest that Bewick's earliest work has a strong affinity with that of the contemporary chap-books, very many of which were printed in his own town of Newcastle, where he was appren-

[1] Since preparing these notes a most impressive and representative loan exhibition of the work of Blake in illuminated books and engravings has been put on in the National Library of Scotland, with the assistance of the Blake Trust, during the period of the Edinburgh Festival 1969. The exhibition was opened with a lecture by Sir Geoffrey Keynes, and a catalogue has been added to the Collection. See also J21, Irene Langridge, *William Blake: a study of his life and art work*, London, 1904.

ticed to an engraver.[1] Bewick and his associates employed the 'white-line' method, working with a *graver* into the finely polished end-grain of hardwood—such as boxwood—giving much greater versatility in the rendering of tone-values than was possible in the old method of cutting with a knife into side-grain. A book of special interest in relation to Bewick's subsequent career is S57, the little 12mo volume of Croxall's *Fables of Æsop* (London 1794).[2] This work was originally published in 1722 and the 'cuts', by an unknown engraver, served as basic models for many of Bewick's engravings in his Gay's *Fables* of 1779, *Select Fables* of 1784 (D71, referred to later), and Æsop's *Fables* of 1818.

Bewick's association with the eminent printer Bulmer,[3] a friend from boyhood days in Newcastle, was instrumental in bringing about the use of a special series of types in the early 'Modern' design, skilfully cut by the typefounder William Martin, in certain books ornamented with wood-engravings by Bewick and his younger brother John. In fact it may be said that Bewick's life completely coincides with a most important period in British book production and illustration. His earlier books are printed with Old Face types on laid papers, his later works with Modern Face on wove, and the brilliance of Bulmer's productions helped to pave the way for the brief 'steel-engraving' period of the 1820's and '30's, when type and illustration reached a degree of technical brilliance not before attained. The phases of Bewick's work and the printing of his blocks may be well studied in the abovementioned D71, *Select Fables* (Newcastle, 1784, printed by T. Saint; *laid* papers, Old Face type) and E2, Somervile, *The Chase* (London, 1802, printed by Bulmer; *wove* paper, Martin's type) and in the

---

[1] See typographical note under the chap-book E103, on the use of some of Bewick's blocks by the London printer Catnach and his successors, who maintained a supply of chap-books during the first half of the 19th-century. See also E126-8, reprints of chap-books.

[2] Presented by Miss Joan Hassall, A.R.E.

[3] See July 1963 Exhibition Catalogue, *Printing and the Mind of Man*, U119A, British Museum Exhibition Section, p. 41, items 130 and 132, and p. 44, item 138; also Earls Court Exhibition Section, p. 108, item 614.

various editions of *British birds* (S71, Newcastle, 1809, printed by E. Walker; S106, Newcastle, 1832, printed by C. H. Cook) and his *Quadrupeds* (S95, Newcastle, 8th edn. 1824, printed by Walker). E63–4–5 (Newcastle, 1824–4–5, printed by Walker) are volumes of cuts only—See Typographical Notes,[1] including note under E22.

The continued popularity of Bewick's works as source-books for natural history subjects is strikingly shown in S114, Goldsmith's *Animated nature*, Edinburgh, 1835 (an octavo volume of over 600 pages in double-column small type) in which many of the *copper* engravings are copied from Bewick's wood-engravings in his *Quadrupeds*, and are therefore reversed—see, for instance, the well-known Stag, or Red Deer, on plate facing p. 211 in Goldsmith and the original wood-block on p. 135 of the 8th edition of the *Quadrupeds*, S95. Some examples, such as the Mexican Opossum, facing p. 211 in Goldsmith and on p. 436 of the Bewick volume, are not reversed, and may have been traced—although of course much depends on the technique used. The continuance of metal-engraving for certain classes of work during the 19th-century is discussed later, but meanwhile it is of interest to find it following in the *wake* of wood-engraving in a book of this date.

John Bewick, Thomas Bewick's younger brother, also a skilled artist and wood-engraver, died in 1795, and reference to his drawing on wood the illustrations for *The Chase*, which his brother Thomas engraved, is made in the Typographical Notes. While working in London, he made engravings for a number of children's books, and an example is S67, *The Blossoms of morality*, 1806, not his best work, and some of the blocks apparently rather worn in this fourth edition, but none the less still attractive.[2]

The successors of Bewick carried wood-engraving to a high

---

[1] For an edition of Bewick's *Memoir* see E108 (Newcastle, 1862); for *Gleanings* see E134–5 (Newcastle, 1886, 2 volumes); for *a résumé of his life and work* see J33 (London, 1949); and for a *bibliography raisonné* of his principal works see P10 (OUP 1953).

[2] See also footnote on Holbein, p. 412, referring to S48, *Emblems of mortality*, London, 1789.

degree of virtuosity, especially under the rival influence of steel-engraving abovementioned, as may be seen by examining such a book as S101, Northcote's *Fables* (Chiswick, 1829, 2nd ed.) a small volume beautifully printed by the elder Whittingham with very fine engravings in which Northcote's designs have been drawn on wood for various engravers by William Harvey, a notable pupil of Bewick's; and the work of Bewick and other engravers may be compared in S112, *Wood engravings*, London, 1833, 8vo, which shows the work of three well-known artist illustrators, Martin, Westall, and Thurston, engraved by Bewick, Nesbit, and many others, and in S142, *The Entertaining Naturalist*, London, 1843, a small octavo 'illustrated by upwards of 350 accurately drawn figures finely engraved on wood by Bewick, Harvey, Whymper and others'. The influence of Bewick may also be seen in the crisp and spirited wood-engravings made for the Lee Priory Press books— see E32, *The Sylvan Wanderer*, 1813–17; E46, *Woodcuts and verses*, 1820; and the Typographical Notes.[1] Subsequent stages may be followed by comparing Bewick's blocks in, say, his

---

[1] John Johnson, who, with Warwick, was compositor for Sir Egerton Brydges at the Lee Priory Press, later left and became notable for his work *Typographia; or, The Printer's Instructor*, 2 volumes. London 1824, of which there are two issues in the collection (M34). Johnson also devoted much of his time to the use of Printers' Ornaments in 'Type-Pictures', etc., and a remarkable example of his work in this field, framed and glazed, was presented by 'The Scotsman' to the Printing Department of the Heriot-Watt College in 1946. It is in the form of a 'triumphal arch', dedicated to William Caxton and others, is 'composed of Type and Brass Rule, containing upwards of 60,000 movable pieces of metal and above 150 different Patterns of Flowers'. The inscription J. JOHNSON TYP., 1826, is said to be worked into the ornaments at the base of the arch, T54.

Another example, less elaborate, of Johnson's work in type-ornaments, etc, also using an 'archway' design, in the collection (enclosed, flat, in brown paper, in cabinet) is entitled '*The Printers' Address to the Queen, and Her Majesty's Tribute to the Press in Answer* (1820), printed for William Hone and worked at the Stanhope Press' (of which there is an engraving). The columns of the arch are made up of rules, and the border is of typographical ornaments. Worked into the base is the imprint JOHN JOHNSON, PRINTER, BROOK ST., HOLBORN, T53. Johnson worked for a time with the printer Thomas Bensley. For further details relating to Johnson, Northcote and Harvey, and Sir Egerton Brydges, see July 1963 Exhibition Catalogue, *Printing and the Mind of Man*, British Museum Exhibition section, p. 44, item 142, U119A.

British Birds, with those in S143-5, the Yarrell volumes on the same subject (London, 1843, printed by Bentley, Wilson & Fley) in which the wonderful brillance of the engraving becomes almost monotonous and is achieved only at the cost of some inevitable loss in variety of texture. The signs of decline are just becoming discernible.

The skill developed by the wood-engravers during the course of the 19th-century led to the accomplishments of some superb technical illustration, the evolution of which makes a most interesting study in the early numbers of a periodical such as *Engineering*, a complete set of which may be seen in the Cameron Smail Library of the Heriot-Watt University. Both wood- and metal-engraving were assisted, in the later stages of their development, by the invention of engraving machines, but almost inevitably at the expense of some loss of character. With the advent of an increasing volume of cheap printing, which was one of the after-effects of the Industrial Revolution, wood-engraving ultimately lost much of its essential character when employed almost solely as a means of reproduction from other media—sometimes with complete disregard for its own natural limitations. Nevertheless, much admirable and useful work continued to be done, and because of its technical advantages as a relief surface for printing with type, the wood-block held its own as a means of providing illustration in the latter part of the 19th-century, when the great work of Edmund Evans in its application to colour-printing for the service of a wider public inaugurated what was almost a new era in that field.

Some very competent and skilful wood-engraving is associated with the reproduction of work by that group of artists who have become known as the 'illustrators of the sixties', but some of these artists were very hard on their engravers, requiring them to reproduce the most detailed and elaborate pen-and-ink drawings with all their varied cross-hatching and spontaneously scribbled lines, or to interpret equally difficult work drawn direct on the block. Thus the wood-engraver, working under increasing pressure for 'the trade', tended ultimately to become something of a 'hack', and the way was opened for the advent of the process block in line and half-tone. These developments are described more fully later.

Throughout the crowded 19th-century a number of processes, including the newly introduced lithography, may be seen successively jostling one another for supremacy, typically observable in the brief but intense rivalry between wood- and steel-engraving during the 1830s, already mentioned. Line-engraving[1] held its own at first in the face of the developing wood-engraving and lithography, but its disadvantage in involving a separate and expensive process numbered the days of its general use. Although lithography normally had the same disadvantage, it was possible to print both type and illustration lithographically (as described later), and lithography also opened up a new field in colour-printing. The advantage of line-engraving for pure line work (and for lettering) has already been mentioned, and its use in continuing to provide clear detail for technical illustration is shown in S84, Martin, *The Circle of the mechanical arts*, London, 1818, 4to, but, apart from their requiring a separate printing, the plates lack the vigour which the best wood-engraving was later able to bring to such work—as in the journal *Engineering* above mentioned.

Some exquisite line-engraving was accomplished in topographical and architectural work, as seen for example in S94, *Skelton's Engraved Illustrations of the Principal Antiquities of Oxfordshire*, Oxford, 1823, folio, with engravings chiefly after the drawings of F. Mackenzie, in some of which the range of texture and tone-value obtained is almost unbelievable—the engraving of the Norman Doorway of Iffley Church, following p. 12 of the section on Bloxham Hundred is a particularly fine example of craftsmanship. An interesting feature of this book (which is dedicated to the Bishop of Oxford, and the list of subscribers to which is headed by the King) is that of the beautiful little line-engravings, printed direct on the text-paper in the upper part of the page, for which varying spaces have had to be

---

[1] i.e., intaglio metal-engraving generally—the term 'line-engraving' not to be confused with photographic relief process-engraving, introduced later in the century.

allowed in the double-column text-matter into which they are fitted. Their disadvantage is that they have not only caused a rectangular impression in the text of the verses, but the slight overlap of the plates over the text-matter has caused in some cases a blackening and distortion of the letters affected. This might have been avoided by printing these little designs on very thin paper and pasting in, as in the Dibdin books referred to on p. 442, and in S98, the next example. This is Izaac Walton's *Lives*, London, 1825, an octavo dedicated to the Bishop of Winchester and beautifully printed by W. Nicol at the Shakspeare Press, in which all the steel-engraved portraits, etc., have been treated in this way. S108, Cunningham, A., *The gallery of pictures*, London, ?1834, 4to, 2 volumes, shows competent line-engraving by a variety of engravers, some employing mechanically engraved backgrounds. The tendency of line-engraving, as a means of reproducing pictures, to give in some cases a certain brilliant but mechanical uniformity, to the detriment of character is felt when looking over volumes such as these.

The rivalry between wood- and steel-engraving is frankly admitted in the preface by John Martin to S116, the small octavo edition of Gray's *Elegy* (1836) printed in London by S. Bentley and dedicated to the wealthy but unread poet Samuel Rogers; and some of the brilliantly executed wood-engravings in this book make interesting comparison with the steel-engravings, after Turner and Stothard, in such books as E71 and E75, which are actually Samuel Rogers's own author's copies of his expensively produced *Italy* (1830) printed in London by T. Davison and *Poems* (1834).[1] It will be seen that some of the wood-engravings are definitely simulating steel. Wood-engraving used in imitation of etching is referred to in a

---

[1] These presentation copies have elaborate gilt-ornamented light-tan morocco bindings, with goffered edges. E72 is another copy of E71, and E76 another of E75, and these copies have plain dark-tan morocco bindings with painted fore-edges. In E72 it will be seen that the engravings on pp. 88 and 91 have been transposed as compared with their placing in E71, an author's presentation copy of the first issue of this first edition. Pasted on the front endpaper in E71 is a photographic print of Samuel Rogers as a very old man. He lived to the age of 92, despite having been crippled, by a street accident, at the age of 87.

later paragraph concerning the 'Etching Club' and the use of etching in Victorian book illustration (p. 450).

Steel-engraving, introduced in 1823, reached its zenith of virtuosity in the second quarter of the 19th century, especially in the many Annuals, Keepsakes, and other drawing-room books of the early Victorian post-Industrial-Revolution period, of which there is a very representative selection (S92-2x) in the collection. That many of the steel-engravers were overworked and underpaid is affirmed with regret by Fielding on pp. 29-31 of his *Art of engraving* (M16) mentioned above. He states that 'when steel was first applied to line engraving, the immense number of impressions it was found capable of producing enabled publishers to offer to the world works beautifully illustrated, at a much cheaper rate than had hitherto been done. A new class of publications, we mean the annuals, were introduced as a vehicle for spreading more rapidly the impressions from steel plates, and the most beautiful productions of our best engravers were flung with a prodigal hand before the public at a price for which they ought never to have been sold'. In a later paragraph, referring to the then 'depressed state of the art' arising from over-production, he also deplores the fact that technical skill alone tended to be valued higher than artistic sensibility. He writes, 'When the hardness of the metal was found to admit of finer work, then came in fashion the excessively finished style of the present day, which . . . tends to reduce all engravers to the same level, or what is still worse, allows some whose only merit consists in a capability of laying lines closer than others, to usurp the place of real talent.' The process of steel-engraving was of short duration. Apart from the fact that, as a line-engraving process it required a printing separate from that of the letterpress, the discovery and development of electrotyping at the middle of the century led to the possibility of working in the easier copper or zinc, which was afterwards 'steel-faced' (actually the deposit was iron) to increase durability. For brilliant examples of steel-engraving see, for instance, *The Bijou* of 1828, which includes illustrations and head-pieces after Thomas Stothard, one of the most prolific illustrators of the late 18th- and early 19th-centuries. Many of these 'annuals' above referred to are interesting for their bindings, employing a great variety of stamped designs on leather, cloth, paper-boards, etc., some highly moulded with composition-finishes resembling present-day plastics, which appear almost indestructible.[1] But Victorian bookbinding is a study in itself.[2]

A notable character of the early 19th century is the Rev. Thomas Frognall Dibdin (1776–1847), bibliographer, traveller, and one of the initiators, in 1813, of the Roxburghe Club, the first true book-club to be founded. Dibdin's most important publications are exquisitely printed by Bulmer at the Shakspeare Printing Office and employ the greatest variety of illustration techniques available at the time, including the finest metal-engravings printed on tissue and so skilfully pasted in as to appear printed on the paper of the text. Dibdin's misgivings concerning the newly-introduced lithography, expressed on p. 513 of his *Bibliographical tour in France and Germany*, 1821 (S89), are significant, and on pp. 610–11 of his *Northern tour*, 1838 (S124-5), he records an interesting interview with the engraver Lizars of Edinburgh in which he describes the hand-colouring, by young ladies (previously referred to under aquatint) of engravings printed in enormous quantities for various publications (such, for instance, as S111, *The Naturalist's Library*, referred to in the next paragraph). The beautifully printed and bound books of this whimsical if inaccurate scholar, to be seen

[1] See, for examples, *The Bijou* and *The Comic Offering*, bound respectively in brown and maroon stained full sheep, treated and heavily stamped with all-over ornament (giving effect of plastic), spine gilt-lettered; *Fisher's Drawing-Room Scrap-book* (1836), quarter sheepskin binding, treated and heavily stamped on side with elaborate all-over design, gilt-lettering and ornament full length of spine; *The Ladies Cabinet*, half-calf bindings, patterned stamped cloth sides, spine gilt, raised bands; *The Keepsake* (1830), binding magenta moiré or watered silk; *The Comic Almanack*, binding half red lined skiver, marbled paper sides, spine gilt-lettered with ornament; *The Christmas Box*, paper boards imitating vellum, red leather-gilt label; and S126, *The Book of Gems* [1838] which has a truly remarkable binding, brown morocco, gilt design and lettering on spine, side treated with shellac hand-marbled, gilt-stamped with ornament and glazed to an astounding glacial finish.

[2] See illustrated and excellently documented summary in chap. 17 of Ruari McLean's *Victorian Book Design*, London, Faber, 1972, U99.

in the collection, will repay study for their range of subject-matter and the variety of reproductive techniques employed. S79-81 is his celebrated *Bibliographical Decameron*, issued in three volumes in 1817.

Although during the course of the Victorian era metal-engraving was largely eclipsed by wood-engraving and lithography, both of which had made progress in the printing of colours, it was nevertheless maintained to a limited extent, especially for such books as those on natural history and other subjects requiring fine detail in the reproductions—which were generally hand-coloured. A typical example is S111, Jardine, Sir W., *The Naturalist's Library*, Edinburgh, 1833, volume I of a work with plates of birds, beasts, and fishes, engraved and well hand-coloured by Lizars abovementioned, which was produced in many volumes in pocket size and ran into many editions. In the later editions (not in the collection) backgrounds of trees, flora, landscape, seascape, etc. have been added (which somehow seem to detract from the original vividness and simplicity of the various subjects) and the hand-colouring can be seen going sadly downhill until it becomes quite crude and perfunctory.[1] Other examples are S130, *Edinburgh Journal of Natural History and of the Physical Sciences*, 1839–40, Fol., with some good hand-colouring; S136, *The Spirit of the Woods*, London, 1841, 8vo, with rich hand-colouring on fine aquatint base; S150, *Les Fleurs animées*, Paris, 1847, 8vo (also interesting for its typography by Lacour et Cie, showing a variety of early 19th-century decorative types); and 11A, Astle, *The Origin and progress of writing*, London, 1876, a large quarto volume which has some affinity in its style of production with that of S54, Dallaway's treatise on English Heraldry, of the previous century, above-mentioned. S146, Goethe's *Reineke Fuchs*, illustrated by

---

[1] An earlier example of Lizars' work in a broader field is E52, Sir D. Lyndsay, *Fac Simile of an ancient heraldic manuscript emblazoned by Sir David Lyndsay . . . Lyon King of Arms, 1542*, Edinburgh, 1822, Fol., but this employs etchings, freely drawn and hand-coloured (largely illuminators' opaque colours) with blazons reproducing the script of the original MS. The Royal Arms of Scotland on Plate 2 is largely line-engraved and includes gold in the colours. The plates are interleaved with thinner paper.

Wilhelm Kaulbach, Stuttgart, 1846, also large quarto, is an example of highly accomplished steel-engraving (not hand-coloured); and S134, *Pictures of the French*, London, 1840, 8vo, printed by T. Baker & Co. for Wm. S. Orr & Co., is of interest in that it shows *wood*-engraving printed on thin paper and pasted in (a treatment more frequently accorded to line-engraving), while in S135, the 1841 issue, London, printed by Balne Bros. for T. Tegg, the wood-engravings are printed direct on to the text paper.

A late example of 19th-century steel-engraving is S194, Tennyson's *Idylls of the King*, London, Moxon [1868], a folio with illustrations by the enormously prolific and—at that time —very popular Gustave Doré (1832–83). This is a typical expen-sively produced 'Doré Gift Book' (the advertisement at the end gives £6,000 as cost of production) and it is essentially a picture book built on extracts from the epic poem. The illustrations, printed on a pale buff toned ground and laden with a heavy atmospheric gloom, have both the sentimental and sinister quality characteristic of much of Doré's work. The pretentious Victorian binding has disintegrated and all the plates are falling out. Doré was born in Strasburg, gained his experience in France and worked for some years in England, where his great *Bible* of 1866 (with wood-engraved pictures—E117-8 in the collection) brought him such fame that a Doré gallery for the exhibition and sale of his works, including his religious paint-ings, was opened in London and maintained for many years. Doré had ambitions of becoming an historical painter, but his work in this field lacked a painter's quality and his large canvases found little acceptance in France. He normally employed wood-engravers to reproduce the wide range of tones required in the reproduction of his drawings, which he made direct on the block himself, with results much more successful than those obtained with these engravings on steel made from his drawings in pen-and-wash. Doré certainly possessed quite unusual gifts of dramatic invention, which have made much of his work memorable, and his earlier books are better than the great folios by which he became so well known, but his effect on illustration and engraving was definitely 'mixed', tending to overstress the exploitation of tone, at the expense of the simpler and more direct techniques.

Interesting but short-lived processes of the 19th-century are the 'Glyphography' of Edward Palmer and the 'Acrography' of Louis Schönberg, both introduced *circa* 1840 and both used for the purpose of producing metallic engravings *in relief* for letter-press printing. In glyphography, U117, the artist works with a needle into a white composition evenly spread on a metal plate which has been specially blackened to enable the work to be visible at all stages as the composition is cleared away by the needle, and the final result is converted into a relief block by an electrotyping process. In acrography the artist may draw with a point on a variety of materials, the most favoured being an ordinary lithographic stone, and the result is translated into a metal relief block by Mr Schönberg's 'secret process'. Glyphography appears to have given much the more satisfactory results, and in a most instructive booklet entitled *The Author's Handbook: a complete guide to Publishing on Commission*, written and published by E. Churton in London in 1844, U56, which includes details and costs of all the principal illustration-processes then in vogue, the author expresses his regret that it was not available for his publication of Westall and Martin's *Illustrations to the Bible*, for which he estimates that it would have saved him no less than £1,594 : 4s. as compared with the cost of the wood-blocks. But it is undoubtedly just as well that he did not have recourse to either of these processes, since neither approaches the quality of original metal- or wood-engraving, and neither appears to have become successfully established.[1] Wood states that glyphography 'ruined its inventor, who gave up a good business as an optician to attend to it, and shortly afterwards found himself in the Bankruptcy Court'.[2] The results given by

---

[1] For fuller details of the origin and development of these processes see article by Elizabeth M. Harris, 'Experimental Graphic Processes in England, 1800–1859', in *Journal of the Printing Historical Society*, No. 4, 1968, pp. 33–86, and No. 5, 1969, pp. 41–80 and No. 6, pp. 53–89.

[2] See pp. 219–20 of Wood, *Modern Methods of Illustrating Books*, London, Elliot Stock, 4th ed., 1898 (first publ. 1887), one of the little books in the 'Book-

acrography (which was originated in Aberdeen before being taken to London) tend to look both coarse and scratchy.[1] Glyphography was improved upon by the 'Typographic Etching' process,[2] patented in 1872 by A. and H. T. Dawson, who used a white wax on the blackened base and devised a better method than Palmer's for building up the white spaces to give greater depth before electrotyping. Type matter could also be impressed into the wax—a useful additional facility for such work as maps and diagrams. Alfred Dawson was the inventor of a very successful swelled gelatine process (referred to later), which was founded on the earlier work of the Austrian, Paul Pretsch, and others, and which preceded the general adoption of line-etching and was in use from the 1870s until about 1895. In this the electrotyping principle was also used to obtain the printing surface, but the basis of the process was photographic, which typographic etching and its abovementioned precursors were not.[3]

Another quite remarkable invention, associated with the illustrated book now also apparently passed into oblivion, is Francis Paul Becker & Co.'s 'Omnigraph', which was capable of perfectly engraving text matter in *any* character, on the same intaglio steel plate as that bearing engraved illustration or decoration, so that both text and illustration could be printed

Lover's Library', edited by Henry B. Wheatley, recently added to the College Library.

[1] A copy of each of the original pamphlets (now very rare) issued by the patentees, advertising and describing, with examples, the processes of Glyphography and Acrography, together with a copy of Mr Churton's valuable 'Author's Handbook' mentioned above, were presented to the Printing Department of the Heriot-Watt College by the late Mr John Grant of Edinburgh, and have now been added to the Clark collection. The Glyphography pamphlet, 2nd ed. 1844 (1st ed. 1843), bears an inscription on the cover in Palmer's own hand.

[2] Not a very satisfactory term, since true etching is not involved—see pp. 215-219 of the Wood volume abovementioned. On p. 219 Wood gives full credit to Palmer's process as a predecessor, 'though unsuccessful', to Dawson's. For further reference to Typographic Etching see A. J. Bull, *Photo-Engraving*, London, Edward Arnold & Co., 1934, p. 94, W43.

[3] Again see Bull, *Photo-Engraving*, pp. 93-4 and 96. See also—for note on the work of Pretsch—Jan Poortenaar, *The Technique of Prints*, London, John Lane, 1933, p. 134—also in Printing section of the College Library.

together *in one operation*. A glowing account of this invention is also included in Churton's handbook, which in addition heralds the publication by the patentees of 'a most beautiful edition of Moore's *Irish melodies*, highly illustrated by Daniel Maclise, R.A., the whole of the text of which is engraved on the Omnigraph'.

This volume (S170 in the collection), published by Longmans and dated by hand [1856] on the letterpress title, is an example of the most sentimental Victorian illustration, but is technically of great interest. A note following the preface states that Maclise's designs are 'a facsimile of his original drawings, and the text is engraved by Mr Becker's process'—and this text is in a delicate open-face letter showing a sound knowledge of letter-forms. The engraved title bears, at the foot, Becker's name and the words, 'The Plates Printed by McQueen'. The inscriptions on the designs on some of the earlier pages show them to have been both designed and etched by Maclise, but other names appear with his on a number of pages. Most pages bear the names of Maclise and Becker only, and on many the text is enclosed within rustic, arboreous, or garlanded borders. The printing is evidently by lithography from copperplate transfers, as there is no visible 'impression'. The letterpress portion of the book (chiefly notes at end) is printed by Spottiswoode & Co., London, and the binding, in green cloth, with elaborate gilt design, is by Leighton Son & Hodge. It is evident that Becker was in touch with the Ordnance Map Office in the late 1840s, in the hopes of their arranging for him to install and operate an Omnigraph on their premises, but the terms offered were considered inadequate. Mr James Mosley, Librarian of St Bride Printing Library, has shown the writer of these notes a pamphlet addressed by Becker to the Board of Ordnance in 1849 making 'respectful remonstrance' at the terms offered, but more information about the Omnigraph is obviously very desirable.

Mention must again be made of etching, so popular, for reasons already given, with the caricaturists and illustrators of the greater part of the 19th-century. Phases in the work of

George Cruikshank (1792–1878), the great pictorial satirist, whose career as an illustrator extends for over 60 years to the 1870's, are amply represented. In his early work he used aquatint, notable among which are his illustrations to S90, Pierce Egan's *Life in London*, 1821, already referred to, but he soon turned to etching for its uninhibited line. Many of his drawings were also engraved on wood, and S105, *Three Courses and a Dessert*, London, 1830, shows faithful wood-engraved reproductions of his spirited sketches.[1] *The Comic Almanack* for 1837, London, printed by Vizetelly, Branston and Co., No. 6 of the 'Annuals', S92-2x, 8vo, includes the liveliest full-page etchings, wood-engraved silhouettes in the text, and excellent typography, all of which combine to make it an outstanding production of its kind.[2] Of the same date is S119, *Sketches* by 'Quiz'. Cruikshank's full-page etched plates— some almost horrifying—to *The Tower of London*, S132, London, 1840, are among the most dramatic in book illustration. His equally famous illustrations to *Oliver Twist* (1838) belong to the same period, and those for E97, *Memoirs of Joseph Grimaldi*, London, 1846, have the same quality of greatness (see Typographical Notes).[3] Another famous Scottish caricaturist, whose work occupies a rather different field, is John Kay (1742–1862, born in Dalkeith), who, after practising as a barber, opened a print-shop in Edinburgh in 1785, where he sold sketches of local celebrities, etched by himself. These etchings, which are not skilful but possess character, and represent over half-a-century's work were published in 1838, and a four-volume edition of 1842 is in the collection (S140); but Kay's work, like

[1] The Introduction states that 'the purveyer is deeply indebted to Mr George Cruikshank for having embellished his rude sketches in their transfer to wood, and translated them into a proper pictorial state'.

[2] Philip James writes, 'For a sustained effort . . . the *Comic Almanack* is unsurpassed, and as a visual record of London life in the first years of Victoria's reign it is a fascinating document' (*English Book Illustration*, 1800–1900, King Penguin series, 1947).

[3] See Ruari McLean, *George Cruikshank*, in series *English Masters of Black and White*, London, Art and Technics, 1948, one of six volumes in this series presented by W. B. Hislop, W24–9.

that of his famous English contemporary, Gillray, belongs to the domain of the print-seller and not to that of book-illustration.

Etching is frequently combined with other forms of engraving, sometimes including the mezzotint principle, which can greatly extend the range and subtlety of the tones. Some of the illustrations by H. K. Browne ('Phiz': 1815–82) to Dickens's *Little Dorritt*, S171, 1857, such as that facing p. 96 in Vol. I, and employing the freest of etching on a mechanically ruled and hand-burnished plate, appear almost stereoscopic, with a darkness that can almost be felt, and it is doubtful whether any present-day process could give such an eerie and dramatic effect. Churton refers to this form of illustration in his pamphlet as 'a superior form of etching', but the example he shows is much more ordinary.[1] S156, *Sketches in London*, London, 1850, 8vo, illustrated with etchings by 'Phiz' and others, has a note in the preface on the promise of 'Phiz', then a young artist. This book, as many other illustrated books of the period, shows something of the poverty existing in 19th-century London.

The genial and lively illustrations of John Leech (1817–64), whose work covers every phase of English life, are well represented in the full-page hand-coloured etchings in S148-9, *The Comic History of England*, London, 1847, printed by Bradbury and Evans for the *Punch* office, and in S182, the Surtees novel *"Plain or Ringlets?"* London, 1860. Each of these books contains many reproductive wood-engravings in the text, skilfully interpreting Leech's expressive sketches. The illustrations of 'Dicky' Doyle (1824–83), a most graceful and sensitive artist—whose cover design for *Punch* was in use for over 100 years from 1849 —may be seen in S166, Thackeray's *The Newcomes*, London, 1855, and it is of interest to compare these with those of Thackeray himself in S155, *Pendennis*, London, 1849, each employing etching on steel for the full-page plates, and wood-engraving for the initials and illustrations in text—as in the

[1] Concerning this 'form of etching' Churton also adds, 'it is a wonder that it is not more generally used in place of Lithography', and his further observations on this subject are mentioned on p. 458 under chromolithography and book-illustration.

Leech books previously mentioned.[1] But the illustrations to S185, *Our Mutual Friend*, London, 1865, by Marcus Stone, another artist typical of this period, whose work possesses a certain natural simplicity of composition, are not etchings, but are wood-engraved by Dalziel and Greene, and with the name of the Dalziel brothers there began in England an important period of reproductive wood-engraving. The full-page illustrations to such books as the novels abovementioned are separate plates inserted and are therefore not physically related to the type-page.

An outstanding draughtsman and illustrator of the period who, like Leech and Doyle, also contributed to *Punch*, and whose power of observation has made his work historically interesting, is Charles Keene (1823–91). After essaying careers in law and in architecture, he was apprenticed to the Whympers (referred to later) as a wood-engraver, an experience which undoubtedly later helped him as an illustrator through that medium. He also did admirable work as an etcher. Various amateur bodies, such as the Etching Club already referred to (p. 441), had helped to maintain the use of etched illustration in bookwork, and in this connexion the illustrations 'by the Etching Club' to S164, a crown octavo edition of Goldsmith's *The Deserted Village*, London, 1855, published for Cundall by Samson Low & Son, and printed by R. Clay, have particular interest in that they show wood-engraving employed in slavish imitation of etching. A paragraph in the prefatory note reads, 'The illustrations in this volume are copied by permission from a series of Etchings published some years since [in 1841] by the "Etching Club". Only a few impressions of that work were printed, the copper plates destroyed, and the book, except in very expensive form, has long been unobtainable. Great care has been taken to render the present woodblocks as like the original Etchings as the different methods of engraving will allow.' Referring again to etchings on steel, some of the most beautiful examples in English book illustration, by Birket Foster, may

[1] For monograph on Doyle, see J9, Daria Hambourg, *Richard Doyle, his life and work*, in series *English Masters of Black and White*, London, 1948.

be seen in S165, *L'Allegro*, London, 1855, described below under the 'illustrators of the sixties'. Before leaving the subject of etching, mention may be made of the excessive discoloration or 'foxing' which sometimes disfigures etched and occasionally other intaglio printed plates in books, and which can be the result of a variety of causes. Extreme examples may be seen in the little annual *The Remembrance*, Edinburgh, 1846—in list S92-2x.

Although wood-engraving had had to face the rivalry of steel- and copper-engraving abovementioned, it maintained its position principally because of its technical advantages, and during the second quarter of the 19th-century its field was greatly enlarged by the introduction of magazines, such as the *Penny Magazine* (1832), *Punch* (1841), and the *Illustrated London News* (1842), using wood-engraving for the widest variety of subjects and employing the services of some leading contemporary artists.[1] From this expansion of the graphic arts there emerged the group of artists, already referred to, who have become known as the 'illustrators of the sixties' (actually covering a period from the 'fifties to the 'seventies) and the reproductive wood-engravers associated with them.[2] A dominant influence in this group was that of the Pre-Raphaelites—notably Holman Hunt, Millais, Rossetti and Hughes—and their importance was that, although professional painters, they approached illustration as a separate activity and generally drew direct on the block, thus calling for facsimile rather than interpretive reproduction. This sometimes gave much trouble to their engravers, particularly in the case of Rossetti. On the other hand, Frederick Sandys, an artist who has some affinity with this group, but whose output as a designer for wood-engraving was small, had an instinct for the engraver's problems, and some of his drawings are actually enhanced by reproduction.

A wood-engraver presented with a painting, pen-and-wash

[1] See July 1963 Exhibition Catalogue, *Printing and the Mind of Man*, Earls Court Exhibition section, p. 108, item 616.
[2] See J41, Gleeson White, *English illustration*, 'the sixties': 1855–70, London, 1906.

or other drawing, or a photograph for reproduction can choose his own technique more or less unhampered, and much of the work of a popular artist such as Birket Foster abovementioned is really translation of painting into wood-engraving within the engraver's own terms; and on p. 81 of L74, *The Charles Whittinghams Printers*, N.Y., 1896, can be seen a typical and very successful wood-engraved reproduction from a photographic subject—'The Old Composing Room'—in which the technique is entirely the engraver's own.[1] It is only when the use of the wood-block, as of any other reproductive medium, is pushed outside its natural limitations that trouble begins.

With regard to the contribution made by the artists of this period to book-illustration, Rossetti was an imaginative designer, whose work exerted considerable influence on his contemporaries, although some of his interpretations of poetry may seem a little strained. Millais, perhaps the outstanding artist of the group, had a natural instinct for illustration and some of his work is most impressive. Foster and Creswick, in an earlier tradition, were not innovators in design, but their rural vignettes are more companionable to the type-page than the rectangular compositions so often favoured by the Pre-Raphaelites. S159 *Hyperion*, London, 1853, has nearly one hundred typical examples of Foster's work beautifully engraved on wood by Henry Vizetelly—who printed the book—and S165 *L'Allegro and Il Penseroso*, London, 1855, mentioned in a previous paragraph, is a handsome large octavo consisting of 24 pages of thick plate paper with Foster's own etchings on steel, most beautiful in their richness and range of tone, and further enhanced by the unusual treatment of printing the accompanying poems (set in Caslon) entirely in red. Both these books were published by David Bogue, and the *L'Allegro* volume has a strong Victorian stamped cloth-gilt bevel-edged binding by Leighton, Sons & Hodge, with the paper gilt-edged all round. S176, *Kavanagh*, London, 1858, is a similar production to

[1] Incidentally this book (which is beautifully printed by the De Vinne Press) shows on p. 197 a portrait of Mary Byfield who worked as a wood-engraver for the Chiswick Press for 43 years—see Typographical Notes.

Hyperion, also printed by Vizetelly, but with the blocks engraved on wood by N. Woods, and the book published by W. Kent & Co.—'late D. Bogue'.

Other notable illustrators of the sixties are George Pinwell, Arthur Boyd Houghton, and Frederick Walker. Pinwell tended to ask too much of his engravers in the almost over-refined drawings for his detailed compositions, which consequently suffer in reproduction. But J. Mahoney, remembered for his illustrations to Dickens and largely self-taught as an artist, showed understanding of the wood-engraver's technique, which he probably acquired from Whymper, who 'discovered' him. George Du Maurier (1834–96) became in his day a leading black-and-white artist and social commentator. He illustrated Thackeray and contributed to various magazines before joining the staff of *Punch*, in which his best-known work appeared.[1]

John Tenniel, whose career began before the period of the 'sixties' and extended well into the present century, is best remembered to-day for his successful collaboration with the fastidious and exacting 'Lewis Carroll' in his illustration of the 'Alice' books.[2] This task gave scope for his talent for whimsical humour, and during his long life (1820–1914) he became well known as leading cartoonist to *Punch*, for whom he worked for 50 years. His experience made him a competent draughtsman for the wood-engraver and his 'Alice' drawings are beautifully reproduced by the Dalziel brothers, but much of his great output, employed in work for which he was not well suited, has been forgotten.[3]

A book, not in the collection, which is representative of the work of the Pre-Raphaelite illustrators, and other of their

[1] For further comment on the black-and-white illustrators of the British School see J32, Henry Reitlinger, *From Hogarth to Keene*, London, 1958, and other books in the same section.

[2] *Alice in Wonderland*, 1865; *Alice Through the Looking-Glass*, 1871. A full and interesting account of 'the genesis and parturition of these two books' is given in G82, Percy Muir, *English Children's Books 1600–1900*, London, 1954, pp. 137–42.

[3] See Frances Sarzano, *Sir John Tenniel*, in series *English Masters of Black and White*, London, 1948—one of the six volumes from this series presented by W. B. Hislop, Sept. 1969, W24–9.

contemporaries in an earlier tradition, is Moxon's *Tennyson* of 1857, well printed by Richard Clay & Sons and like most of such books of the time, providing a full list of the artists and engravers. David Bland has observed that the undistinguished typography and general design of many of the books of this period are partly accounted for by the fact that much of the illustration had appeared previously in magazines and was not specifically designed for the books in which they later appeared. The inherent hardness of the actual line given by wood-engraving (as by any form of engraving) is generally best offset by a vignetted or irregular edge-treatment, whereas many of the blocks of magazine origin were monotonously rectangular and were used in bookwork with border rules or 'Oxford' borders surrounding them and the text, as if endeavouring to contain what is often inevitably a 'miscellany'. (It will be noticed that of Millais' many illustrations those without defined edges sit more happily on the page than those which are strictly rectangular.) Nevertheless, some of the Victorian ruled borders of this period, when combined with a moderate use of ornament—an inheritance from the more elaborate wood-engraved or lithographically drawn borders of the first half of the century—and printed in tints or colours (including gold and silver) for use in books illustrated with colour wood-blocks, do possess a certain appropriateness—or even charm—especially when used in conjunction with the rather thin 'old style' types which had come back into favour since the 'fifties.

Characteristic examples of the illustrators of the 'sixties will be found in S179, *Favourite Modern Ballads*, London, 1860, containing some extraordinary skilful reproductive wood-engraving, with secondary grey tint-blocks, all beautifully printed by Edmund Evans; S181, *Poems and Pictures*, London, 1860, printed by Clay; S186, *Dalziel's Illustrated Goldsmith*, London, 1865, showing much of Pinwell's best, printed by Dalziel Brothers and a monument to their patient craftsmanship—see, for instance, p. 241, the illustration of a 'pious matron', a wonderful reproduction of an almost impossible technique; S188, *Ballad stories from the Scandinavian*, London, 1866, showing a very interesting 'continuous-line' technique in Dalziel's wood-engravings, anticipating that of some present-day electronic engraving; S191, Ingelow's *Poems*, London, 1867; and S193, *North Coast Poems*, London, 1868.

The various phases of the wood-engraver's reproductive technique, including those used for pen, chalk, wash, or actual photographs, may be amply studied in the magazines S187, *Good Words*, London, 1865; S190, a miscellany of Christmas stories from various annuals, 1867–8, printed by various printers, and including a few wood-block colour plates by Edmund Evans; S192, *The Quiver*, London, 1867; S211 *St. Nicholas*, N.Y., 1882–3; and S212, *The English Illustrated*, London, 1883–4.[1] An earlier example, anticipating the above, is S147, Milner, T., *The Gallery of Nature*, London, 1846, an octavo 'serial production' of 804 pp. in magazine format, with two-column text within rules, wood-engraved illustrations and decorative initials in text, and full-page line-engraved plates on plate paper, some employing mechanical engraving for background skies, etc.

Before proceeding with the development of colour wood-block printing—and its special application to children's books—mention must be made of Lithography, which, discovered and invented by Aloys Senefelder in Bavaria during the years 1797 to 1800, was not used to any extent in bookwork until after the 1820's.[2] Senefelder discovered that a form of limestone could be made 'selective' as a printing surface by application of the

---

[1] W. B. Hislop is of the opinion that wood-engraving in this field reached its highest point, technically, in some of the American magazines of the period, such as *Harper's* and *Scribner's*—not represented in the collection. In a larger scale the amazing reproductive wood-engravings, after paintings by Old Masters, by the American Timothy Cole, show a high degree of virtuosity, and an example, (after a portrait by El Greco) presented to William Maxwell by the late W. E. Rudge of Mount Vernon, N.Y., is in the Collection (in cabinet with other specimens) T52. See also Bland, *A History of Book Illustration*, pp. 300, 304, 307.

[2] Senefelder's own interesting account of the origin and development of his invention was published in Munich and Vienna in 1818. A copy of the first edition of the English translation published by Ackermann in London as *A Complete Course of Lithography*, 1819 (printed by William Clowes) is a valued possession of the Printing Department of the College.

principle of the mutual antipathy of grease and water. The design to be reproduced was drawn on the prepared surface of the stone in a greasy ink, and in printing, the surface was first dampened with water which was absorbed by the 'blank' or non-printing parts of the stone, thus causing them to repel the printing ink, which the water-repellent image received, and from which the ink was transferred to the paper under pressure. It was thus a 'planographic' process, in that both the printing and non-printing portions of the surface were in the same plane, although present-day methods and developments have made refinements on all this. Drawing on the stone could be made with pen, brush or chalk with much less effort than that required for the various methods of engraving and much larger work could be produced in quantity. The surface of the stone was 'grained' or polished according to the nature of the work, chalk-work requiring a grained finish. Drawings could also be made in greasy ink on special papers and transferred to stone, and it was found that engravings on copper could also be similarly transferred, a facility which found very useful service in map-work, music printing, and other applications; and more copies could be printed than was possible from the original copper before it wore out.

W. B. Hislop has pointed out that the freedom of draughtsmanship offered by lithography, without requiring the laborious mastery of a special tool, largely accounted for its extraordinary rapid spread over the globe within Senefelder's lifetime.[1]

Although lithographic stone could give the finest results, its cumbersome nature had various disadvantages, particularly in the kind of printing machinery it required, and after experimenting with various metals, Senefelder discovered that zinc had similar properties to stone and could be substituted for it, a discovery which foreshadowed the use of rotary machinery towards the end of the century. The discoveries of the Scot,

[1] For some notes on the invention and development of lithography, see July 1963 Exhibition Catalogue, *Printing and the Mind of Man*, Earls Court Exhibition section, p. 109, paragraph 'Lithography', and items 622–7.

Mungo Ponton, concerning the light-sensitive properties of a bichromate, referred to later under photography, led to the application of photography to lithography as early as 1840. Direct photo-lithography with gelatine film was invented by Poitevin in 1855 and the first photo-litho transfer was introduced in 1859.[1] During the present century aluminium plates have been introduced, and the use of anodized aluminium is now general. The use of multi-metal plates has also been developed. The offset principle, evolved during the 1870s, by which the inked image was transferred to a rubber blanket cylinder from which it was impressed on the paper, led to a number of far-reaching developments in machine design, and the slight 'give' introduced by the rubber blanket enabled printing to be made on matt or rough-surface paper and other materials. Before the introduction of offset presses the necessity of bringing every portion of the plate or stone into intimate contact with the paper called for enormous pressure, and greatly limited speeds of running.

The early lithographic book-illustrations, as in the case of the copper and steel engravings of the same period, were frequently hand-coloured, and provided a rival to the well-established aquatint—see, for instance, S93, the little *Treatise on the carnation*, London, 1823; *The Bouquet of Melody*, N.Y., 1848, No. 4 in S92–2x, the series of 'Annuals'; and S157, *Voices from the woodlands*, London, 1850, a modest but effective later example.

Senefelder actually printed in colour from about 1800, but after many experiments C. J. Hullmandel[2] (one of the earliest lithographers in London, who learned the craft from Senefelder) in the 1830's developed a technique of printing in various neutral tints from which the white highlights were scraped out. This technique is known as 'lithotint', and examples may be seen in

[1] See Bull, *Photo-Engraving*, London, 1934, pp. 63, 92, and 96. For early experiments by Niepce, the inventor of photography, and others, again see July 1963 Exhibition Catalogue, *Printing and the Mind of Man*, Earls Court Exhibition Section—p. 110, items 632 and 637.

[2] For further details of this early experimental period of lithography and of the work of Hullmandel and others, leading to the development of 'chromolithography', see McLean, *Victorian Book Design*, pp. 54–5.

S167, *Explorations in S.W. Africa*, London, 1856, printed by M. & N. Hanhart, and in S175, *Scotland delineated*, London, 1858, printed by Day & Son, Lithographers to H.M. the Queen. Full colour effects soon followed and 'chromolithography' began to take over from the earlier applications of colour wood-block printing developed by the inventions of George Baxter and Charles Knight in the second quarter of the century, finding a special field in larger books devoted to such subjects as topography, architecture, palaeography, and illuminated manuscripts, bringing these subjects for the first time within a wider range of study.

This development is both anticipated and corroborated by Churton in some interesting observations on p. 18 of his pamphlet *The Author's Hand-Book* (1844) referred to on p. 445, in which, after setting out some of the advantages which he considers the use of the intaglio steel plate has over lithography, he writes, 'But I must not say too much, or it will be thought I have some prejudice against Lithography, which is not the case; for, although I do not admire it for literary illustrations, it is valuable for large plates, and even for books, when coloured illustrations . . . are required'. E83, Westwood, *Palaeographia Sacra Pictoria*, London, 1843–5, Fol., is an example of the kind of book soon to be generally produced entirely by chromolithography. In this volume the lithographed plates have some of the colours and tints added by hand, and Mr Carter states that the gold and silver are overprinted by letterpress.[1]

Towards the end of the century the most elaborate work was being accomplished by chromolithography and although it has to be remembered that a separate stone was required for each colour, as many as twenty printings for one subject was not uncommon. Printed on hand presses or by flat-bed machines

---

[1] The plates in S178, Charles Kingsley's *Glaucus; or the Wonders of the Shore*, 1859, are printed by W. Dickes, a lessee of the Baxter process (referred to under Baxter). For the advance of chromolithography, again see McLean, *Victorian Book Design* above mentioned, p. 81 and elsewhere, U99.

See Typographical Notes and the reference also to M57, William Savage's work on *Practical hints on decorative printing* (1822), of which further details are given on p. 465.

on heavy plate paper the books containing these illustrations tended to be weighty and cumbersome and unless the plates were specially 'guarded in' they had a tendency to fall out.[1] Also with the great number of printings the ink tended to pile up and become unpleasantly 'soapy' or 'oleographic', and any facing plates were very liable to stick together.[2] While some remarkable and sometimes beautiful work was accomplished in this field, showing a high degree of craftsmanship and skill in printing, particularly during the 'forties and 'fifties, chromolithography was inevitably forced to give ground before the great developments in the application of wood-block colour printing initiated largely by Edmund Evans (following upon pioneer work by George Baxter and Charles Knight) in the second half of the century, and it was later readily superseded by the four-colour half-tone photo-mechanical methods of reproduction. All the phases of book production during the Victorian period are amply and discerningly described—and illustrated—by Ruari McLean in his *Victorian Book Design*[3] (London 1967) from which some of the material in the following paragraphs has been condensed. Examples of chromolithography in the collection are referred to later.

An important name in connexion with the early application of chromolithography to the printed book is that of Henry Shaw (1800–73), scholar, draughtsman, and engraver who, over a period of nearly 40 years, produced a number of books—some of them magnificent—on medieval art and illumination, mostly published by Pickering and beautifully printed (as far as text and wood-block printing is concerned) by Whittingham at the Chiswick Press. His earlier books employ a variety of processes, including copperplate hand-coloured, and colour wood-blocks, and thus cover the interesting transitional period during which these processes were being generally supplanted by lithography.

[1] A tendency aggravated by the use of unsewn gutta-percha bindings for many of these books.

[2] See, for instance, S203, Walton, *The Bernese Oberland*, London, 1874, a book which exhibits all these faults, although the actual compositions are attractive.

[3] U99 in the Collection is the second edition of 1972.

His *Hand Book of mediaeval alphabets and devices*, Fol., London, Henry Geo. Bohn, 1856, N61 in the collection, shows wood-engraved alphabets and initials in colour, some very well executed, and J36, his *Art of illumination as practised during the middle ages*, Fol., London, 1870, has fine monochrome wood-engraved illustration, printed, with the text, at the Chiswick Press, and coloured plates chromolithographed by Vincent Brooks, Day & Son. Unfortunately this book is an example of inadequate binding already referred to, and all the plates are loose. An earlier and more elaborate treatise on the same subject is J39, Tymms, *The Art of illuminating as practised in Europe*, London, 1860, with colour plates chromolithographed by 'Day & Son, lithographers to the Queen' (before their amalgamation with Vincent Brooks) and an introduction by Digby Wyatt[1] which refers to the work of Owen Jones and Noel Humphreys, the subjects of the following paragraph. This book is excellently bound in a Victorian 'grolieresque' binding; it opens well and the plates have no tendency to become loose. It is unfortunate that this type of book frequently has—as in this case—indifferent 'gothic' lettering on the lithographed title. Incidentally this book contains some interesting Victorian type-ornament.

But the most influential pioneers in the endeavour to use chromolithography in conjunction with the printed page are Owen Jones and Noel Humphreys—both, like Henry Shaw, particularly interested in ornament and illumination. Owen Jones (1809–74), an architect, made a special study of the decoration of the Alhambra Palace in Spain, of which he made systematic drawings. For the publication of these in two folio volumes between 1836 and 1846, he used various contemporary processes, including chromo-lithographs in six or seven printings from the stone and zinc,[2] having set up his own press with help from the lithographic firm of Day & Haghe. He also

---

[1] For the importance of Digby Wyatt—more especially his *The Industrial Arts of the Nineteenth Century*, 1853—see McLean, *Victorian Book Design*, pp. 86–9; also p. 83, pl. 33, and elsewhere.

[2] 'The first of their kind to be produced in England, the forerunners of a great new industry'—McLean, *Victorian Book Design*, p. 57.

produced illuminated gift books, but his great work was his *Grammar of Ornament*, superbly lithographed, and published by Day & Son in 1856. A copy of this outstanding production has now (1969) been added to the collection, splendidly bound in full levant, with double raised bands and linear decoration in gold and blind, by A. W. Currie of the Department of Printing and Publishing, Napier College, from whom the volume was acquired (S167A). Other of Owen Jones's activities included his contribution to the decoration of the Great Exhibition of 1851 and to that of the Crystal Palace.

Henry Noel Humphreys (1810–79), author and illustrator, whose work, like that of Owen Jones, is essentially 'decorative', spent some years in Italy, where he became greatly influenced by Italian art, especially the illuminated manuscript. His first published book, *The Coins of England*, 1849, included chromolithographed plates of coins against a royal blue background. This was followed by other books, some on biblical subjects, such as *The Parables of Our Lord*, 1847, and *The Miracles of Our Lord*, 1848, in which he endeavoured to make the most appropriate use of illumination, beautifully chromolithographed. He also produced designs of characteristically studied intricacy for woodcut ornament and initials, mainly used in books printed by Vizetelly Brothers and Edmund Evans, and he took great interest in the binding and decoration of his books, some of which were most elaborate. An outstanding example of his 'derivative' work is the gift book, S154, *A Record of the Black Prince*, 1849, which contains six very finely executed chromolithographed plates, and beautifully wood-engraved borders and initials in black and red. The text, printed by Vizetelly Brothers in a Figgins black-letter, and the elaborate moulded papier-mâché binding, simulating carved ebony (and adapted from one of the compartments of the prince's tomb at Canterbury) are all characteristic features of 'Victorian Gothic'. Noel Humphreys was also very interested in natural history (especially in entomology), which was one of the many subjects which he recommended for study by all interested in illumination, and in 1851 there was published by Wm. S. Orr & Co., in two quarto volumes, his *British Moths and their Transformations*, 'arranged and illustrated in a series of plates by H. Noel Humphreys, Esq., with characters and descriptions by J. O. Westwood, Esq.' (author of E83, *Palaeographia Sacra Pictoria*, referred to on p. 458, and other works on illuminated manuscripts). The illustrations are superbly lithographed by Humphreys, with a precision which has almost the appearance of metal engraving, and most of the hand-colouring is of the very highest order, although a few colours have suffered some change over the years. This work was followed, within the same decade, by *The Genera of British Moths and Butterflies*, 'popularly described and arranged according to the System now adopted by the British Museum, illustrated by a series of picturesque plates, exhibiting the insects in their different stages, with the caterpillars and the plants on which they feed'. This was published in three small-folio volumes, by Paul Jerrard & Son—the *Butterflies* in one volume, perhaps in 1859, and again the plates, 96 in all, are perfectly lithographed by Humphreys, but the hand-colouring is a little uneven in quality. In these two works the species, with the caterpillars and their respective plants, are beautifully arranged on each plate, and the labour involved in their compilation must have been prodigious, but Humphreys appears to have been quite undaunted. In the preface to the earlier *Moths* volumes he writes, 'The number of moths greatly exceeds the butterflies, which will oblige me in the present work frequently to give as many as twenty species upon a single plate; a labour which I cheerfully undertake, in order to produce a more complete and at the same time more accessible work than has hitherto appeared on the subject.' The printer of the letterpress for the two Moths volumes (1851) is Thos. Harrild, and, for the three-volume work, Bradbury & Evans, but of the lithographic plates no printer is mentioned.[1]

---

[1] In this connexion it is also of interest to note that, concerning Humphreys' *illuminated* books, McLean writes, 'No lithographer is mentioned in any of them (italics ours): but most of them were probably printed under the supervision of Owen Jones at 9 Argyll Place' (off Regent Street, London)—*Victorian Book Design*, p. 78.

Humphreys' little book *River Gardens*, S172, 1857, contains full-page wood-engraved plates, printed in black with buff-tinted background, and colours added by hand, and also typical decorative wood-engraved initials.[1]

But Humphreys' historical interest in book decoration embraced the whole craft of printing as well as that of illuminating, and his work reached a wider public than that of his abovementioned contemporaries; and in drawing inspiration from medieval book-illumination his work—as that of Owen Jones—to some extent anticipates that of William Morris. It also represents a significant phase in the era before colour wood-engraving took over the ascendancy from lithography. A copy of the second Issue of his *A History of the Art of Printing*, M31 in the collection, is a folio published by Quaritch, London, 1868, 'illustrated by 100 facsimiles in photolithography [by Day & Son] executed under the direction of the author'. In the preface Humphreys refers to the 'sudden winding-up' of Day & Son, which preceded their being taken over by Vincent Brooks as 'Vincent Brooks, Day & Son'—a sign of the times, for sales of chromo-lithography were dwindling. N43 is a copy of Humphreys' *Masterpieces of the early printers and engravers*, Fol., Sotheran, London, 1870, with facsimile plates by Vincent Brooks, Day & Son, and descriptive text facing, printed by Wyman's, each commentary opening with a reproduction of a decorative initial. Humphreys states in the preface and on the title that his endeavour has been 'to exhibit the best examples . . . combining the labours of printer and engraver . . . remarkable for illustrative devices, beautiful borders, decorative initials, printers' marks, elaborate title-pages . . . the greater part of the examples now published for the first time'. These two books are characteristic of Noel Humphreys' painstaking endeavours to popularize knowledge of printing and illustration.

But, for all their interest in decoration and illumination, it cannot be said that either Owen Jones or Noel Humphreys ever

---

[1] Companion volumes (not in the Collection) are *Ocean Gardens*, 1857, and *The Butterfly Vivarium*, 1858.

attained to a perfected sense of letter-forms, and it was also inevitable that the interest in illumination which their work engendered in the Victorian era did lead to some debasement of lettering in its popular use on music covers, religious mottoes, Christmas cards, etc. It remained for Edward Johnston, at the end of the century, following the impetus given by William Morris, Emery Walker, and the Arts and Crafts movement, to 'rediscover the whole craft of lettering' as referred to later. But, by their great energy and devotion, Jones and Humphreys did much to spread a genuine scholarly interest in the decorative arts, and they opened up completely new fields in the application of lithography. Of the two men, Jones, as an architect, had the better sense of design for the book as a whole, in which Humphreys' work is in some ways more naive—but for a full appraisal of their respective attainments, reference is recommended to Ruari McLean's *Victorian Book Design*, U99, especially chapters 8, 9 ,and 10.

Typical examples of the larger book with elaborate chromo-lithography are S189, Lose, *Terra cotta architecture of North Italy*, London, John Murray, 1867, printed by Spottiswoode & Co., and S230, Gibb, *The Royal House of Stuart*, London, Macmillan, 1890, with colour plates printed in Edinburgh by McLagan & Cumming and text printed by R. & R. Clark, a work dedicated to Queen Victoria. Both these weighty volumes—the first of which is essentially a book of plates with ancillary text—are examples of fine lithographic draughtsmanship and printing, yet each shows in different ways the limitations as well as the possibilities of chromolithography. In the Lose volume the illustrations are technically competent, showing fine detail printed in excellent register, but the colours tend to be flat and lifeless, with some soapiness of finish. In the Gibb volume as many as twenty printings have been used for some plates (the late Mr Charles Cumming informed the writer of these notes that for work of this kind as many as three different 'whites' were sometimes required) and, although some of the results are beautiful, the excessive overprinting has tended in some cases to produce a rather unpleasant sheen. In the Lose volume the illustrations on heavy plate paper are pasted in, and the book requires great care in opening. In the Gibb volume, which has a handsome half morocco and vellum-gilt binding, the plates have all been carefully guarded in, and the book opens beautifully.

Chromolithography is also associated with the illustration of certain English sporting books of the 'sixties and 'seventies, such as some of the Surtees novels illustrated by Henry Alken with full-page plates chromolithographed by Hanhart. Typical of these are S202, *Jorrocks' Jaunts and Jollities*, London, 1874, 4th ed., and S204, '*Down the Road*', London, 1875, in the latter of which it will again be noted that the illustrations, on heavy paper, tipped in, are becoming loose and the whole book, printed on paper with the 'grain' the wrong way, is difficult to open and is beginning to disintegrate. These books are *not in any sense* examples of integration of illustration with text.

S196, *Miss Kilmansegg*, London, Moxon, 1870 ($8\frac{1}{2} \times 6\frac{1}{2}$ in.) is of interest in that the illustrations (by Thomas Seccombe, R.A.) together with the script for the text (stanzas) have been copper-engraved and transferred to stone for printing by lithography, and in S199, Mercier, *Mountains and Lakes of Switzerland*, London, Bell & Daldy, 1871, while the plain pages of text have been printed by letterpress, those portions of the text which appear on the same pages as the chromolitho illustrations have been transferred to stone or plate for lithographic printing—a procedure which must have involved very careful make-up.

Before the development of chromolithography, a pioneer experimenter in colour printing in the early 19th-century was William Savage (1770–1843). Savage, whose work anticipates that of George Baxter described later, made use of colour wood-blocks, and his work on *Practical hints on decorative printing*, London, 1822, 'printed in colours at the Type Press' Fol., (M57 in the collection), is of both technical and general interest in that it not only contains reproductions from a variety of subjects (one plate printed from no less than twenty-nine wood-blocks) but the author describes his methods and materials. He also published in 1832 a work *On the Preparation of Printing Ink* and, in 1841, his carefully compiled *Dictionary of the art of printing* (M56 in the collection) which still contains much of interest.[1]

Examples of an interesting and in some ways unique process of colour printing in the early 19th century will be found in the plates of tartans in volumes I and II of S121–1C, Browne, J., *A history of the Highlands and of the Highland Clans, c.* 1838, 4 volumes, printed in Edinburgh by Fullarton & Macnab, employing 'Mauchline Machine Printing' which is described as 'weaving with colours'. A typewritten extract, taken from another book not in the collection, and describing the process which is carried out by paper-ruling machine, is inserted in Volume I.

But the name of one whose work exerted a far-reaching influence on the development of both wood-block colour printing and chromolithography is that of George Baxter (1804–67). The son of a printer in Lewes, Sussex,[2] he showed considerable artistic ability and, having early learned both lithography and wood-engraving, he patented in 1835 a process which had an almost immediate effect on the reproduction of pictures in colour.[3] Up to that time the main method of colouring prints made by the various forms of metal-engraving or by lithography had been by hand, but Baxter substituted a series of wood-blocks or metal relief blocks (from ten to twenty or even more, for one subject) printed by letterpress in oil inks on a key impression made from an intaglio steel or copper plate or from a lithographic stone or plate—most frequently intaglio, including aquatint and mezzotint, as these

[1] For a full and interesting note on the work of William Savage, see July 1963 Exhibition Catalogue, *Printing and the Mind of Man*, British Museum Exhibition Section, p. 44, item 141.

[2] John Baxter, printer, publisher, bookseller, and co-inventor with Robert Harrild of the composition-roller.

[3] The work and influence of George Baxter and his pupils is summarized by Ruari McLean in *Victorian Book Design*, Chapter 5. A well produced little booklet, *Early Colour Printing and George Baxter*, 'a monograph by James Cordingley', produced in the Printing Department of the North-Western Polytechnic, London, 1948–9, is in the Printing Department of the College. It includes four attractive reproductions of Baxter prints, printed from electrotypes in eight workings.

gave the widest range of texture and tone. The key impression was usually printed in a neutral grey, but sometimes in terra cotta. 'Baxter prints', which have a subtlety and richness of colouring all their own, became very popular at the middle of the century, and an exceptionally fine series, selected by the late Dr Cameron Smail, framed and glazed, and covering a very wide and representative range of Baxter's work, was added to the collection during the war period (1940 et seq.). An examination of these prints reveals not only Baxter's extraordinary skill and patience as a printer but also his very real ability as artist and draughtsman. Some of the prints in the series are from aquatint base only, others also include fine line-engraving as well as stipple. Descriptions of the prints, sometimes giving the number of blocks used, are in some cases given on the backs of their respective mounts.[1]

Among Baxter's pupils when he set up his business in London were Harrison Weir, who later became noted for his fine illustrations of animals, and George Cargill Leighton (1826–95) who, when out of his apprenticeship in 1843, joined with other pupils of Baxter to set up a separate firm which in 1849 he finally took over as 'Leighton Brothers'. In that year Baxter's patent expired, but he was granted an extension of five years. Leighton, who had unsuccessfully challenged the renewal, was therefore obliged not to infringe Baxter's patent, the essence

[1] The series comprises the following (the descriptions of basic plates given are conjectural, and subject to verification): *fine aquatint base*—'Four Scenes: Ascent of Mount Blanc', in one frame, each $4\frac{1}{4} \times 6$ in.; *coarser grain aquatint base*—'Winter Scene with Farmhouse' and 'The Swan Inn', each $10\frac{1}{2} \times 15$ in.; *very fine line- and stipple-engraved base*—'The Pompeian Court of the Crystal Palace', $7\frac{3}{4} \times 11\frac{1}{2}$ in., eleven blocks; 'The Bridesmaid', $15 \times 10\frac{3}{4}$ in. not less than nine blocks. It is interesting to compare these Baxter prints with a fine framed print, of historical and technical interest, in the Heriot-Watt University, entitled 'The Queen's Birthday, 1856', and showing 'The "James Watt" man-of-war, colours flying and manned at the yard'. This print has been made from wood-blocks by George C. Leighton, a pupil of Baxter's whose work is referred to in the paragraph following that on Baxter above. Among the framed prints referred to above will also be found a title-page design, 'Mansions of England, by Joseph Nash', (n.d.), $11 \times 7\frac{1}{4}$ in. This is a lithographic chalk drawing with colour added by water-colour tints, but it is not known whether it has anything to do with Baxter.

of which was the use of an intaglio plate for the key, but he appears to have substituted quite successfully a wood-block for this key impression also, and he produced some very interesting work by the Leighton 'Chromatic Process'. An outstanding example of this process in the collection is S161, *The Poultry book*, 1853, published by W. S. Orr, containing some splendid pictures by Harrison Weir 'printed under his superintendence', in which it is very interesting to note that, whatever restrictions Leighton may have been under, some of the skies (e.g. in the 'Bantams' plate, following p. 190) show distinctly a mottled or 'mezzotint' technique, including parallel streaks such as are obtainable by a graining tool—although Leighton may have been able to get this effect from wood. Another broken-tone effect for skies and other tints is seen in S163, *Stories about beasts*, London, 1854, a little book for children, also including some vigorous illustrations after Harrison Weir, and published by Darton (a name associated with the earliest books for children with coloured illustrations). This little book bears a letterpress imprint of J. O. Clarke, but the technique of the plates appears to be identical with that of Leighton, the mottled tones being particularly noticeable in the plates for the Elephant, the Cow, and the Dog. At this period it is sometimes difficult to say exactly how some colour prints were produced, as various mixed methods were used. It was also possible to treat relief blocks with a resinous 'dust-grain', giving a broken tone like aquatint, and in this connexion it is of special interest to note that Edmund Evans actually employed a grain similar to that used in aquatint for some of the tints in his reproductions of Caldecott's pictures[1]—see especially S222, his *Graphic* contributions, referred to later.

After the expiry of his patent in 1854, Baxter found himself in financial difficulties. He granted licences of his process

[1] Mr Rex Evans, grandson of Edmund Evans, informed the writer of these notes that his grandfather 'used aquatint' in reproducing much of Caldecott's later work, but from an examination of the impressions it would appear that the aquatint grain was used as a *relief* printing surface, as abovementioned, since the grain is the reverse of that appearing in a normal aquatint print, which is, of course, made from an *intaglio* plate.

to others, among whom—besides Leighton—was the artist, engraver, lithographer, and printer William Dickes (1815–92), an excellent example of whose use of the process may be seen in Charles Kingsley's little book, S178, *Glaucus; or The Wonders of the Shore*, London, 1859, 4th ed. in which an aquatint base is used for the plates—some of which are really beautiful—if one can overlook the overprint 'sheen' in a few places.[1] Another and less successful example of the use of the process by Dickes—in this case apparently combined with lithography—is S201, *Beauty in Common Things*, London, 1874; and the printer of the illustrations to S209, Cook, *Three voyages*, London, 1882, evidently employs the process, but the plates do not bear an imprint. Another noted lessee of the Baxter process was J. M. Kronheim (referred to later under 'Toy Books' and Kate Greenaway) who, like Dickes, was also a lithographer, but his work does not appear to be represented in the collection.[2]

In 1885 Leighton (who in 1858 had become printer and publisher of the *Illustrated London News*—for which two years previously he had printed from wood-blocks the first colour illustrations to appear in a journal) sold his business to Vincent Brooks, Day & Son, so that some of the Baxter 'know-how' was handed on to a leading firm of lithographers. Baxter is therefore important in that not only was his process followed up by various of his pupils and lessees, becoming also the basis of the first experiments by Edmund Evans, the great Victorian colour-printer, but also because his work had a transmitted influence on the development of chromo-lithography which, after being eclipsed by the success of wood-block colour-printing, came into its own again in the era of poster printing which followed, reaching its zenith in the

[1] As already mentioned, a more distinguished example of Dickes's use of this process, Philip Gosse's noted book, *A History of Sea-Anemonies and Corals*, 1860, demy 8vo, has recently been added to the collection by W. B. Hislop—see footnote on p.458, directing comparison of this use of the Baxter process with work (in similar books) by Leighton's modification of it, and with work in early chromolithography by Hanhart and others.

[2] For details of Kronheim's work see McLean, *Victorian Book Design*, pp. 33, 142–4, and (re 'Toy Books') pp. 135–6, 138.

succeeding century, notably during the 1920's and '30's, when Vincent Brooks, Day & Son were among the eminent firms who became engaged in this work. An example of Victorian chromolithography by Vincent Brooks, Day & Son is S195, *Canaries and Cage Birds*, London, [1870], the plates of which show fine rendering of colour and detail, while at the same time exhibiting most of the characteristic shortcomings of chromolithography already mentioned. Compared with the better examples of the Baxter and other wood-block processes of the same period, such as in *The Poultry book* above described, the plates, some of which have gathered fluff from the text-pages opposite, appear somewhat lifeless.

After Baxter the second early letterpress colour printer was Charles Knight (1791–1873), important as a pioneer of cheap literature and also as the patentee of an interesting and original method of printing in colours from wood and metal plates. There does not appear to be an example of his printing in the collection but his work is fully described in Chapter 5 of Ruari McLean's *Victorian Book Design*, above mentioned.

A vogue for children's books began in the late 18th-century and was considerably developed during the 19th. Characteristic examples of early 19th-century works intended for the 'improvement of young people' may be seen in S67, *Blossoms of morality*, London, 1806, which includes engravings by John Bewick, and in the neat little books of 'Peter Parley's Tales' on historical subjects, with wood-engraved illustration, soundly printed by Whittingham the elder of the Chiswick Press—see S117, *Tales about Great Britain*, 1836, and S127, S131 (1838 and 1839 respectively) companion volumes about Greece and Rome. 'Peter Parley' is the editorial name adopted by Samuel Clark, a partner in the well-known firm of Darton and Clark, and the earliest of the Parley books for children in the collection, S104, *Wonders of Art*, London, 183–, is printed and published by that firm.[1]

A rival to 'Peter Parley' was Henry Cole (1808–82) who,

[1] *Peter Parley's Annual*, believed to be the earliest boys' annual, was started in 1839—McLean, *Victorian Book Design*, pp. 34, 39, 45.

in 1840 under the pseudonym of 'Felix Summerly', launched the very successful 'Home Treasury' series of books for children, also beautifully printed at the Chiswick Press, and published by Joseph Cundall—a name associated with excellence in book design. McLean states that the illustrations to the earlier titles in the series were usually by lithography, the later ones cut in wood, and some were hand-coloured. When colour printing was introduced it was all from wood, and it is of interest to note that it was carried out by Gregory, Collins & Reynolds, the firm set up by some of Baxter's pupils in 1843 and later taken over by Leighton, as already mentioned, but unfortunately this series is not represented in the collection.

To this period belongs Edward Lear (1812–88), important as an illustrator and in many ways unique. His prime interest was in painting (he became a regular exhibitor at the Royal Academy) and he first attracted attention by his paintings of birds. He travelled widely and became better known through his travel books with his own illustrations, for some of which he used lithotint. His famous *Book of Nonsense* (1846) was printed entirely by lithography, later books with wood-blocks. Through this book and others in the same vein Lear became perhaps the first to introduce entertainment into children's books in place of 'moral instruction'.[1]

A very skilful wood-engraver and printer who produced some beautiful work in colour, of greater delicacy than the vigorous and sometimes rather 'impressionist' work of Leighton, was Henry Vizetelly (1820–94), printer of the text of S154, the *Black Prince* volume already described. Other examples of his work in the collection (not in colour) are S159, *Hyperion*, London, 1853, also previously mentioned, which includes his engravings on wood after Birket Foster, and S162, Tupper, *Proverbial philosophy*, London, 1854, which contains illustrations after various artists reproduced by several engravers including the Dalziels, and elaborate woodcut floral initials designed by Noel Humphreys. Henry Vizetelly's other and wider

[1] F139, *Edward Lear's Nonsense Songs*, London, 1938, No. 8 of the Zodiac Books has line-block reproductions.

activities are mentioned in a later footnote, under Edmund Evans.

But it was Edmund Evans (1825–1905) who in the latter half of the century made the greatest advances in the printing of colour wood-blocks on a commercial scale, especially through his books for children, by which his name is probably best remembered. As his work extends from the period of the heyday of Victorian wood-engraving to the decades during which photo-mechanical methods took over in the field of illustration, it covers a most important and significant era in the history of printing. Concerning this period, Ruari McLean writes, 'It might be expected that the commercial wood-engravers, who merely engraved an artist's original drawings on wood, would be humble down-trodden creatures. In fact, the opposite was the case. The leading wood-engravers were men of great character and originality who initiated the work that kept them busy. Many became publishers. Ebenezer Landells, to whom Edmund Evans was apprenticed in 1840, was one of the founders of *Punch* and the *Illustrated London News*; Henry Vizetelly, who began as a wood-engraver and printer, and was extremely skilful as both, became a leading publisher, editor, and foreign correspondent; the Dalziel brothers commissioned many of the finest illustrated gift-books of the 'sixties. The skill of the wood-engravers was often much greater than that of the artists whose work they were responsible for reproducing: their profession was at the very heart of the Victorian book and magazine world.'[1]

Evans's greatest contribution, apart from his own skill and resourcefulness, was undoubtedly the courage and discernment he showed in his 'discovery' of artists whose work he was prepared to back wholeheartedly in enterprises in which he was personally very much involved. The most notable of these are Walter Crane (1845–1915), Kate Greenaway (1846–1901), and Randolph Caldecott (1846–1886), and their success, especially perhaps Kate Greenaway's, was very much bound up with his own. By his ability and sound judgment Evans built up a

[1] See Ruari McLean, *The Reminiscences of Edmund Evans*, Oxford, 1967, Introduction, p. vii.

unique position, so that publishers—especially Routledge—came to rely on his advice, and even to entrust him with commissioning work for them.

Edmund Evans was apprenticed to Landells (who, with Luke Clennell and William Harvey, had been one of Bewick's leading pupils) in 1840, and a year later he was joined by Birket Foster, who was apprenticed as an artist, and the two became lifelong friends, their work taking them on many expeditions together. Birket Foster's pictures and vignettes of English rural landscape and village life still have their appeal to many, as they did in the earlier years of an urban and commercial age. When out of his time Evans set up on his own, moving in 1857 to Racquet Court, Fleet Street, where he remained for nearly fifty years. His skill in colour work soon became known and his commercial success began with a commission to print book covers ('Yellow Backs') with illustrations by popular artists of the day, for the new railway bookstall market, which was sustained for many years. Much of his early work in book printing was in association with Foster, and a splendid example of this collaboration is S177, *The Poems of Oliver Goldsmith*, published by Routledge in 1859 with colour illustrations by Foster from blocks engraved by Evans, and decorations by Noel Humphreys in black and varying tints of pale grey, giving an effect simulating line-engraving. The blocks have been cut with great skill and delicacy and the 'register' is perfect throughout.[1] Another fine example of Evans's work, with several artists including Foster, is S179, *A Book of Favourite Modern Ballads*, referred to under the 'sixties'. This was published by W. Kent & Co. (late D. Bogue) in 1860, and contains some of the most skilful reproductive wood-engraving, with secondary tints in light warm greys, giving a wide and subtle range of tone. The decorative floral ruled borders, headpieces and tailpieces are by Albert Warren, once assistant to Owen Jones, and designer of various decorative Victorian bindings. Again all is beautifully engraved and printed by Evans.

[1] McLean is of the opinion that this book was probably planned by Joseph Cundall.

According to McLean it seems to have been in 1865 that Routledge and Warne began to publish 'Toy Books', from which date the enormous output of colour-printed books for children really begins. The Routledge Toy Books measured $10\frac{1}{2}\times9$ in., and consisted of six pages of text and six pages of coloured illustrations, printed one side only, bound in paper covers. They were sold at 1s., or mounted on cloth at 2s. Warne's first Toy Books, in similar style, were the 'Aunt Louisa' series, and Evans's part in the printing of these early Toy Books is related in *Victorian Book Design* (1963), pp. 133–8.

Evans's first discovery was Walter Crane (1845–1915), who had been apprenticed to the wood-engraver W. J. Linton, where he learned to draw on wood before he turned his attention to illustration. In 1866 Routledge began, with the publication of *Sing a Song of Sixpence*, Crane's first series of sixpenny Toy Books which, after a slightly slow start, grew steadily in popularity. The series, which was much more elaborate and sophisticated in design than the other Toy Books, were designed throughout by the artist and printed in three colours by Evans, thus marking a new step forward in design and simplification of colour. Crane was essentially a designer and decorative artist, who preferred to give an 'all-over' treatment to the entire book —including cover and title—which he sometimes accomplished very successfully, as may be seen in S227, *The Baby's Bouquet*, 1890, and S252, *The Baby's Opera*, considered by many his best work in this series, the latter showing successful integration of music with the other motifs in the design.[1] Evans's collaboration with Crane gave ample scope for his skill in colour work, and Crane is important in that during his lifetime his work was successively reproduced by both autographic and photo-mechanical methods. For instance, in the collection S253, *A Floral Fantasy*, 1899, which shows Pre-Raphaelite influence, is printed by letterpress from three-colour half-tone process-blocks, but S256, *A Masque of Days*, 1901, is printed by lithography, with decorative paper-board cover design and

[1] See July 1963 Exhibition Catalogue, *Printing and the Mind of Man*, Earls Court Exhibition section, p. 108, item 617.

end-papers all in keeping. Both books are printed by the firm of Edmund Evans. Crane exhibited at the R.A., wrote books on design,[1] and from 1898 to 1899 was Principal of the Royal College of Art, London.

Evans's next discovery was Kate Greenaway (1846–1901) with whom he began work in 1877. According to Muir,[2] her first book commission was in 1871, by the firm of Kronheim & Co., an 'Aunt Louisa' Toy Book, published by Warne, who, with Routledge—both helped by the impetus given through the work of Evans—had by this time opened up a new market in children's books, and it has highly coloured illustrations, very different from her later style. Kate Greenaway's father was employed as an engraver at Landells, and showed some of his daughter's drawings to Evans. In 1877 she took a book of her drawings and verses to Evans, who boldly decided to publish them and, without consulting Routledge, to that publisher's dismay printed 20,000 copies to sell at 6s., but they sold out immediately and Kate Greenaway's success was assured. The book, *Under the Window*, was still in print, from electros made from the original blocks, in the 1960's.

Kate Greenaway's drawings of children, whom she clothed with costumes of her own devising, have both delicacy and charm, but even when pictured in action, the figures appear a little 'posed', and the faces she gave them have a certain marionette-like vacancy, as though the artist was shy of portraying any emotion. Her collaboration with Evans was most successful, especially in the use and choice of colour. In his *Reminiscences* Evans states that he developed a procedure of sending his artists proofs, engraved from their key drawings made on wood, to colour with simple washes, and, after colour separation, printing in colours prepared from pigments similar to those used by the artist.[3] He also describes how, for Kate Greenaway's work, he used the new technique of *photographing*

[1] See J7, Walter Crane, *Of the decorative illustration of books*, London, 1896.
[2] See G82, Percy Muir, *English Children's Books, 1600 to 1900*, p. 184.
[3] See McLean, *The Reminiscences of Edmund Evans*, pp. 61–5.

the drawings on to wood, engraving them and transferring the wet impressions on to other blocks for engraving the colours —'a costly matter, but it reproduced the colours very well indeed'—surely a foreshadowing of the day of photo-engraving.

Evans also records a very interesting technical point about paper, which shows his characteristic courage and resourcefulness. Kate Greenaway particularly wanted one book (*Mother Goose*, 1881) to be printed on 'rough paper'. Evans states that it was impossible to print in colours on rough paper 'like drawing paper', he had the rough paper which he had supplied rolled on both sides in copper plates, printed when smooth and then, when quite dry, dipped in water, which completely restored the rough surface so that 'it looked exactly as if it had been printed on rough paper', after which it was dried again, 'and the colours had not suffered by this method'.

Kate Greenaway is well represented in the collection by four books, in each of which her work, engraved and printed by Evans, is differently deployed. S215, *Language of flowers*, Routledge [1884], is a charming little book, with colour wood-blocks, text in a harmonizing brown ink, and a sap green rule round all pages. An almost half-tone effect is obtained in the blocks by skilful cross-cutting. The book has brown endpapers and a beautifully designed paper-board binding printed in flat colours. S219, Mavor, *The English Spelling Book*, Routledge, 1885, is a small narrow octavo with wood-engraved illustrations in pure line printed in sepia ink and including the oft-reproduced alphabet-letters with children's figures.[1] S232, *Marigold Garden*, Routledge (n.d., before 1890) is a quarto with Kate Greenaway's pictures and verses, and its colour wood-blocks are fine examples of Evans's technique of engraving and printing, showing the great variety of tints he obtained by the successive

---

[1] In his *Reminiscences* Edmund Evans writes, 'I particularly wanted R. Caldecott to join with Kate Greenaway in illustrating this book, but K.G. was dead against it, so, as usual in such cases, I had to give way: K.G. got her way! I still feel sure R.C. would have been of immense value and the Public would have taken cheerfully to this book, which, I am sorry to say, they did not. This was one of my failures . . .'. McLean, *The Reminiscences of Edmund Evans*, p. 58.

overprinting, on smooth paper, of cross-line 'grids' and dots in subtly differing colours. The cover-design is in keeping, and the whole book gives an impression of a most successful collaboration between artist and printer. S233, Bret Harte's *The Queen of the Pirate Isle* (c. 1890), a quarto published by Warne, is printed on a toned laid paper of fairly soft surface. Margins are spacious and some of the colour-effects on this paper are most pleasing—see for instance page-opening 28–9—again the result of the same effective collaboration. It is only unfortunate that some of the illustrations are somewhat marred by the very heavy impression of the backing letterpress. S234, *The Old farm gate*, Routledge, 1890, is a quarto containing twenty-five full-page pictures, and text illustration, in black only, by various artists, including Kate Greenaway.

A book printed by Evans for the Religious Tract Society, probably before any of the Kate Greenaways abovementioned, is S207, *Story-Land* (n.d., c. 1880), a quarto with thirty-two illustrations by Robert Barnes, wood-engraved and printed in colours. The illustrations in this book are not in any way stylized as those of Greenaway and Crane, but are delightful observations of childhood in the country and by the seaside, and they are engraved and printed with consummate skill by Evans, showing particularly clearly his technique 'anticipating half-tone'. The cover has a cloth gilt spine and bevelled varnished-paper boards bearing a full colour text-picture, re-engraved with an extra black printing, within a lively border of daisies, forget-me-nots and ferns, designed by Noel Humphreys and printed with a black key-plate background. S237, Watts, I., *Divine and Moral songs for children*, London, c. 1890, a little 16mo printed by Evans from colour wood-blocks on smooth paper, is another example of his technique anticipating half-tone or the use of shading media. Another decorative children's book printed by Evans is S250, *Book of Nursery Rhymes*, London, 1897, published by Methuen, illustrated and ornamented by Francis Bedford, who was once Owen Jones's assistant, and who lithographed 100 plates for his *Grammar of Ornament*. This book gives the impression of being a little taut and over-designed—and again the typography is in brown.

In the late 'seventies Evans was looking for a successor to Crane for the Routledge Toy Books, and in 1878, a year after he had commenced work with Kate Greenaway, he chose Randolph Caldecott (1846–86) who began by producing *John Gilpin* and *The House that Jack Built*, which led to his providing two annually until his early death.[1] More than a million copies of these books have been sold and they are still being printed. Caldecott, who began life as a bank clerk, was commissioned by J. D. Cooper, a wood-engraver, to make sketches for Washington Irving's *Old Christmas*, 1875, and also for *Bracebridge Hall*, 1876, of which an 1882 edition, printed by R. & R. Clark of Edinburgh, with wood-engraved illustrations in black, is in the collection (S210). Caldecott's work is very different from Crane's, being freer and more literal, with a kindly humour all his own, and it can be studied at its best in S222, *The Complete collection of Randolph Caldecott's contributions to the 'Graphic'*, 1888, the large volume already referred to, which includes a brief biography in Arthur Locker's preface. The dust-grain ('aquatint') technique employed by Evans for the tints in some of these sketches makes an interesting study. A Caldecott Toy Book is S226, *Babes in the Wood*, 1890.

Before leaving Edmund Evans mention must be made of the enduring and inimitable series of children's books by Beatrix Potter, which began with Peter Rabbit in 1901. These were printed by Edmund Evans's successors in four-colour letterpress half-tone.[2]

Another notable Victorian colour printer was Benjamin Fawcett (1808–93) of Driffield in Yorkshire, bookseller, stationer, designer, engraver, and publisher. He collaborated with the Rev. Francis O. Morris in the production of works on natural history, to the study of which they were both devoted. Some of Fawcett's wood-engraving was superb and he gave the greatest care to printing. There is only one example of his work

[1] See G82, Percy Muir, *English Children's Books, 1600 to 1900*, p. 183.
[2] See U118B.

in the collection but it is outstanding. It is S238, Hibberd, *New and rare beautiful-leaved plants*, London, 1891, 2nd ed., a truly remarkable achievement in wood-block colour printing. Unfortunately Fawcett was not a typographer and the rest of the book is ordinary.

During the early part of the second half of the 19th-century a number of books were published illustrated with actual photographs, pasted down. The pioneer work in photography by Fox Talbot and others during the second quarter of the century was partly instrumental in bringing this about. For his work *The Pencil of Nature*, 1844–6, Fox Talbot employed this method, which was inevitably a laborious one. An example in the collection is S183, Wordsworth, *Our English Lakes . . . as seen by William Wordsworth*, London 1864. The introduction states that '. . . the Reader will be able, with the assistance of Photographic illustrations, which have been taken . . . specially for this work, to appreciate more fully Wordsworth's wonderfully true descriptions of the beauties of Nature . . .' The photographs, which have protecting flimsies, have faded little considering that they are well over a hundred years old, but fading, generally caused by the adhesives, did give trouble, and various patent processes were developed in the endeavour to get over it. This particular book has an elaborate stamped gilt leather 'gift-book' binding, but the stiff wove paper used makes it difficult to open.

An important name in connexion with early photography and printing is that of Joseph Cundall, author, publisher, and book designer (mentioned under Edmund Evans), who in the middle of the century became a founder-member of both the Photographic Club and the Photographic Society, and whose premises in New Bond Street were named 'the Photographic Institution'.

Although in the early days of photography it was naturally thought that photographic prints might provide a new and ready means of book illustration, their limitations soon became obvious, but the carbon method of photographic printing——'carbon printing' as it was called—invented in 1865 by Sir

Joseph Swan, was to some extent used in the illustration of books. As early as 1839 the Scot, Mungo Ponton, had made the important discovery that paper, immersed in a solution of potassium bichromate and dried, became very sensitive to light, giving a darkened image which could be preserved by washing with water. This led to the application of various films such as bichromated albumen (used in early photo-lithography) and bichromated gelatine which Swan used in perfecting the carbon process. When treated with cold water, gelatine, as other similar colloid substances, swells, but in hot water it dissolves. In the carbon method a 'tissue' is prepared with a coating of bichromated gelatine charged with carbon or other finely ground pigment, exposed to light under a negative, mounted face-down on paper or other suitable support and developed in hot water. The tissue base is then removed, leaving on the support a gelatine film which has been hardened in varying degrees or depths according to the action of the light.[1] The gelatine unaffected by light and still soluble is washed away, leaving an insoluble pigmented film whose varying thickness will reproduce the tones of the original. Carbon prints, or 'autotypes', are permanent and the best are very beautiful, but as each print is the result of a separate series of operations, their use in bookwork was inevitably confined to limited editions.[2]

But the ingenious process devised and worked out by W. B. Woodbury in 1864 by which numbers of what were really carbon prints could be reproduced mechanically, while still not a true printing process, is much nearer to it than a process such as ordinary carbon printing, in which each print is produced separately from a negative. Woodbury found that under great pressure in a hydraulic press it was possible to make lead moulds from specially hardened high gelatine reliefs (up to 50 or 60 from one film) and to use these 'reverse' moulds to make

---

[1] The principle of the 'carbon tissue' was utilised by Karl Klič in 1879 in the development of photogravure, as described later.

[2] See also M25, G. L. Hawkins, *Pigment printing*, London, 1933, of interest in this connexion.

casts in pigmented gelatine giving very faithful reproductions of the original. He also experimented with a process which he called 'Stannotype', devised to dispense with the use of the hydraulic press. The Woodbury process could give most beautiful results, but unfortunately it was not commercially successful.[1]

But in the early 1850's the important discovery had been made that it was possible to photograph drawings down on to the wood[2] (the technique successfully employed by Edmund Evans some 30 years later in making the blocks for Kate Greenaway's illustrations above mentioned) and it was inevitable that endeavour should be made to extend the use of photography in the preparation of printing surfaces, from the various types of original, by photo-chemical means. In evolving the most successful procedures every possible permutation and combination of method was tried.[3] The ultimate success of these experiments led quickly to the supplanting of hand-engraving by chemical etching, a process which, at least in its earlier applications, could never have quite the same selective capacity in *interpretation*, and which imposed its own particular limitations on the techniques for the preparation of originals. But although one therefore leaves with some regret the age of the preparation of the printing surface by hand, since it produced results which, even if laborious in attainment, had in some cases a subtlety and richness not since surpassed, one cannot force comparison too far between methods so essentially different, and it must be fairly stated that the new techniques opened up new worlds of delightful possibility in the hands of those who knew how to use them. For instance, Beatrix Potter's exquisite water-colours in the 'Peter Rabbit' series were made available to generations of children by four-colour letterpress half-tone, and from the 1940's the lovely work of such illustrators as

[1] Examples of Woodburytype and the early processes of carbon printing may be seen in the early volumes of Penrose Annual, in the collection U117A.

[2] See Bland, *A History of Book Illustration*, London, 1958, p. 270.

[3] Much of the pioneer work is admirably summarized in Wood, *Modern Methods of Illustrating Books*—see footnotes under 'Glyphography' and 'Typographic Etching', pp. 445–6.

'Lewitt-Him' (the two Polish artists later referred to) has been beautifully reproduced by photo-litho offset, a process which does not require recourse to shiny 'art' paper, and has made possible some of the most delightful children's books of the post-war period. Every new process brings with its new possibilities a new set of limitations and it is only those who have understood the process who have exploited it to the full. The phases of these technological changes are discussed further under the Arts and Crafts Movement and the Design and Industries Association.

An early form of line-etching for relief printing was of French origin. Poortenaar states, 'Gillot, about 1858, made drawings in a greasy ink and transferred these to a zinc plate by pressure, making the ink into an acid-resist by dusting it with asphaltum and melting it. His plate was then ready to be etched.'[1] But the letterpress line-block, as we know it to-day, was largely perfected in the 1880's and had generally replaced Dawson's swelled gelatine process, already mentioned, by the end of the following decade. It introduced a new, quick and satisfactory method of reproducing pen-and-ink drawings, provided the originals were truly 'black and white', but because of its very facility process line-engraving was at first often grossly abused in the reproduction of inferior or unsuitable drawings. Philip James has stated that it was in the *English Magazine* of 1886 that a drawing by Hugh Thomson was first reproduced by this process, which was soon taken up by a new school of pen-and-ink draughtsmen, notable among whom are Hugh Thomson, Hubert Railton, and the Brocks. They illustrated several series of the novels of Jane Austen, Mrs Gaskell, and others, but a tendency to over-use the facility by which it was possible to

[1] Jan Poortenaar, *The Technique of Prints*, London, 1933, p. 111; see also July 1963 Exhibition Catalogue, *Printing and the Mind of Man*, Earls Court Exhibition section, p. 110, item 628, which describes an exhibit of Firmin Gillot's relief printing plate, the date for which is given as 1850. On p. 299 of Bland's *A History of Book Illustration*, London, 1958, is an example, dated 1882, of a pen drawing 'reproduced by gillotype, an early form of line block', but it is not stated whether this is Firmin Gillot's process. All these books are in the Printing section of the College Library.

reduce drawings photographically imparted a slightly artificial fineness into much of their work as reproduced in illustration. Typical of this work are S224, *Coaching days and coaching ways*, London, 1888, illustrated by Railton and Thomson, S247, Jane Austen, *Pride and Prejudice*, London, 1894, and S255, *A Kentucky Cardinal*, Edinburgh, 1901, both illustrated by Thomson—the latter beautifully printed by R. & R. Clark and bearing an interesting pencil note by Dr Maxwell on the flyleaf.

Thomson also made many illustrations for the *Highways and Byways* series of English guide-books, to which the American Joseph Pennell (long domiciled in England) also contributed. Pennell, one of the original members of the Senefelder Club, is remembered for his work in lithography; and his contributions to the ordinary editions of the *Highways and Byways* series were by process blocks reduced from the lithographs made for the limited editions—see S259, *Highways and Byways in Devon and Cornwall*, London, 1904, with illustrations by Thomson and Pennell, printed by Richard Clay & Sons. Pennell's useful work on *Pen drawing and pen draughtsmen*, London, 1894, J26 in the collection, is referred to below. He also produced similar books on Lithography and Etching. S212, the *English Illustrated Magazine* for 1883–4, also printed by Clay, and interesting for its variety of reproductive wood-engraving of the period, shows on p. 731 an illustration by Thomson from a wood-block engraved by Dawson, and on p. 109 of the Pennell volume (J26 abovementioned) is shown for comparison two reproductions of an illustration by Linley Sambourne, the '*Punch*' artist, from Charles Kingsley's *The Water-Babies*, one a wood-engraving by Swain and the other an early line-block by Dawson. A copy of the original *Water-Babies* volume, Edinburgh, 1886, printed by R. & R. Clark, with illustrations from the wood-blocks by Swain, is also available in the collection—S221.

It is interesting to examine the work of the wood-engravers in reproducing pen-and-ink drawings during the period of the development of the line-block—see for instance S210, *Bracebridge Hall*, Edinburgh, 1882, illustrated by Caldecott, already referred to, S220, *Days with Sir Roger de Coverley*, London, 1886, illustrated by Hugh Thomson with wood-blocks printed by Richard Clay & Sons and published during the same year as that of Thomson's first illustration by line-block, and S228, *The Owls of Olynn Belfry*, London, c. 1890, also illustrated by wood-engravings, from sketches by Caldecott, and printed by Field & Tuer. For comparison, see S223, 'Petrel', *In Southern Seas*, 1888, printed in Edinburgh by J. & J. Gray, shows early use of line-blocks, during the same decade.

Although not represented in the collection mention should be made of the illustrations by H. J. Ford, in letterpress-line and colour half-tone, to Andrew Lang's widely read series of Fairy Books, published by Longmans, which belong to the following decade. These show some William Morris and Pre-Raphaelite influence, with that loving attention to detail which seldom fails to delight children; and the stories, culled from the folk-lore of many countries, gave the widest scope in subject matter for the illustrator, including costume and architecture. The series began in 1899 with *The Blue Fairy Book*; and others, in different coloured gilded bindings, followed at every Christmas for twenty-five years. They were printed in London by Spottiswoode's (later Spottiswoode, Ballantyne) and reprinted in the 1930's in Edinburgh by Neill & Co., and the Darien Press, and in Glasgow by MacLehose.[1]

In reproducing the work of the artists abovementioned the line or other process blocks were used simply as a means to translate their uninhibited pen-and-ink, pencil, or other drawings into something printable. Within a few limitations the technique of the process engraver was ancillary to that of the artist, but Aubrey Beardsley (1872–98) was the first artist to recognise both the limitations and the possibilities of the line-block as a new medium, turning both to their fullest advantage. In the technique which he ultimately evolved he drew *for* the line-block, producing effects not before obtained, the nearest perhaps being those of the wood- and metal-cuts of late

[1] Some details in this paragraph have been kindly provided, from Messrs Longmans, by Mr P. C. B. Wallis, late production director.

15th-century. In his designs for *Le morte d'Arthur* (London, J. M. Dent & Son, 1893) drawn during what has been called his Pre-Raphaelite period—although his work appears effeminate and out-of-character compared with the Pre-Raphaelites' treatment of the same subjects—he made use of heavy black masses and a simple line. These may be seen in S261, 1909, 2nd ed., in S265, 1927, 3rd ed., large paper (with foreword on Beardsley by Aymer Vallance) and in S266, 1927, one of a limited edition of 300 copies—all printed in Edinburgh by Turnbull & Spears.

In his next phase Beardsley came under the then current influence of the Japanese print, as is seen in his designs for *Salome*, S248, London 1894, printed in Edinburgh by T. & A. Constable, in which line and solids are still used but the line has become precious and over-fine. His last and 'perfected' phase, in which he, like Hugh Thomson, also turns back to the 18th-century for his theme, is shown in his designs for Pope's *Rape of the Lock* (1896) and his own romance *Under the Hill* (1903), the latter of which appeared in the periodical *The Savoy*. These books are not in the collection but characteristic reproductions from them may be seen in any of the well-known reference books (Aldis, Bland, James, &c.). In these designs Beardsley invents a new technique, pressing the resources of the line-block to the very full and producing an extraordinary range of tone and texture by his use of fine line-work and intricate dotted patterns which could be obtained as relief surfaces by no other means, and which anticipated the mechanical tints which followed later. The technical skill and unerring precision of his draughtsmanship in these designs are truly amazing, and all entirely within the range of line-block reproduction.

Various ephemeral and experimental annuals and quarterlies were sponsored by artists and bibliophiles during the 1890's, and of these Beardsley contributed to the *Savoy* abovementioned, and to the *Yellow Book*—see S249, which consists of volumes 1, 2, 4, 6, 8, and 9 of the latter (1894–6), volumes 1 and 2 of which have cover designs by Beardsley, compared with which the designs by other artists for the subsequent covers show a sharp decline. These volumes are of interest for their asymmetrical typography, in the development of which the lively personality of the artist-etcher J. M. Whistler was a leading influence, their early process work and their 'art nouveau' influence. Beardsley's letters to his publisher Smithers, which reveal various details as to the course of his work and his outlook upon it, as well as of the characters of these two extraordinary men, are available in F103, *Letters from Aubrey Beardsley to Leonard Smithers*, First Edition Club, London, 1937.

With further reference to pattern and texture in black-and-white work for process reproduction, it is of interest to note that various papers with artificially grained surfaces were introduced towards the end of the 19th-century. The most popular was *Papier Gillot*, with horizontal lined screen, the resultant process reproduction from which has something of the effect of half-tone or of mechanical wood-engraving, and it is this very mechanical effect which is its limitation. These papers are referred to on p. 419 of Pennell's book on pen drawing, J26 abovementioned,[1] which also reproduces and describes examples of work on *Papier Gillot*—see pp. 46, 47, 98, 100, 101, 140 and 263. Examples in the collection will be found in S236, Walter, *Shakespeare's true life*, London, 1890[2] (see, for instance, title, pp. 1, 161, 168–9, and the zinco on the parchment-paper binding) and in the full-page illustrations to S240, Oscar Wilde, *A House of Pomegranates*, London, 1891, designed by Ricketts and Shannon and printed at the Chiswick Press, in which the artificial grain is partly disguised by the very faint sepia printing. Pennell states that these papers could also be obtained with dots or 'chalky' finishes, all of which could be scraped to produce 'whites', in the manner of present-day scraper-board—as will be clearly seen in the above examples.

[1] The copy of this book in the collection has been faultily bound, and p. 419 is out of sequence.

[2] This book is also of interest in that the imprint states that it has been 'composed on the "Thorne" machine', a machine for composing and distributing type patented in U.S.A. in 1880 It is described on p. 87 (exhibit 467) of the Catalogue of the Exhibition at Earls Court, London, 16–27 July 1963, *Printing and the Mind of Man*, U119A.

The letterpress half-tone block was established by the early 1890's,[1] and it is interesting to compare the printed results of the early efforts of the process-engravers with those of the wood-engravers of the same period—sometimes appearing in the same work. The mechanically even half-tone screen produced results which (especially in the early stages) look very characterless next to the subtle rendering of form and texture of which the best engravers were capable—see, for instance, pp. 222–3 of S229, Darwin, *Journal of researches* (Edinburgh, 1890) on which an early half-tone and in this case a very ordinary woodengraving may be compared, and S241, Wordsworth, *A Selection from the Sonnets* (N.Y., 1891) in which some of the full-page plates are half-tones and compare unfavourably with the remainder, which are wood-engraved.

The techniques naturally evolved by the wood-engravers in making reproductions from photographs and other media have already been referred to, and S216–7, Mayer, *Sport with gun and rod* (N.Y., 1884, printed by De Vinne) are volumes which show examples of the highest virtuosity in purely reproductive wood-engraving, in date near to the half-tone period, the most delicate examples being on rice-paper, pasted in; and a particularly fine example of the wood-engraver's skill, analogous to half-tone in its relief-dot technique, but superior in rendering tone, form, and texture, is shown in the enlargements from an illustration in *The Girls' Own Paper* of 1890 on

---

[1] Max Levy patented an etched half-tone cross-line screen in 1891. Interesting and successful experiments in the making of relief half-tone blocks without the use of a half-tone screen had been carried out by Charles G. Petit and by F. E. Ives some twenty years earlier, and are described by Bull in his *Photo-Engraving*, London, 1934, pp. 94–5. Vol. 1 of the *Yellow Book* (1894) abovementioned, has frontispiece half-tone employing Meisenbach's single-line screen of 1882. The subject is a draped figure study by Sir Frederick Leighton, P.R.A. and is reproduced by the Swan Electric Engraving Co. See also July 1963 Exhibition Catalogue, *Printing and the Mind of Man*, Earls Court Exhibition section, p. 110, item 630 (Ives) and 631 (Meisenbach). Item 629 is an exhibit described as 'The First Relief Half-tone, 1854' by Paul Prestch, already mentioned as a pioneer of the swelled gelatine process. The invention of three-colour photography by Clerk Maxwell in 1861 led to the development of three-colour printing processes—again see Bull, *Photo-Engraving*.

pp. 146–7 of John Farleigh's *Graven Image*, (London, Macmillan, 1940) in the Printing section of the College Library.[1] It is also instructive to compare the wood-engravings made from Whymper's own sketches in S200, Whymper, *Scrambles amongst the Alps*, Edinburgh, 1871, with those in S244, the fourth edition of 1893 in which they have been revised or re-engraved and are harder, sharper, and less subtle than those in the first edition. S243, Whymper's *Travels amongst the Andes*, Edinburgh, 2nd ed. 1892 includes some wood-engravings made from photographs. All these three books are beautifully printed by R. & R. Clark.

In addition to the regular cross-line half-tone screens, some screens giving an irregular grain have been employed, the best known of which is the metzograph[2] screen which gives a characteristic 'dust-grain' effect in the impression. Another such screen is the Irwin (stated by Bull[3] to be later than the metzograph) which gives a result having resemblance to the grain of collotype. Mr Reddell of the London College of Printing states that although Wheeler marketed his metzograph screen in 1897 it is evident that experiments with this type of screen must have taken place some time prior to that date, and many of the half-tone portrait illustrations in S235, Paton, *Scottish National Memorials*, Edinburgh 1890, a weighty folio printed by T. & A. Constable and dedicated to Queen Victoria, are from a metzograph type of screen. This volume is of further interest in that it employs collotype, 'heliogravures' (photogravures) and lithographs for the plates, in addition to wood-engravings and letterpress half-tones in the text—and the names of the various printers are given on p. xiii of the preliminaries.

While Beardsley was perfecting his decorations for the printed book, the same quest was being pursued in a very different spirit by a very different man, William Morris, whose

[1] Farleigh's legend to the larger of the two reproductions refers to the 'sad struggle to see on the part of the engravers, for their blocks are so much more beautiful than the drab half-tones of this date and the line-blocks from careless pen-drawings'.

[2] Sometimes called mezzograph.

[3] A. J. Bull, *Photo-Engraving*, London, 1934 p. 31, W43.

work in printing, which he took up in later life, was ultimately
to exert an influence so much more far-reaching than he could
possibly have contemplated at the time.[1] The work of the
Private Presses, as part of the reaction from the effects of an
industrial age, has already been described in the Typographical
Notes, and although much of their work may now appear
precious or artificially archaic, it nevertheless contributed
immeasurably to the restoration of an enthusiasm for good
workmanship and the reassessment of the whole printed book
as a unit of design. The beauty of really black type on white
paper—and good paper— had been almost forgotten by many
engaged in book printing and publishing, as also such matters
as marginal proportions and the satisfactory distribution of
white space, and the enthusiasms of the Private Press Movement engendered a new spirit of enquiry into all the arts, crafts
and processes involved in the making of books.

The work of Emery Walker as a key-figure behind the most
important Private Presses has already been mentioned, together
with that of the L.C.C. Central School of Arts and Crafts
which, under W. R. Lethaby from 1894 to 1912, and F. V.
Burridge during the immediate post-1914–18 war period,
became a nursery and training ground for the revived crafts.
It was with Lethaby's encouragement that Edward Johnston,
who rediscovered the whole craft of writing and illuminating,
held his first lettering class at 'the Central' in September 1899—
probably the first of its kind since the Middle Ages—the
beginning of a revival which was to expand from England to
the Continent, there to exert an influence on almost every form
of lettering—including type-design.[2] His handbook *Writing and*

---

[1] A perfect copy (with its own special box) of the Kelmscott *Chaucer* (Fol., 1896),
F 308 Morris's great masterpiece, with illustrations engraved on wood by Mr Hooper
after drawings by Burne-Jones, and borders by Morris, is one of the most treasured
possessions in the collection. The entry under F308A covers six leaves only from
this great work, in slip-in cover, an additional item provided specially for lecture
or class use. The illustrations (by process line block) in F307, Morris's *The Story
of the Glittering Plain* are by Walter Crane—see Typographical Notes.

[2] The books which Johnston used during his previous years of study, some
bearing his own notes, are also in the Clark Collection, a unique and personal

Illuminating and Lettering, in the Artistic Crafts series of Technical Handbooks edited by Lethaby, first published by John Hogg in 1906, and from 1918 by Pitman, has gone into innumerable editions and has been described as 'the perfect craft text-book'. It includes beautiful line illustrations by Noel Rooke made from Johnston's own hands at work in the many operations from the preparing of quills to the actual writing.

Two numbers of *Die Zeitgemässe Schrift*[1] now in the collection, No. 32 January 1935 and No. 38 July 1936, published by Heintze & Blanckertz (Berlin-Leipzig) the notable firm built up in Berlin to meet the needs of scribes and letter-artists on a commercial scale, are largely devoted to the work of the Arts and Crafts Movement in England and Edward Johnston in particular, and show convincingly the extent of the renaissance in letter-design in Germany which stemmed from his work. The articles are in German and English and that in No. 38 on 'Edward Johnston and English Lettering' is by Prof. Anna Simons, a German lady who came to England to study under Johnston, became one of his most distinguished pupils, translated his text-book into German and was the leading influence in disseminating Johnston's teaching throughout Germany.[2] No. 38 also includes portraits of William Morris and Johnston, the first from a photograph, the second from the well-known drawing by Sir William Rothenstein. Another original portrait of Johnston by Rothenstein is included in the series of four (framed and glazed) in the Clark Collection, the other subjects being Count Kessler (referred to under the Cranach Press), Cobden-Sanderson, and Douglas Cockerell—all by Rothenstein.[3]

---

group of *reliquiae,* recorded in the Calligraphy section (index letter I) with the suffix JOH.

[1] I 31-2.

[2] See also I20, Anna Simons, *Titel und Initialen für die Bremer Presse,* sheets in portfolio (in cabinet).

[3] For further records of Johnston's life and work see Priscilla Johnston's *Edward Johnston,* London, Faber, 1959; *Tributes to Edward Johnston, Calligrapher,* privately printed under the direction of Charles Pickering at the Maidstone College of Art, 1948; *Lettering of today,* special autumn number of *The Studio,*

Another event which was ultimately to exert a profound influence on the typography of the printed book, and also upon that of general printing at this critical time, was the founding of full-time Day Technical pre-apprenticeship classes for compositor students at the Central School in 1909 and the appointment of J. H. Mason (who had been conducting evening classes at London centres during the previous five years) as teacher-in-charge. Having worked for Cobden-Sanderson at the Doves Press, Mason had become imbued with an enthusiasm for both scholarship and design, and brought (to borrow one of his own expressions) a new 'energy of thought' to his task, much of which he imparted to his students. He became a self-taught Oriental scholar, his classes being the only ones in London (and probably in Britain) in which the setting of Greek and Hebrew was taught at that time. Above all he was a pioneer in the teaching of absolute accuracy in typographical layout, the value of which the more far-seeing London printers soon became aware, so that his influence spread far and wide in industry through the work of his students, some of whom became leading teachers in the period between the wars. In his classes he also built up a collaboration with the classes in Book Illustration under the direction of Noel Rooke, the classes through which the important revival of wood-engraving, which was to play such a significant part in the reintegration of type and illustration, was largely inaugurated. In the well-attended evening classes in lithography, developed by F. E. Jackson, one of the founder-members of the Senefelder Club, artists and art students drew direct on the stone, and these classes were also to extend their influence very widely in book-work and commercial printing, particularly through the work of Barnett Freedman, referred to later, and under the Typo-

1937 (I12 in the collection); *Alphabet and Image*, Spring 1946, pp. 52–8; *The Art of the Book*, special number of *The Studio*, 1914, pp. 11–12; Noel Rooke's broadcast, 'A Great Calligrapher and his Work', printed on pp. 583–4 of *The Listener* of 22 November 1945, with portrait on cover-page—all in the College—and other works given under 'Illustrations' on p. 14 of Priscilla Johnston's book mentioned *above*.

graphical Notes. During the same period the classes in Book-binding, under the great craftsman Douglas Cockerell (who also learned his craft under Cobden-Sanderson) assisted by G. McLeish, became an important influence in both the craft and industrial branches of the trade.

But one of the most important influences emanating largely from the Central School was the journal *The Imprint*. In 1911 Jackson introduced Mason to Gerard Meynell (cousin of Sir Francis Meynell) at the Westminster Press, and in their sub-sequent informal meetings the idea of a journal 'of wider outlook than any existing' and devoted to raising the whole status of printing, was brought to birth. It was to deal with every aspect of printing and the making of books, including calligraphy and illustration. Edward Johnston was invited to contribute and joined with Meynell, Mason, and Jackson to make up an editorship of four, backed by an advisory com-mittee including many names distinguished in the graphic arts. Only nine issues of this journal were issued, between January and November 1913, yet it has been truly said that 'the influence . . . of this brave vision is still to be evaluated'.[1] The highest and most critical standards were set by its sponsors, whose ideals ranged from such aims as the 'imposing and spreading technical knowledge' to that of lending their 'sympathy and full encour-agement to the revival in wood-engraving'. For this journal a new type-face, the design of which was largely the outcome of the plans and policy of Mason, was produced and cut by the Lanston Monotype Company in a remarkably short space of time, and was used by Meynell at the Westminster Press where *The Imprint* was printed. Although cut for *The Imprint*, the type was made available 'to the general public' as 'Imprint Old Face' and, because of its firmness of 'colour' and total lack of any eccentricities, it is still widely used as a book face.

[1] See 'Fifty years on'—the excellent leading article in *Monotype Newsletter* 71, Oct. 1963—which is entirely devoted to providing a summary of the inception and history of *The Imprint*. It includes some well-selected illustrations. (It was for *The Imprint* that Stanley Morison wrote his first article to appear in print. For Morison's connexion with *The Imprint* see *Stanley Morison 1889–1967*, by James Moran, *The Monotype Recorder*, Vol. 43, No. 3, 1968).

Volume One of *The Imprint*, Jan.–June 1913, and also separate copies of Nos. 6 (June) and 8 (Aug.) are in the collection, and show the extraordinarily wide range of subject-matter covered and appropriately illustrated.

It was at this time that Frank Pick, then responsible for the advertising policy of the London Underground Railways, and later to become Vice-Chairman of the unified London Passenger Transport Board, was endeavouring to raise the whole standard of the companies' publicity, giving opportunity to both leading and lesser-known artists and printers,[1] and it was also in 1913 that Meynell introduced Edward Johnston to Pick, an event which led to Johnston's designing of the famous 'block letter', a letter-form which, completed in 1916 during the darkness of the war-period, was in after-years to have such a far-reaching effect on type-design in Western Europe.[2]

There was thus brought about at this critical period a revived consciousness of the necessity and efficacy of good design in all fields of production, including that of printed matter—a movement which gathered impetus during the reconstruction years following the 1914–18 war and which played its part in the designing of the illustrated book.

But the success of the revival of the arts and crafts had also a

[1] Pick, among whose many visions was that of a better and cleaner London, also gave attention to redesigning the Underground's stations, with 'front windows' inviting attention to the many amenities which the system offered. This led to the famous era when Underground posters—to quote Mr H. S. Hutchison, later the Executive's Publicity Officer—'fashioned a new tradition'. Many of the most notable of these posters were printed at the Baynard Press, where Tom Griffits, already referred to in the Typographical Notes (para preceding F20) led the field in interpretive lithography, contributing also to book illustration, as will be seen from examples in the collection—some referred to later in these notes. See *Art for All: London Transport Posters* 1904-49, London, Art and Technics Ltd, 1949, with 68 plates, and articles by James Laver, Hutchison, and Griffits—in College Library.

[2] Photo-litho copies of the first experimental pulls showing the various trial letters made in the evolution of this alphabet (signed and dated by Johnston, February and March 1916) and also of the fount as finally cut, are in the Printing Department of the College, printed in the Lithographic Section. Johnston also designed the all-familiar red ring which, with label across it, forms the basic badge of London Transport.

most unfortunate effect in some sections of industry, where its origins were not understood. Various unenlightened manufacturers, seeing a new market in hand-produced goods, began to use their machines for the mass-production of artificial imitations of hand-craftsmanship and 'period' styles—such as 'stamped-out' furniture—with the most deplorable results. It was to combat this tendency that the Design and Industries Association—the DIA (actually founded in 1915 during the war period[1]) raised its voice as 'a propaganda body engaged in spreading a knowledge and appreciation of contemporary design'. A number of the more far-seeing designers, manufacturers (which included printers) and departmental stores became members, and exhibitions were held up and down the country.[2] Their great theme was that the machine had come to stay, that it was foolish to rebel against it, since rightly used it could confer great benefits on the greatest number. Their prime endeavour therefore was to harness the machine to the doing of that which it could do well and appropriately, and not

[1] By the turn of the century the influences of the Arts and Crafts movement had spread to Germany where, largely through the ardent work of the *Werkbund*, founded in 1907, its idealism was translated into practical applications in the widest fields of industrial design, and, as a result of its progress, the *Werkbund* was able to hold a large exhibition in Cologne seven years later—shortly before the outbreak of the First World War. Some of the members of the Arts and Crafts movement, who had been dissatisfied with the progress and results of the Arts and Crafts Exhibition Society's four-yearly exhibitions, attended the Cologne exhibition, and their impressions led to the founding, in May 1915, of the DIA, after the pattern of the German *Werkbund*.

[2] It is of special interest that on the first working committee leading to the foundation of the DIA were Ernest Jackson and J. H. Mason of the Central School, with Lethaby, its Principal, giving his powerful support in the background, and in October 1915, within five months of its foundation, the Association was able to mount its first exhibition, in the Whitechapel Art Gallery, the subject of which was *Design and Workmanship in Printing*, in which England was the leading influence at that time. During 1916–18, in spite of the war, this exhibition travelled to leading cities in Britain, including Edinburgh, Dublin and Belfast, and finally as far afield as to Johannesburg and Cape Town, doing much to make the work of the Association known. It is also significant that the first address of the new body was at 6 Queen Square, London, the premises of the Art Workers' Guild. These details have been summarised from Sir Nikolaus Pevsner's history of the DIA which appeared in the Association's 1964–5 Yearbook, the jubilee issue.

to the making of bad imitations of hand-made articles. One of their early pamphlets bears the title 'Nothing need be ugly'. The idealism of the Arts and Crafts Movement was thus translated into realistic and everyday application in contemporary industrial techniques, as had already taken place in Germany, and much of the work inaugurated by the DIA, whose activities now cover a greatly extended field, has been further developed through the complementary policy and operation of the Council of Industrial Design, set up by the Board of Trade in 1944, and through other associations or individuals sharing the same aims.[1] A few DIA pamphlets of the 1930's, together with examples of work by early members, such as the fine 1937 and 1938 furniture catalogues for Bowmans (London) designed by Stuarts and printed by Curwen, with auto-lithographic covers in colour by Barnett Freedman, are in the Printing Department of the College.

The study of the 'Old Masters' of printing induced by the Private Press Movement was an influence in formulating the policy of the Monotype Corporation and other typefounding concerns in recutting and making available for machine-composition the leading type-faces of the past which had stood the test of time (with their appropriate ornament) and to these were added others by contemporary designers, important among whom was Eric Gill. Gill, once a pupil of Johnston's, became both type-designer and wood-engraver, and by these means a designer and decorator of books; and the work of Robert Gibbings, who in 1924 took over the Golden Cockerel Press—the private press for which Gill's best work was done—aroused the interest of general publishers and was instrumental in bringing wood-engraving out of the domain of the limited

[1] Mr R. S. Hutchings, past-editor of 'The British Printer', in his foreword to Jack Deller's *Letterpress Machine Problems*, London, Pitman, 1963, writes, 'The role of craftsmanship in Printing has always been subject to confused thinking, and at the present crucial stage of the industry's history, is in danger of being sentimentalized. Printing is intrinsically a multiplication process, and there can be no special virtue in doing by hand anything that can be performed more precisely and speedily by mechanical means'. In its right context this statement can be regarded as ancillary to the policy of the DIA.

edition into general circulation. Gibbings's famous 'river books', *Sweet Thames run softly* (1940), *Coming down the Wye* (1941) and *Lovely is the Lee* (1945) were printed many times despite wartime difficulties of production, and enjoyed exceptional sales in America. These books were printed for J. M. Dent & Sons by the Temple Press, Letchworth.[1] The work of the Golden Cockerel Press is summarised in the Typographical Notes and is very fully represented in the collection (F232–F260).[2] Famous examples of Gill's work in wood-engraved illustration and decoration are seen in F238, *Bible—Matthew* [Latin.] 1926, and F242, *The Canterbury Tales*, Vol. III, 1930; and typical illustration by Gibbings of nautical subjects are his wood-engravings in F248–50. The work of John Nash, Lynton Lamb, and others is also included, and F251 and F256 show Lettice Sandford's engravings—in pure line on copper and zinc.

John Farleigh, one of the group of post-1914–18 war students at the Central School, where he studied drawing, painting and lithography—and finally wood-engraving under Noel Rooke— was originally apprenticed to a firm of engravers and was thus well equipped to turn his talents to practical use. It was Rooke who introduced Farleigh to Newdigate, which led to his first major essay in book illustration, Pindar's *Odes of Victory*, Oxford 1928–30, imp. 8vo (F446 in the collection), printed by Newdigate at the Shakespeare Head Press, and showing a very successfully established harmony between the black line of the engravings and the text in Poliphilus and New Hellenic Greek. But in F112, Bernard Shaw's *The Adventures of the Black Girl in her Search for God*, 1932, Farleigh uses the reverse technique of white-on-black to exploit to the full the rich blacks obtainable

[1] See Thomas Balston, 'The River Books of Robert Gibbings', *Alphabet and Image 8*, Dec. 1948.

[2] See also J5, Thomas Balston, *The Wood-engravings of Robert Gibbings*, London, 1949; and L27, *Chanticleer: a bibliography of the Golden Cockerel Press, 1921–36*, London, 1936, and L27A, *Pertelote: a sequel to Chanticleer, 1936–43*, London, 1943. For later information see 'The Wood Engravings of Robert Gibbings', *Book design and production*, Vol. 3, No. 1, 1960, pp. 32–4, in which reference is made to the lavishly illustrated *The Wood Engravings of Robert Gibbings*, edited by Patience Empson, and published by Dent in 1959.

by wood-engraving. This little octavo, the format of which was designed by John Farleigh in collaboration with its author (who indulgently gave him a very free hand, in addition to providing the liveliest of roughs for the designs) is an outstanding example of a book entirely decorated by wood-engraving, including endpapers and cover, and it reached a wide public at the astounding price of half-a-crown. As usual with Bernard Shaw's works, it is beautifully printed by R. & R. Clark and published by Constable, and once again the recommendation of Farleigh to the author was made by Noel Rooke—through the mediation of his printer, William Maxwell, the inaugurator of the Edward Clark Collection.[1]

A folio volume of interest in this connexion is F447A, *Paradise regain'd*, Cresset Press 1931, also printed at the Shakespeare Head Press, with wood-engravings by D. Galanis employing a 'white-dot-on-black-ground' technique similar to that used by Farleigh for the *Black Girl*, which was published in the following year. Another large folio printed by Newdigate[2] for the Cresset Press in F442–5, *The Pilgrim's Progress*, 2 volumes, showing the very accomplished wood-engraving of Blair Hughes-Stanton and Gertrude Hermes, the former of whom was associated with the Gregynog Press, where R. A. Maynard and Horace Bray had worked prior to 1930—see Typographical Notes.

Other notable artists who contributed to the resurgence of wood-engraving are Gwen Raverat (one of the pioneers of the movement), Ethelbert White, D. P. Bliss, Eric Ravilious (one of the first to put wood-engraving to commercial use), Clare Leighton, who wrote and illustrated books on country matters, Agnes Miller-Parker, who illustrated books on similar themes, and whose work is technically brilliant, but sometimes with a tendency towards a hardness and uniformity of texture, Joan Hassall, whose exquisitely delicate work for such books as

[1] See John Farleigh's *Graven Image*, chap. VIII, pp. 210–71 and James Shand, 'Author and Printer: G. B. S. and R. & R. C.: 1898–1948', *Alphabet and Image 8*, Dec. 1948.

[2] For further reference to Newdigate's work, see L68, Joseph Thorp, *B.H. Newdigate, scholar-printer, 1869–1944*, Oxford 1950.

Cranford (1949), *Our Village* (1946) and other books is well known, and who has also designed typographical and other ornaments, John Buckland Wright, Reynolds Stone, who is also a designer of type and ancillary ornament,[1] and John O'Connor, a pupil of Ravilious—all of whose work is represented in the collection.[2] Mention should also be made of a notable book, almost entirely the outcome of 'Central School' influence, the folio *Hamlet* (F549 in the collection) printed in 1930 by Count Harry Kessler at his Cranach Press in Weimar, with illustrations designed and cut in wood by Edward Gordon Craig and type designed by Edward Johnston. Craig, always original, obtained a black and grey in one impression from these cuts by lowering portions of the block, a technique which he uses with dramatic effect. Some of the two-page openings in this book are very impressive. John Mason acted as adviser to Count Kessler in the latter days of his press. For further details see Typographical Notes.

Before the 1914–18 war Noel Rooke revived the craft of wood-*cutting*, with the knife, on side-grain. This was not taken

---

[1] See J27, Myfanwy Piper, *Reynolds Stone*, in series *English Wood-Engravers*, London, Art and Technics, 1951. Also in the series (but not in the Collection) are Ruari McLean, *Joan Hassall*, and Alec Clifton-Taylor, *John O'Connor*.

[2] The revival of wood-engraving in England (and Scotland) is fully summarized and illustrated in J4, Thomas Balston, *English wood-engraving, 1900–1950*, London, 1951 (a republication of the study which appeared originally in *Image 5*, Autumn 1950). Incidentally this review refers to and gives examples of the work of the 'independent artist', Edward Wadsworth, mentioned later under the Dadaist publication, *Blast*, begun by Wyndham Lewis in 1914. The example shown of the work of G. W. Lennox Paterson is lively in design and interesting in its natural exploitation of the use of the wood-engraver's principal tools. A note is also given on coloured wood-engraving (of which examples are shown), re-inaugurated before 1900 by Lucien Pissarro (who was attracted to it by the work of Edmund Evans) and successfully pursued during the subsequent revival by various distinguished wood-engravers, including the woman artists Gwen Raverat and Joan Hassall. See also Stuart Rose, 'The Engravings of John O'Connor', *Image 1*, Summer 1949; Thomas Balston, 'The wood-engravings of Ethelbert White, *Image 3*, Winter 1949–50; John Lewis, 'The wood-engravings of Blair Hughes-Stanton, *Image 6*, Spring 1951; Charles Mayo, 'Recent wood-engravings by Joan Hassall', *Motif 2*, Feb. 1959; and articles on other engravers in these periodicals— all presented to the collection in 1969 by W. B. Hislop. See also J42, *The Woodcut: an annual*, Nos. 1–4, London, 1927–30.

up to any extent by his pupils, but Fritz Kredel, the German artist and illustrator, and pupil in Offenbach of the great craftsman Rudolf Koch, successfully revived the use of the woodcut, very notably for *Das Blumenbuch*, published by Insel-Verlag in three folio volumes in 1930, with its brief text in Koch's Jessen type. Re-issued in the famous pocket-size series (using 58 of the plates, reduced by photo-litho offset) it attained, according to Paul Standard, 'a vast popularity'. After 1938 Kredel did much work in America.[1]

Before the work of William Morris, other printers had interested themselves in earlier styles of printing. Andrew Tuer, who founded the Leadenhall Press ('Field and Tuer') in 1880, affected a deliberate archaism in chap-book styles which he accomplished with both humour and genuine typographic feeling, especially in books illustrated by Joseph Crawhall with zincos or wood-cuts from his bold drawings—see E133, Crawhall, *Old tayles newlye relayted*, London, 1883, and the accompanying typographic notes on its manner of production. Tuer's interest in the more naive forms of printing is shown in G100, his *History of the horn-book*, London, 1897. He also started the *Printers' International Specimen Exchange* in 1880, the volumes of which are made up of contributions by compositors and printers, chiefly British and German, in the field of jobbing work, which give a remarkable insight into what was accomplished under the heading of 'artistic printing' at that period. A complete set is in the Collection.[2]

An important artist-illustrator also in the chap-book style at the end of the century was William Nicholson (associated with his brother-in-law James Pryde as the 'Beggarstaff Brothers', pioneer artists of the poster) whose bold wood-cut illustrations were hand-coloured for limited distribution but printed by lithography for ordinary editions; and in the 1920's Claud Lovat Fraser followed a similar style, enhancing his bold

[1] See Paul Standard ('calligrapher, New Yorker'), 'Fritz Kredel, artist, wood-cutter, illustrator', an interesting and well-illustrated article in *Motif 4*, March 1960, which shows the wide range of Kredel's work and the liveliness of his illustration.

[2] See McLean, *Victorian Book Design*, p. 162, U 99 and U118D–Q.

drawings by a generally restrained use of very bright colours.[1]
His poster for *The Beggar's Opera* is still remembered. The work
of the three abovementioned artists was generally characterised
by a bold or thick line, such as obtained by the use of quite a
broad pen or a brush, but the technique of enlivening black-
and-white work by the juxtaposition of bright colours was
further developed by Albert Rutherston and others in the
1930's, applying it to the more delicate drawings made with a
fine pen.

Appropriate to the bolder chap-book style, and very suitable
for broad colour and tint effects is the linoleum-cut, the use of
which was stimulated by the wood-engraving revival, and
which has found successful if limited use in certain printed
books—see, for instance, S267, McDowall, *Peaks and frescoes*,
printed at the University Press, Oxford, in 1928, in which the
12-pt Plantin type on antique laid paper has the necessary
richness and density to hold its own opposite the colour lino-
blocks, and also F396, the Nonesuch Press *Mask of Comus*, 1937,
described in the Typographical Notes and showing the most
exquisite use of lino-cut illustration (by Mildred Farrar) printed
by the Curwen Press. The text, beautifully printed by the
University Press, Oxford, seems a little high on the page for
the illustrations. Another example is F416, *Fifteen Old Nursery
Rhymes*, Perpetua Press, 1935, a quarto printed on hand-made
paper, in which the spirited lino-cuts by Biddy Darlow are
delightfully coloured by hand.

The popularisation of wood-engraving not only contributed
to the extended use of the lino-cut—particularly as a craft for
schools—but it also led to the introduction of the woodcut's
humbler offspring, scraper-board, which has enjoyed wide use
commercially as it can be worked more easily and quickly than
the wood-block. As its surface is more friable than boxwood,
and after working has also to be translated into a process line-
block, it cannot give quite the same fineness and precision as
wood-engraving, but rightly used it can produce useful and

[1] See Gerard Hopkins, 'The Sketchbooks of Claud Lovat Fraser', *Alphabet and
Image 7*, May 1948.

attractive work. The surface may be black, exposing a white composition-base when scraped, or it may be white, on which the design may be made in black, and then modified as required by scraping. It can also be obtained with various artificial finishes, yielding 'half-tone' and other effects when worked. Its leading exponent in book-illustration in this country is C. F. Tunnicliffe, and S288, *The Seasons and the Woodman*, and S289, *The Seasons and the Fisherman*, both 1941, are two from a series of four delightful little quartos published by the Cambridge University Press, each with 50 illustrations from scraper-board drawings by Tunnicliffe, printed 'in an ink intended not to dazzle' (the jacket to the second of these two books is an excellent example of the use of this medium); and almost all the beautiful illustrations by Rex Whistler for F450, Hans Andersen's *Fairy Tales* (1935), finely printed by the Shenval Press (and bound in gilt-on-white buckram by Leighton-Straker Bookbinding Co., with Whistler's decoration) are also from drawings on scraper-board[1]—and there are other examples in the collection.

The line-block has been well used in book-illustration and decoration in Great Britain in the years between the wars in a variety of styles by such artists as D. P. Bliss, Rex Whistler, Osbert Lancaster, Thomas Lowinsky, Barnett Freedman, Edward Bawden, Edward Ardizzone, Lynton Lamb, Leonard Rosoman, David Knight, Mervyn Peake, Robin Jacques and others, many of whom have continued their work in the decades following—see for instance F39 (Lancaster), F45 and F226 (Lowinsky), F372-5 (Bliss), the monographs J11, J24, and J40 on Bawden, Freedman, and Rex Whistler respectively[2] and

---

[1] For the interesting subsequent printing history of this book, see *Book design and production*, vol. 2, No. 3, 1959, p. 62.

[2] These three books are in the series *English Masters of Black-and-White*, already mentioned. The work of the following artists, much of whose work has been reproduced by line-block, may be seen in the periodicals (which are among those presented by W. B. Hislop in 1969) given herewith after their names: John Minton, *Image 1*; Ben Shahn, *Image 2*; Leonard Rosoman, *Image 3*; Ardizzone, *Image 6* and *Motif 1*; Lynton Lamb, *Motif 1*; Bawden (line-blocks from lino-cut prints in colour) *Motif 9*.

various articles in *Alphabet and Image* for 1948. After various experiments Freedman very successfully further developed and extended the use of chalk drawings made on rough or grained paper, or of chalk-drawn lithographs—both amplified by line where necessary—for the making of line-blocks. The first examples of the former (using grained paper) are his tailpieces for *The Post Office*, published in 1934 by the GPO, a copy of which is in the Printing Department of the College. Later, and very distinguished examples are his drawings for S301, *Love*, the anthology made by Walter de la Mare, printed by Mac-Lehose and published by Faber in 1943—described by McLean as 'a superb unlimited edition'. It is interesting to compare these illustrations with those using the same method in the 1890's. For an example of a line-block made from a lithograph by Freedman (for a Double Crown Club menu in 1956) see *Motif* 1, Nov. 1958, p. 75. 'Starved-brush' drawings on rough paper may also be used for line-block reproduction, and a variety of textures and tone values can be obtained by the application of mechanical tints already mentioned. F674, *Candide*, N.Y., 1929, designed by Elmer Adler, is an interesting experiment in the harmonising of Rockwell Kent's line-illustrations and ornament with the typeface (Garamond). The line-block's resources have also been extended in the reproduction of multi-colour work, that is in designs made up of several colours, each employing a separate block—see for example S277, *Seven Simeons*, U.S.A., 1937, and S286, *Quetzal Quest*, OUP, 1940, and other examples already referred to.

The skilful use of tinted paper to lower the tone of the page bearing type and line-blocks, opposite bled-off half-tones on the normal white paper of the facing page, is shown in S292, *Polish Panorama* (1941) an oblong quarto cleverly designed by the talented Polish artists, Le Witt and Him ('Lewitt-Him') and printed by the Munro Press, Perth. Characteristic line work reproduced by line-block, and line with single tints or colour washes reproduced entirely by half-tone are shown in Hugh Casson's delightful sketches of architectural subjects in *Alphabet and Image* 6, 1948; and the important contribution to topographical (and architectural) illustration by the distinguished artist John Piper, using both letterpress and lithographic methods, is referred to later under auto-lithography. S281, Woodruff, *The story of the British Colonial Empire*, issued in 1939 by the Empire Marketing Board and published by the Stationery Office at the outbreak of war at the price of 2s. 6d., is of interest in that it employs line, line-and-wash and colour half-tone all made from artists' drawings. A brilliant exponent of line-and-wash illustration is Feliks Topolski, and among his most vividly expressive drawings are those for Bernard Shaw's *In Good King Charles's Golden Days*, 1939. The illustrations in the text, from Topolski's drawings in pen-line or chalk, or a mixture of both, are printed in terra-cotta ink from line-blocks, and the full-page drawings in line-and-wash, chalk-and-wash, or chalk only have been reproduced by photo-litho offset with an exquisite softness and subtlety of tone and texture.[1]

A brilliantly satirical artist of the post-war period who has used line-and-wash with devastating effect is Ronald Searle (of 'The Girls of St Trinians' fame), whose drawings show great sensitivity and exceptional powers of observation. Much of his most notable work has been reproduced by photo-litho offset.[2] In the same stream of starkly discerning levity, bordering on the grotesque, are Rowland Emett, André François, and Gerald Hoffnung, but none of these artists is represented in the collection.

Mention should also be made of the illustrations made by McKnight Kauffer for reproduction by the stencil process successfully employed by Harold Curwen and referred to in the Typographical Notes under F180, the Nonesuch Press *Benito Cereno* (1926). F181, Arnold Bennett, *Elsie and the Child*,

[1] The text and illustrations in text are printed by R. & R. Clark. It has not been possible to trace the printer of the full-page illustrations. For some further details of Shaw's working with Topolski and William Maxwell, again see James Shand's Article in *Alphabet and Image 8*, Dec. 1948.

[2] See, for instance, Ronald Searle and Kaye Webb, *Paris Sketchbook*, Saturn Press, London, 1950, printed by Straker Brothers Ltd, and the 'Penguin' paperback, *Searle in the Sixties*, printed by Hazells Offset Ltd.

London, Cassell, 1929, also illustrated by Kauffer, is a particularly beautiful example of this process, making use of opaque colours. Other examples of the use of water-colour stencils by the Curwen Press are in the Nonesuch books F315, Thomson, *The Seasons*, 1927, and F316, *The Pilgrim's Progress*, 1928, in the first of which the stencils are applied to illustrations (by Jacquier) printed from copper engravings, and in the second to illustrations from wood-blocks. Both books are printed by the Kynoch Press—again see Typographical Notes.

As, from the late 1920's, wood-engraving enjoyed a period of revival, so there was also inaugurated a corresponding resurgence in auto-lithography. A pioneer in this field in Britain was Barnett Freedman, who brought lithography back into both commercial work and book work. He even used it to make basic prints for postage-stamp designs to be reproduced by photogravure. An important example of his work in book-illustration is F328, Sassoon, *Memoirs of an Infantry Officer*, London 1931, for which the colour has been added to his line drawings by lithography, and the cloth case lithographically printed. This book was published by Faber and Faber, for whom Freedman designed and lithographed a series of dust jackets, and these have been recorded in the Typographical Notes under books printed by MacLehose. F319, de la Mare, *Early One Morning*, London 1935, is another example of Freedman's lithographic book-illustration. Freedman also produced some remarkable and original lithographic posters for the London Underground Railways, printed at the Baynard Press— some examples of which are in the Printing Department of the College—and he did outstanding work as a war-artist during the Second World War.

An interesting if somewhat precious little book, chalk lithographed in bright colours and printed on Chinese paper, with printed silk binding case, is F577, Okakura, K. *Das Buch vom Tee*, printed at the Staatliche Akademie, Leipzig, and published by Insel-Verlag in 1922. Another, a children's book already referred to, is F20, *This year: next year*, 4to, published by Faber in 1937 and printed at the Baynard Press with colour-lithographs by Harold Jones for which Walter de la Mare provided the ancillary verse.

At this time books, especially children's books, began to be produced hand-lithographed throughout. This involved the artist's drawing direct on a separate plate for each colour required in the illustrations, a job sometimes calling for considerable energy and application, but the result, cutting out all the current photo-chemical processes, could be sold very cheaply— an important factor during the war-period. These experiments originated in Russia in the 1920's and were taken up in France, where the delightful series of Père Castor books, with illustrations by 'Rojan' (F. Rojankovsky), were published by Flammarion in the 1930's.[1]

In Britain the Puffin Picture Books, edited by Noel Carrington and published by Penguin Books Limited, are an attractive and successful series begun during the war and employing this technique for the earlier numbers. They were mostly printed by W. S. Cowell & Sons, but some were by the Baynard Press and other printers. Artists who understood the limitations of the technique produced some delightful work—see, for instance F21, Badmin, *Village and town*, 1942, in the Puffin series, and S317, *Ming*, 1944, a Baby Puffin, both printed by Baynard, and the gay *Orlando* books by Kathleen Hale, printed by Cowells, of which F171 (1942) is in the Puffin series, and S302 (1943) and S320 (1944) are in the large folio size published by Country Life Limited. In all these books the overprinting from chalk-drawn colours is carefully limited and controlled. S290 and S291 are early and more roughly executed wartime examples in the Puffin series. Other attractive books showing skilful use of auto-lithography are the octavos S324, *Sea Poems*, 1944, with illustrations by Mona Moore, printed by Cowells, and S363, *Travellers' verse*, 1946, with illustrations by Edward Bawden, printed by Curwen—both published by Muller. For each of these books the binding case is lithographically printed with a design which is repeated on the jacket. S336, *Babar's Travels*, 1945, is one of Jean de Brunhoff's famous

[1] Examples are in the Printing Department of the College.

Babar series, printed by Cowell's and employing a hand-written text.

Reference has already been made to the important topographical illustration of John Piper, the distinguished artist who, as a result of a carefully established understanding with plate-maker and printer, has used a variety of reproductive methods—including autolithography—to their best effect. In an illustrated contribution to *Image 2* (Autumn 1949)[1] S. John Woods writes, 'John Piper admirably suggests the conditions of mutual respect which should exist between creative printer and creative craftsman in an article in *The Penrose Annual* 1949 on "Book Illustration and the Painter-artist",' and from this article Mr Woods gives the following extract 'When a painter's work is reproduced in colour, by whatever method, he should ask for a lively parallel to his work, not for an imitation of it . . . He should ask, in fact, for the same kind of result he would get if he translated a work of his own into another medium'. Later in his monograph Mr Woods adds the words: 'he (John Piper) has simply used half-tone, line, mechanical tints, printing inks, instead of paint and canvas. An obvious enough thing for an artist to do—but rarely done!'

Early in the century some exquisitely hand-drawn lithographic work was accomplished for some of the Insel-Bücherei, the attractive series of little books published in Leipzig by the Insel-Verlag, the text of which was printed by Poeschel and Trepte with some of the best lithographic work printed by H. F. Jütte, and with paper-board covers also printed in colours—see F565–F569 and the Typographic Notes. Count Kessler (referred to under the Cranach Press) was also concerned with these publications. In the 1940's the King Penguin series was begun in Britain in similar format to that of the Insel-Bücherei. The text for most of this series is printed by R. & R. Clark of Edinburgh and the illustrations are for the most part photo-litho offset from plates made and printed by Baynard, Swain, Cowells, and other firms. Many of the cover designs in colour are letterpress printed—see S308A–S313, in the last of

[1] *'John Piper as a Topographical Illustrator'*.

which the plates, by letterpress half-tone, appear somewhat 'hard' compared with those in the series by litho offset.

For furthering various forms of autographic work Messrs W. S. Cowell developed a process, known as 'Plastocowell',[1] by which the artist can draw (the reverse way round) on a transparent sheet of plastic grained like a lithographic plate, the drawing being printed down on a lithographic machine plate in the ordinary way for printing in quantity. Machine plates can be duplicated from the plastic original without loss of quality, and colour separation is easier as the plastic sheets can be super-imposed. Graduated washes can be used, the break-up into irregular dots being achieved by the actual particles of pigment which lodge in the grain of the Plastocowell. If chalk work or washes are not too fine, Plastocowell can be used for making line-blocks; also etchings and other intaglio work can be proofed and photographed, and offset on to Plastocowell, if necessary as a key for colour separations. Probably the most widely known book-illustrations made on Plastocowell are those by Anthony Gross for Heinemann's edition of *The Forsyte saga* published in 1950 (S368). The intensely sensitive pen-and-ink drawings with washes of the most subtle transparent colours are extra-ordinarily expressive, and there are other line drawings and vignettes in black only. The text (which is not printed by Cowells) is in a Modern type, which is not inappropriate, but is rather unevenly printed.

The lively incursion of 'auto-lithography' into the field of book-illustration was an influence in raising the standard and increasing the variety of work done by photo-lithography—again with the collaboration of those artists who understood the essentials of the process. Diana Ross's *Little red engine*, 1942 (S294) designed and illustrated by the Polish artists 'Lewitt-Him', abovementioned, is a perfect example in which the inherent softness of offset litho is skilfully countered by a simplified and disciplined contour in the drawing of figures, buildings, etc., and the potential of beautiful colour-effect

[1] See John Lewis, *A Handbook of Type and Illustration*, London, Faber, 1956 (printed by W. S. Cowell Ltd), pp. 57-61, 63-4, 101, 103-4.

and texture is fully explored. It is interesting to compare this book with the autographically produced *Orlando* (F171) in the Puffin series, which was sold at about one-fifth the price, yet each is excellent value in its class. Many other delightful children's books were produced by photo-litho offset at this period, of which a number of examples are in the collection. F576, the Hans Andersen *Märchen*, Th. Knaur, Berlin, 1938, 8vo, entirely lithographically printed, is an attractive example of line-and-water-colour illustration. The publishers must have had sufficient confidence in its attractiveness to print in quantity for wide distribution, even with German text untranslated, as it sold at the remarkable price of 4s. 6d. Other examples are S308, *Amanda*, 1943, printed by Collins, Glasgow; S338, *Jack Robinson,* 1945, with pictures by John R. Parsons, printed by Dugdale Printing Ltd—an example of most happy collaboration between author, artist, publisher and printer, as described in its introduction; S358, Diana Ross's *Whoo, whoo, the wind blew*, 1946, printed by the Baynard Press, in which Leslie Wood's pictures follow the style of Lewitt-Him in the renowned *Little red engine* by the same author (S294 above mentioned); and S360 and S361, 1946, two delightful little books printed in Haarlem by the distinguished firm of Enschedé.

A point of note is the employment of an *oblong format* for so many of these books or series of books intended for children, which allows for much more dramatic illustration and the use of larger type or lettering than is possible when the format is upright. To meet the same requirements of spaciousness, quartos and folios, or their general sizes and proportions, are also much employed. Among the latter are the *Orlando* and *Babar* books already referred to; and a very popular series, in a size approximating to crown quarto, are the *Little Tim* books, published by the Oxford University Press and also printed by Cowells, with story and pictures by that excellent illustrator Edward Ardizzone; but even in this size it is interesting to note how frequently an action-picture spreads across the two page opening, which provides the necessary large-scale oblong. For this series Ardizzone drew his water-colour sketches in full colour to a pencil key, omitting the black line which is drawn separately on Kodatrace, thus saving its photographic separation from the colour positives.

By the use of photolithography and photogravure it became possible to produce books in which the text, photographically reproduced, and the illustrations, were laid down together, and the principle of the rubber offset-blanket enabled printing to be made on a wide variety of papers and surfaces. It was thus possible to produce books printed throughout—including binding and jacket—by litho offset, and examples have been already given under auto-lithography. An outstanding example, from the pre-war period, of a lithographically printed book, for which illustrations, case, endpapers and jacket are printed by photo-litho offset, is F644, W. H. Hudson's *Green mansions*, published by the Heritage Press, N.Y., 1936. The Curwen Press used offset very successfully for the cloth case of their *Miscellany* of 1931. Photo-litho offset also provides a useful means of reproducing originals which have been made in a variety of media, and this is well shown in such a book as S298, Tunnicliffe, *My country book*, 1942, printed by Balding & Mansell for The Studio Ltd, in which the illustrations from water-colours, chalk drawings, wood-engravings and scraper-board are all—together with the text—reproduced and printed by this process.

A very notable book, printed by Cowells, in the collection is S370, *The Royal philatelic collection*, 1952, published, by permission of the late King George VI, by Viscount Kemsley at the Dropmore Press Ltd, London. The prefatory note states that 'reproducing a number of stamps on one plate has involved many separate colour printings, one pair of plates necessitating as many as forty-five'. A more recent example of delightful and accurate illustration by photo-litho offset is Vedel and Lange, *Trees and Bushes in Wood and Hedgerow*, a very compact crown octavo, 'prepared by a brilliant team of Danish foresters and artists', first published in English translation by Methuen in 1960, with the plates superbly printed in Denmark and the text printed by the Shenval Press.

But special mention should be made of the publisher Paul Hamlyn, who from small beginnings has, especially since the late 1950's, built up a vast international publishing concern which has produced books, many of outstanding design (especially in the field of books on art subjects, popular technical books, and books for children) printed in various European countries—notably in Czechoslovakia—but some as far away as in Singapore. They include the large-paper illustrated Encylopaedias in the 'Golden Pleasure' series for children, and, as in the case of the pre-war Phaidon Press books, referred to on p. 513, the colour work is printed in great quantity by photo-litho offset, with text added afterwards in the languages of the respective countries in which the books are circulated. Hamlyn has recently taken over (and redesigned) the famous Larousse publications, originally printed in France.

Other publishing concerns dealing with large editions, especially of children's books (such, for instance, as the Oxford University Press) now have much of their colour work printed in Europe—in Holland and Austria, for example. Miroslav Sasek's famous impressions of the world's cities (*This is Paris, This is London*, etc.), printed in Italy and published by W. H. Allen, are also notable examples of the liveliest illustration beautifully printed by photo-litho offset. It is hoped that representative examples from all the abovementioned series may be added to the collection.[1]

Also of interest are the *Gumdrop* ('vintage car') books begun in 1968, with delightful stories and pictures by Val Biro. These are published by the Brockhampton Press and printed by Fletcher & Son of Norwich, using what is described on the jacket as the 'fluoro-graphic half-tone process' in which the artist paints each of the four primary colours with special inks

[1] A particularly beautiful example of a children's book published by Hamlyn is *Sing a Song of Everything* by Rosemary Garland, designed and produced by Artin, illustrated by Mirko Hanák and printed by photo-litho offset in Czechoslovakia by Svoboda, the English text copyright by the Hamlyn Publishing Group, 1968, from the original edition published in Czechoslovakia in 1963. Hanák's illustrations (copyright 1964), made in gouache water-colour wash with all the directness and spontaneity of Chinese painting are exquisite.

on to special pieces of plastic sheet—apparently a technique similar to that of Plastocowell.

It has been shown above that both wood-engraving and auto-lithography have enjoyed a period of revival in the period between the wars, finally winning acceptance from general publishers, and in so doing have exerted an appreciable influence on the design of books produced by contemporary technological processes. But a corresponding revival has not been experienced by the third group of graphic reproduction methods, that is the intaglio craft processes—including essentially etching and copper-engraving—on account of the difficulty in applying mass-production procedures for their multiplication. They have therefore remained largely within the domain of the limited edition. Exponents in this country have been Stephen Gooden, who designed and engraved the fine copperplate titles and ornaments for the four-volume Nonesuch folio *Bible*, 1925–7 (F363–6) and *Apocrypha*, 1924 (F362), and David Jones, whose copperplates are seen in F223, the folio *Rime of the Ancient Mariner*, 1929, printed by the Fanfare Press for Douglas Cleverdon, Bristol. In France, J. E. Laboureur is among the artist-illustrators who have specialised in copper-engravings, and his work may be seen in S270, Farquhar, *The Beaux Stratagem*, 1929, a small octavo also published by Douglas Cleverdon, with text printed by Cambridge University Press and the copper engravings printed in France. In France particularly, etching has found favour among the painter-illustrators, such as Segonzac, Matisse, Picasso and Chagall—referred to later under the *livre d'artiste*.

Photogravure, invented and developed between about 1875 and 1890 by Karl Klič, a native of Bohemia (who was both artist and photographer), is a photo-chemical method of intaglio etching in tone—a logical development from aquatint. It made use of Mungo Ponton's pioneer discovery of the light-sensitiveness of potassium bichromate, already described under photography. Interesting experiments in the 1850's by Fox Talbot (who developed a process closely resembling photogravure) and by Sir Joseph Swan in 1865 led to the use by

Karl Klič in 1879 of a tissue coated with bichromated gelatine, in conjunction with a dust-grained copperplate. The gelatine tissue was exposed to light, pressed down on to the plate, the backing-tissue removed, leaving the gelatine film adhering, through which carefully controlled etching was made by solutions of perchloride of iron which penetrated the gelatine-resist in inverse proportion to its light-hardness, thus etching the plate through the interstices between the grain particles. By this hand-method of preparing the plate and subsequent printing on a copperplate press, the most exact and beautiful gradations of tone were possible, as may be seen in such a relatively modern example as the frontispiece portrait medallion of Robert Foulis, printed by Emery Walker for James MacLehose's *The Glasgow University Press, 1638–1931*, Glasgow, 1931 (text printed by MacLehose) a copy of which is in the Printing Section of the College Library.[1]

In rotary photogravure, also developed by Karl Klič, the printing impression is from an etched copper cylinder in the preparation of which the 'carbon tissue' is exposed in contact with a mechanical screen before its exposure to the original. Volatile inks are used and a 'doctor' blade rides on the cylinder removing the ink from the surface and leaving it in the etched recesses only. In conventional photogravure the printed 'dots' are theoretically of equal size but, through the varying depth of the etch, of different tone (best discernible in the lightest tones of the print). In half-tone photogravure the dot varies in size and the impression is much more brilliant—especially in high-speed colour work. This may convincingly be seen in comparing copies of the late *Picture Post* (conventional photogravure) and *Illustrated* (half-tone photogravure) which are in the Printing Department of the College.

Because of the high cost of preparing the cylinder, but with a relatively low subsequent running cost, photogravure

[1] Some notes on the beginnings and early development of photogravure are given under the exhibits 632–6 listed under 'Intaglio' on p. 110 of July 1963 Exhibition Catalogue, *Printing and the Mind of Man*, Earls Court Exhibition section.

is more suitable for magazine work than for bookwork unless the edition is large, as in the case of the Phaidon Press art books, in which the monochrome plates are by photogravure, the coloured illustrations by offset litho, bound up with an introduction in the particular European language of the country of distribution—see F578, *Vincent van Gogh*, Vienna, 1936, described in the Typographical Notes. Photogravure can yield a certain richness and softness comparable with that of mezzotint, but the heavy shadows sometimes tend to appear 'sooty' and the highlights chalky—although these characteristics are less in evidence to-day. The process also has the advantage of not requiring coated paper.

Successful use of photogravure in book-work is seen in F391, Clunn, *The Face of the Home Counties*, a royal octavo with text printed by letterpress at the University Press, Oxford, and bled-off photogravure illustrations printed by Vandyck Printers Ltd, Bristol, published in 1937 by Simpkin Marshall at the extraordinary price of 7s. 6d. (the author regarded this book, with its companion volume, *The Face of London*, as a labour of love for the benefit of the citizens of Greater London); and F596, Kleyn, K., *Het landschap, foto's*, 1948, a large quarto printed by Enschedé in Haarlem, with typography by van Krimpen, has good photogravure reproductions, although even in some of these the blacks are a little too dense. But an outstanding example of photogravure in a superbly designed and printed book is I10F, Dr Gerard Knuttel, *The Letter as a Work of Art*, Amsterdam, 1951, centenary volume of the typefoundry vorheen N. Tetterode, produced with the help of Dr G. W. Ovink 'Aesthetic Adviser to the Typefoundry'. The photogravure plates, printed in the Netherlands, show examples of letter-forms—manuscript, incised, or printed—opposite examples of architecture or objects of art of the corresponding period. An attractive example of the use of colour-gravure in book-work is S366, *Our Bird Book*, published by Collins in 1947, in which the colour-plates by Tunnicliffe have been printed by Bemrose of Derby. It is of interest to compare the illustrations, from Cecil Beaton's photographs, in S348, *Face to face with China*,

1945, in which they are printed by photogravure, with those in S353, *Indian album*, 1946, in which they are letterpress half-tone printed in a deep sepia ink, giving, at first glance, the appearance of photogravure; and F637, Newberry, *Mittens, N.Y.*, 1936, is a pre-war example of a child's book with delightful brush drawings successfully reproduced by photogravure.

One of the most beautiful and sensitive of printing processes is collotype—developed largely during the 1860's and '70's—in which printing takes place direct from the photo-sensitive gelatine emulsion which has been evenly spread on a thick glass plate.[1] It is thus a planographic process having some affinities with lithography, and is capable of reproducing faithfully the finest gradations of tone and colour. But it is slow and expensive,[2] calling for the most careful control of temperature and humidity, and is therefore most suitable for smaller editions dealing with subjects requiring the finest reproduction, such as paintings, illuminated manuscripts, ceramics, coins, textiles, etc. It also has the advantage that printing can be done on hand-made paper. After exposure in contact with continuous-tone negatives the plate is immersed in a solution of glycerine and water which penetrates the gelatine coating in inverse proportion to the amount of hardening produced by the action of the light, so that after inking it will hold both ink and moisture together in suspension in complementary proportions, the greater amount of ink being retained in the harder portions, which have received the lesser amount of moisture. The plate is printed on a machine similar to a lithographic press, but without the damping rollers, since the plate normally only requires redamping after about every 200 copies. By careful control of exposure and colour-filters, some of the finest reproductions of paintings have been made by collotype, such as those of the Marées Society before the war, and the Ganymed prints of to-day.

[1] For some brief notes on the Earliest use of the collotype process, again see July 1963 Exhibition Catalogue, *Printing and the Mind of Man*, Earls Court Exhibition section—pp. 110-11, items 638-9.

[2] The maximum yield of the average plate is about 1,500 impressions, after which a new plate is required.

The Oxford University Press possessed a fine collotype department, which was wound up only as recently as 1968 and taken over by the department of lithography, with which its work had frequently been combined. Beautiful examples of colour collotype may be seen in some of the reproductions of textiles in volumes V and VI of S279, Pope, *A survey of Persian art*, published by the OUP in six folio volumes in 1938, but in this case the colour work is from different sources (acknowledged in the Preface) and not printed at Oxford. This great work, with text in 18-pt Caslon and footnotes in 12-pt double-column, was designed by the late James Shand, and the text printing and the binding are by the University Press. The line illustrations in the text were made at the Press from photographs and other material provided by the editor [1] Other examples of collotype in the collection are F485, the Noncsuch Press *La Divina Commedia*, 1928, Fol., with text printed at the Westminster Press and collotype reproductions (reduced) from 42 drawings by Botticelli printed by Daniel Jacomet; F24, Sackville-West, V. *Some flowers*, London, Cobden-Sanderson, 1937, 8vo, with full-page bled-off monochrome photographic illustrations; F261, *Cecil Beaton's Scrapbook*, London, 1937, 4to, printed by Graphic Arts Ltd, in which some of the pen-and-

---

[1] But the most lavish and expensive example of collotype book production ever made is Muirhead Bone's *Old Spain*, in this case entirely the work of the University Press, Oxford, and published by Macmillan in 1936 at 100 guineas a copy. The format of this astonishing two-volume folio ($13\frac{3}{4}$ in. by $20\frac{1}{2}$ in.) was also designed by the late James Shand, with double-column text in 18-pt Baskerville, and the production is a supreme example of collaboration between artist, author and printer. Three of the 120 full-page plates occupy double pages. In addition there are 34 half-page plates and headpieces, and 27 tailpieces; and the make-up, for which a complete mock-up was made, ensured that no letterpress ever backed a collotype—many of which are in colour. Mrs Bone, who provided the 'copy' for the text, was always ready to revise it to ensure that the space for a tailpiece was adequate or an awkward blank filled. Among *The Connoisseur's* comments on this great work were, 'This two-volume folio must surely be awarded pre-eminence among publications of the century . . . we shall assuredly never see its like again'. Other fine examples of colour collotype are seen in some of the OUP Almanacks, also in the College. In a few of these collotype is used for the black only, the colours being by photolithography, which later took over the whole printing.

wash sketches and photographs are reproduced by collotype and others by letterpress half-tone; and J1, Abbey, J. R., *Scenery of Great Britain and Ireland in aquatint and lithography, 1770–1860, a bibliographical catalogue*, 1952, 12½ × 9¼ in., a beautiful book privately printed by the Curwen Press, with monochrome collotype reproductions (frontispiece in colour) and including a brief note on the original aquatint engravers' technique. A small collotype plate of a pen-and-wash subject, with accompanying proofs, made by the late Edinburgh Zinco-Collotype Company, is in the Printing Department of the College. The illustrations to F643, Van Gogh, *Letters to an artist*, N.Y., 1936, are by aquatone, an interesting process analogous to collotype, which has been successfully used in the U.S.A. It is worked by the Aquatone Corporation.[1]

*   *   *

The foregoing notes have dealt principally with printers, artists, engravers, and printing processes, but not specifically with *design*—especially the more recent trends. Mention has been made in the Typographical Notes of the work and influence of the Bauhaus founded in 1919 in Weimar by Professor Walter Gropius. Probably the chief influence of this school is that derived from their complete substitution of asymmetrical or dynamic forms of design in typography in place of the conventional, symmetrical and static form inherited from the Renaissance. The many influences, from Morris to Dadaism, via Futurism, Constructivism, and other 'revolutionary' movements, which led to the founding of the Bauhaus and gave direction to its development have been fully analysed elsewhere[2]

[1] According to Bull, in this process the bichromated gelatine is said to be coated upon thin zinc plates, and the surface of the gelatine is smooth. The negatives used are either line or very fine half-tone of about 400 lines to the inch. By not having to take into account the intermediate tones between black and white, which renders the true collotype process a somewhat delicate matter to operate, it is possible to obtain extremely good effects and to print upon matt papers, using rotary machinery. See A. J. Bull, *Photo-Engraving*, London, 1934, pp. 73–4.

[2] See, for instance, F331, Gropius, *The New Architecture and the Bauhaus*, London, Faber, 1935; 'A Note on Modern Typography' by Bertram Evans, pp. 167–9 of

but certain subsequent trends which are in a large part its legacy must be referred to in their effect on the design and presentation of the printed book—in particular the book carrying illustration.

Broadly speaking, the conventional, symmetrical form of design, being static and 'reposeful', is still quite naturally maintained in a large proportion of day-to-day books, especially those uncomplicated by illustration, while the more dynamic, asymmetrical forms of presentation, designed to rouse attention —often by *optical* rather than literary impact—naturally find their employment in the more ephemeral kinds of printing, such as advertising matter or other 'utility' work which, for its success, must be effective during a relatively short lifetime. This kind of work may also include brochures, catalogues, bulletins or other such periodicals, especially where a variety of illustration has to be effectively assembled, and from this class of printing it has naturally extended to bookwork, where the same problems frequently exist. If, in typographic work, a group of lines of varying length are given a centred treatment, as in the conventional title-page, they cannot be so quickly or easily read (or set up) as when the beginnings of the lines are ranged on the left on an imaginary vertical line to which the eye constantly returns. But the advent of asymmetrical typography has brought with it a complete reorientation of the distribution of white space. Balance still remains the basis of design, but

Tarr, *How to Plan Print*, Pageant of Progress Series, OUP, 1945; and Lewis, *Typography: Basic Principles. Influence and Trends since the 19th Century*, Studio Books, 1963, pp. 22–41—to quote references easily available in the College. In addition, a copy of *Blast*, No. 1, June 1914, the Dadaist magazine edited and published by Wyndham Lewis at the 'Rebel Art Centre', 38 Great Ormond St., London, referred to in Bertram Evans's article abovementioned, and in the footnote on p. 498 relating to the artist and wood-engraver Edward Wadsworth, has been presented to the collection by W. B. Hislop in Sept. 1969, and can be examined for the deliberately aggressive impact of its heavyweight typography. A thick quarto, with text printed on antique wove paper, and plates on calendered paper, it includes Wadsworth's woodcut 'Newcastle' mentioned by Thomas Balston in his review (J4 before mentioned), and it is characteristic that the artists or sculptors whose work is reproduced include Epstein, Gaudier-Brzeska, and the cubist William Roberts (W3).

whereas in traditional bookwork it is achieved with type-area and marginal proportions symmetrically planned—illustration conforming to type-area as far as possible—in asymmetrically designed books text, illustration, and white space are dynamically distributed, with particular attention to white space as 'part of the whole picture'.

But there has been another development, which took place principally during the inter-war period, and which has furthered the incursion of asymmetry into book-design, and this is the introduction and rapidly increased use of 'bled-off' illustration —generally photographic illustration. For many years it was customary,[1] when ordering blocks for full-page illustrations to ensure that as far as possible they should conform to the area of the type page. For smaller formats this could not only involve considerable reduction in size, but in a series of say twenty or more subjects provided from different sources it could be by no means uncommon for only two or three to conform to this proportion. Some might be square, others very long and narrow necessitating their being turned to run up the page. But further —and this can be most significant—in photographic subjects scale is an important factor, since photographs too greatly reduced may not only lose essential detail, but will generally lack conviction—facts which have encouraged the use of illustration covering the whole paper-page, especially in the smaller formats. But if the book has many such illustrations, distributed as far as possible to be near their context, the principle of symmetrical balance achieved by twin facing pages is constantly upset by the appearance of a bled-off illustration facing a normally imposed text-page, and this has led in some cases to a more dynamic or 'overall' treatment of the text, with headlines 'skied' and projecting into the margins and folios at the foot of the page, against or in the outer margins, and lower than in the conventional page. The legend to the illustration facing has also generally to be accommodated in the lower margin.

An article by Paul Stadlinger, entitled 'A New Book Style',

[1] In many cases it is still customary.

in *Commercial Art and Industry*, April 1935 (in the Printing Department of the College) presents a most interesting survey of this problem in the early days of its emergence, with illustrations from a lively series of books, published in Berlin, which have a 'family likeness' one with another without being slavishly uniform. The use of photographic subjects for the jackets in this series, with simple binder's zincos for the cloth bindings is both effective and economical. The article also includes an example of a format suitable for a fully illustrated book in which, by treating the legends to the pictures as marginals, the maximum scope is provided for the most varied sizes in the illustrations—printed on the same paper as the text— without ever giving too wide or too short a line for comfortable reading. An example of the importance of scale in illustration may be seen in the little crown octavo S339, Fraser Darling, *Crofting agriculture* (Edinburgh, 1945) in which many of the bled-off plates show topographical detail which would have been completely lost if the subjects had been reduced to conform with the type-area. In this case the full descriptive legends are on flimsies covering the plates. Another small octavo, F331, Gropius, *The New Architecture and the Bauhaus*,[1] printed by MacLehose in 1935, shows the unfortunate effect of a text-page with conventional margins (but in this case imposed too high on the page) when appearing opposite a bled-off illustration occupying the whole of the facing page. A slight but attractive example of the early use of bled-off illustration is F385, *Tintern Abbey* (1935), a slender octavo printed by the University Press, Oxford.

To-day the utmost variety obtains in the integration of text and illustration on asymmetrical principles, especially in the larger formats accommodating many different subjects to the page, and the application of these principles has naturally been brought to bear on all parts of the book, including the preliminaries and supplementaries, with title-pages not only receiving asymmetrical treatment but even extending across the double-page opening where appropriate to the design of the

[1] See footnote, p. 516.

particular book, as also exemplified in the Stadlinger article abovementioned; see also S321, Hill and Tisdall, *Balbus: a picture book of building* (1944), a gay little quarto, printed in Edinburgh by McLagan & Cumming for Pleiades Books Ltd,[1] in which the title (with contents) receives this treatment, and Fuchs and Hillary, *The Crossing of Antarctica*, published by Cassell in 1958, a carefully designed book printed by Hazell, Watson & Viney, with colour plates by Rembrandt Photogravure Ltd, one of which makes a most impressively spacious double-page opening as a background to the title.

These developments in the treatment of the illustrated book are well summarised in a number of books on graphic design,[2] and they are now commonplace. An increasing number of present-day publications are now being printed by photo-litho offset on pleasingly matt-surfaced papers, with text and illustration laid down together, so that the physical and aesthetic unity of the book is preserved. Typical examples are the lively *Looking and Seeing* series (1964 *et seq.*) by Kurt Rowland—of interest to all design students—printed by Cowells and published in quarto by Ginn and Company, in which a great variety of illustrative material is successfully incorporated with the text.

With the progress which has taken place in colour printing by photo-litho offset and photogravure, and the application of synthetic glazes to the finished product—simulating the gloss associated with letterpress half-tone on coated papers—it is becoming increasingly difficult to identify the method of printing of some present-day work without the use of a magnifying glass or even a microscope. Two useful books, between them showing well-selected examples of the various processes up to the late 1950's are J20, Krüger, *Die Illustrations-Verfahren*, Leipzig, 1929, in the Clark Collection, and Kollecker and Matuschke, *Der moderne Druck*, Hamburg, 1956, No. 11820/655 in the Printing Section of the College Library. Although

---

[1] An article by Hans Tisdall, with the subtitle 'Some Pages from my Notebooks', appears in *Motif 13*, 1967.

[2] See, for instance, John Lewis, *Typography: Basic Principles. Influences and Trends since the 19th Century*, in the Printing Section of the College Library.

both are German publications, many of the illustrations are almost self-explanatory and, with the aid of a dictionary or technical 'Wörterbuch' (also in the departmental library) their legends can generally be elucidated, even by a student scarcely versed in German.

Recent technical developments in computer typesetting, photo-composition and electronic engraving have made it now more than ever necessary—and possible—to achieve a unity in the end-product of the various printing processes, a unity which has so often been lost and found again during the many vicissitudes of printing history. Writing in *Typographia 16* (the ultimate issue of December 1967) Herbert Spencer refers to the past two decades as a period 'in which the practice and techniques of typography have changed dramatically, in which technical developments have released typography from the restrictions and discipline imposed by metal type, and have allowed it to become increasingly visual and less linear, less linguistic. The frontiers between graphic design, photography, and typography have dissolved; *the marriage of word and image has been consummated*' (italics ours). It remains to be seen how settled this alliance will prove to be when subject to the impacts of future innovation.[1]

SUPPLEMENTARY NOTE

The references to illustrated books in the foregoing notes are almost entirely to books in the Edward Clark Collection. As already mentioned, few additions were made under this heading during and after the busy post-war reconstruction period of the late 'forties and early 'fifties, but some books representative of the development of book illustration from that time to the present day have been added by normal routine to the Printing and other sections in the College General Library.

The illustrated books in the collection belonging to the

[1] For influences in book design in Western Europe and America, see John Lewis, *The 20th Century Book*, Studio Vista, 1967, printed by Cowells and amply illustrated.

twentieth century are for the most part British, with some American and Continental in addition—generally following a similar tradition. But one particular 20th-century manifestation of the illustrated book is not represented, and that is the peculiarly French contribution through the *édition de luxe* and the *livre d'artiste*. The work of William Morris and the Private Press Movement, with the attendant revival of wood-engraving, re-emphasised the integration of type with illustration, a principle which was in some danger of being lost sight of during the busy late 19th-century period of technical innovation, but the disciplines imposed by the Movement, although ultimately responsible for a great improvement in book-design, tended rather to inhibit the use and experimental development in bookwork of processes not naturally associated with metal type. While the influences of the Private Press Movement spread to Germany, Holland and America, they had little impact in France, where the outlook on illustration was largely unrestrained by what might be called a 'typographic conscience'. Pictures have always been highly regarded in France for their own sake and while, in some of the *éditions de luxe* which began to appear with the opening of the 20th-century, the illustrations employ a variety of processes and reach the highest level of accomplishment, there is little or no attempt to integrate them with the type, which remains a rather static ancillary—sometimes giving the impression that it is something which can be discarded, leaving the illustrations to be treasured separately as 'prints'.

Lithography, which in the previous century had been kept at a higher level in France than it had been in this country, largely through the work of such artists as Delacroix, Daumier, Gavarni, Toulouse-Lautrec and others, became one of the favourite processes of autographic book-illustration, but etching, aquatint, wood-engraving, and other processes such as hand-stencilling were all favoured and developed experimentally at the hands of some of France's most distinguished artists, and in the resulting emergence of the *livre d'artiste*, on which the most devoted care was lavished for very limited editions, new ground was constantly explored and opened up in methods of making printed illustrations, with the relation of word to image now often receiving special attention. In France leading painters and sculptors have always been interested in and taken naturally to the various crafts of graphic reproduction, generally using them with great perception. A pioneer patron in this development from the beginning of the century was the discerning Ambroise Vollard, picture-dealer, print-dealer and publisher, who commissioned such artists as Bonnard, Redon, Denis, Chagall, Picasso, Rouault, Segonzac and others, all of whom have contributed influentially to this genre of the printed book.

The finest and most representative collection of works ever held in this country representing this art form was exhibited for a month in the Scottish National Gallery of Modern Art in Edinburgh in the summer of 1967. Most of the works in this exhibition were from the collection of Mr W. J. Strachan, who also wrote the introduction, entries and technical notes for the catalogue.[1] Four items were on loan from the Victoria and Albert Museum. Mr Strachan writes in his introduction:

'The essential feature of the *livre d'artiste* . . . is that each of the illustrations . . . in a given book is an "original" and not a reproduction. That is to say that the painters, sculptors, *peintres-graveurs* (original print-makers) have themselves executed their designs in one or other of the autographic media . . . on the surface of the wood, linoleum, copper or stone from which the illustrations are ultimately printed. These artists are in no sense professional book-illustrators; their contribution to the book is in addition to their normal activities in painting, sculpture and print-making in which they have made a national and in most cases international reputation. . . . The diversity of individual techniques never ceases to surprise; nor the high standard of production. The role of the specialised printer—most of the books are hand set—and of the printer of the engravings,

[1] See also W. J. Strachan, 'The Book illustrations of André Marchand', *Image 6*, Spring 1951, and 'The Illustrations by Lurçat for the Beau Livre', by the same author, *Motif 1*, Nov. 1958.

etchings and lithographs cannot be over-emphasised . . . Each copy is issued cased and boxed *en feuilles*, that is to say the gathered book sections are not sewn. . . . This enables the individual owner to commission an original binding from a professional designer who will in turn call in the services of a craftsman binder. Such bindings are works of art in their own right and there are of course exhibitions devoted to them'.

The exhibition also included some examples of the *livre manuscrit* in which the text is transcribed by the hand of the artist employing one or other of the autographic media, mostly lithography. The catalogue of the exhibition was printed in Edinburgh by Messrs R. & R. Clark, and is valuable as a record of some of the famous *ateliers* in Paris at which most of these works were made. Such essays by leading artists, covering the widest range and diversity of technique and design in different media (with special attention given to paper) constitute an influence which feeds the main stream of printing and graphic art and has a special interest to the student of the Illustrated Book. It is hoped that despite their costliness it may be possible for selected examples of the *livre d'artiste* to be added from time to time to the Edward Clark Collection. Meanwhile it is of interest that the most representative exhibition of this manifestation of the printed book so far held in this country should have been put on view in an ideal setting in Edinburgh.

F. P. RESTALL

s. *Illustrated Books*

S1

[14—]. *Biblia pauperum, photographed to half the natural size of the original in the Hunterian Museum Library, University of Glasgow.* A photographic reproduction of a Block Book.

S2

[14—]. *Exercitium super Pater Noster: suite de gravures avec légendes, reproduction photographique d'une publication xylographique du XVe siècle; notice par Benjamin Pifteau.*

S3

1499. Venice. [Colonna, Francesco.] *Poliphili hypnerotomachia, ubi humana omnia non nisi somnium esse ostendit, atque obiter plurima scitu sanequam digna commemorat.* Line block facsimile published in London in 1904.

S4

1517. Rome. Fulvius, Andreas. *Illustrium imagines.*

S5

1545. Venice. [Colonna, Francesco.] *La Hypnerotomachia di Poliphilo, cioe pugna d' amore in sogno dov' egli mostra, che tutte le cose homane non sono altro che sogno . . .*

S6

1551. Lyons. Alciati, Andrea. *Emblemata D. A. Alciati, denuo ab ipso Autore recognita, ac, quae desiderabantur, imaginibus locupletata.*

S7

1552. Basle. *Notitia utraque cum orientis tum occidentis.*

S8

1554. Lyons. Obsequens, Julius. *Giulio Ossequente de' prodigii* (and)

Polidoro Vergilio de' prodigii lib. III; per Damiano Maraffi, fatti Toscani.

S9

1557. Venice. Vico, Enea. *Le imagini delle Donne Auguste intagliate in istampa di rame; con le vite, et ispositioni di Enea Vico. Vol. 1.*

S10

1558. Lyons. Alciati, Andrea. *Toutes les emblemes de M. Andre Alciat; de nouveau traslatez en Françoys vers pour vers (par B. Aneau.)*

S11

1565. Antwerp. Alciati, Andrea. *Emblematum clarissimi viri D. Andreae Alciati libri II.*

S12

1577. London H[olinshead], R[aphael]. *The Historie of Scotlande . . . unto the yeare 1571.*

S13

[1592] Rome. Agostin, Antonio. *I discorsi del S. Don Antonio Agostini sopra le medaglie et altre anticaglie; tradotti dalla lingua spagnuola nell italiana.*

S14

1592. Antwerp. *Apologi creaturarum.*

S15

1614. Geneva. Alciati, Andrea. *Clariss. viri Dn. Andreae Alciati emblematum libri duo.*

S16

1618. Padua. Alciati, Andrea. *Emblemata v. cl. Andreae Alciati, cum imaginibus plerisque restitutis ad mentem auctoris.*

S17

1625. Rome. Radi, Bernardino. *Varie inventioni per depositi.* Bound with S19.

S18

1630. Padua. Tomasini, Giacomo Filippo. *Illustrium virorum elogia, iconibus exornata.*

S19

1642. Amsterdam. Passe, Crispin van der. *Oficina Arcularia.* Bound with Radi, B. *Varie inventioni per depositi* (S 17).

S20

1646. Amsterdam. Sichem, Christoffel van. *Bibels tresoor, Ofte der zielen Lusthof, Vytgebeelt in Figueren, ende gesneden.*

S21

1649. Frankfurt. *Dance of death (Todtentanz). Todten-Tanz, wie derselbe in der loblichen und weitberühmten Statt Basel, als ein Spiegel menschlicher Beschaffenheit . . . ; nach dem Original in Kupffer gebracht und herauss gegben durch Matthaeum Merian den Eltern.*

S22

1655. Lyons. Beiard, I. *Recueil des tiltres, qualités, blazons et armes des prelats des estats generaux de la province de Languedoc, Tenus par . . . le prince de Conty en la ville de Montpelier l'annee 1634.*

S23–4

1659–60. Cambridge. *Bible. The Holy Bible, containing the bookes of the Old and New Testament.* 2 volumes.

S25–7

1672. Amsterdam. Mallet, Allain Manesson. *Les Travaux de Mars; ou, La Fortification nouvelle tant reguliere, qu'irreguliere.* 3 volumes.

S28

1673. London. Carter, Matthew. *Honor redivivus; or, An analysis of Honor and Armory*; 3rd ed.

S29

1675. Oxford. Loggan, David. *Oxonia illustrata.*

S30

1694. Amsterdam. Bosboom, Symon. *Cort onderwys vande Vyf Colommen.*

S31

1695. Augsburg. Weigel, Christopher. *Biblia ectypa: Bildnussen aus heilige Schrift des Alt und Neuen Testaments. Historia von Jesu Christi unsers Heylandes Geburt.* 2 volumes in 1.

S32–3

17—. *Views in Scotland.* 2 volumes.

S34

1700. London. Scamozzi, Vincent. *The Mirror of Architecture; or, The Ground-rules Of the Art of Building; whereunto is added a Compendium on the Art of Building, by William Leyburn*; 4th ed.

S35

1707. London. Evelyn, John. *A Parallel of the ancient architecture with the modern*; 2nd ed.

S36

1712. London. Caesar. *C. Julii Caesaris quae extant . . . Accesserunt annotationes Samuelis Clarke . . .*

S37

1716. London. Cave, William. *Apostolici; or, The History of the Lives, Acts, Death, and Martyrdoms of those Who were Contemporary with, or immediately Succeeded the Apostles*; 4th ed.

S38

1732. London. *Amusing and Instructive fables in French and English.*

S39

1745. Venice. Tasso, Torquato. *La Gerusalemme liberata con le figure di Giambatista Piazzetta alla sacra real maestà di Maria Teresa d'Austria.*

S40

1764. Paris. Bonne, M. *Petit Tableau de la France; ou, Cartes Géographiques . . . Description Géographique abrégée de la France.* 2 volumes in 1.

S41

1770. Paris. Sacy, Le Maître de. *L'Histoire du Vieux et du Nouveau Testament, représentée avec des figures & des explications édifiantes.*

S42–2A

1777. La Fontaine, Jean de. *Contes et nouvelles en vers.* 2 volumes.

S43

1782. London. Adams, George. *A Treatise Describing the construction and Explaining the Use of New Celestial and Terrestrial Globes*; 5th ed.

S44

1784. Newcastle upon Tyne. *Select fables in three parts, to which are prefixed, The Life of Æsop, and an essay upon fable.*
See also D71, another copy.

S45–6

1788. London, Gilpin, William. *Observations, relative chiefly to picturesque beauty*; 2nd ed. 2 volumes.

S47

1788. Glasgow. Ramsay, Allan. *The Gentle Shepherd.*

S48

1789. London. *Dance of death* [*Todtentanz*]. *Emblems of Mortality; representing, in upwards of fifty cuts, death seizing all ranks and degrees of people.* (See p. 412)

S49–9A

1790. London. Hassell, J. *Tour of the Isle of Wight: the Drawings taken and engraved in Aquatinta by J. Hassell.* 2 volumes.

S50–1

1791. London. Gilpin, William. *Remarks on forest scenery.* 3 volumes. Vol. 3 missing.

S52–3

1793. London, Cowper, William. *Poems*; 5th ed. 2 volumes.

S54

1793. Gloucester. Dallaway, James. *Inquiries into the origin and progress of the science of heraldry in England with explanatory observations on armorial ensigns.*

S55

1793. London. Gay, John. *Fables.*

S56

1793. Perth. Thomson, James. *The Seasons.*

S57

1794. London. Æsop. *Fables of Æsop and others*; translated by S. Croxall; new ed.

S58–9

1797. Salisbury. Maton, William G. *Observations relative chiefly to the natural history, Picturesque Scenery, and antiquities of the Western Counties of England in the years 1794 and 1796.* 2 volumes.

S60–1

1799. London. Junius. *Letters.* 2 volumes.

S62–3

1799. London. Beattie, James. *The Minstrel, with some other poems, to which are now added, Miscellanies by James Hay Beattie.* 2 volumes.

S64

18—. (Eighteen steel engravings by various engravers after Turner.)

S65–5A

1801. London. Stoddart, John. *Remarks on Local Scenery and Manners in Scotland during the Years 1799 and 1800.* 2 volumes.

(Plate LV)

S66

1803. London. Spilsbury, F. B. *Picturesque scenery in the Holy Land and Syria.*

S67

1806. London. *Looking-glass for the mind,* The Editor of. *The Blossoms of morality intended for the amusement and instruction of Young Ladies and Gentlemen;* 4th ed.

S68

1807. Edinburgh. *The Holy Bible, containing the Old and New Testaments: together with the Apocrypha.*

S69–70

1808–10. London. Hogarth, William. *The Genuine works of William Hogarth; illustrated with Biographical Anecdotes . . .* by John Nichols and George Steevens. 2 volumes.

S71

1809. Newcastle upon Tyne. [Bewick, Thomas.] *A History of British birds.*

(Plate LVI)

S72

1810. London. Beckford, William. *Thoughts on hunting in a series of familiar letters to a friend.*

S73–3A

1812. London. Ackermann, R. *The History of the Abbey Church of St. Peter's Westminster, its antiquities and monuments.* 2 volumes.
(Plates LIII & LIV)

S74

1812. Liverpool. Bible. *The Christian's family bible*; revised by James Wood.

S75–6

1813. London. Porter, Robert Ker. *Travelling Sketches in Russia and Sweden during the years 1805, 1806, 1807, 1808.* 2 volumes.
(Plates LVII & LVIII)

S77

1813. London. Reresby, Sir John. *Travels and memoirs: the former . . . exhibiting a view of the governments and society in the principal states and courts of Europe, during the time of Cromwell's usurpation . . .*

S78

1815. London. Berry, William. *The History of the island of Guernsey . . . with particulars of the neighbouring islands of Alderney, Serk, and Jersey.*

S79–81

1817. London. Dibdin, T. F. *The Bibliographical Decameron; or, Ten Days Pleasant Discourse upon illuminated manuscripts and subjects connected with early engraving, typography, and bibliography.* 3 volumes.

S82

1817–19. London. Gell, Sir William and Gandy, John P. *Pompeiana: the topography, edifices, and ornaments of Pompeii.*

S83

1818. London. Latrobe, C. I. *Journal of a visit to South Africa in 1815 and 1816.*

S84

1818. London. Martin, Thomas. *The Circle of the mechanical arts; containing practical treatises on the various manual arts, trades, and manufactures.*

S85–7

[1819–21.] London. [Combe, William.] *The Tours of Dr. Syntax in search of the picturesque: a poem.* 3 volumes.

S88

[1821.] Blake, William. *Jerusalem, a facsimile of the illuminated book.* Produced in 1952 by D. Jacomet from the only coloured copy.

S89–9B

1821. London. Dibdin, Thomas F. *A bibliographical, Antiquarian and picturesque tour in France and Germany.* 3 volumes.

(Plate LXIII)

S90

1821. London. Egan, Pierce. *Life in London; or, the day and night scenes of Jerry Hawthorn, Esq. and his elegant friend Corinthian Tom accompanied by Bob Logic, the Oxonian, in their Rambles and Sprees through the Metropolis.*

S91

1822. London. Macauley, Elizabeth Wright. *Tales of the Drama.*

1823–55. ANNUALS. Various publishers.

S92–2X

The Amulet.	*The Christmas Box.*
The Bijou.	*The Comic Almanack.*
The Bouquet.	*The Comic Annual.*
The Bouquet of Melody.	*The Comic Offering.*
(Plates LIX & LX)	*Dramatic Annual.*

Fisher's Drawing Room Scrap-book.
Forget me not.
Friendship's Offering.
The Gem.
Heath's Picturesque Annual.
The Iris.
The Keepsake.
The Ladies Cabinet.

The Leisure Hour.
The Literary Souvenir.
The Oriental Annual.
The Pledge of Friendship.
The Recreation.
The Remembrance.
The Scenic Annual.
The Talisman.

S93

1823. London. Hogg, Thomas. *A concise and practical treatise on the growth and culture of the carnation.* 4th ed.

S94

1823. Oxford. Skelton, Joseph. *Skelton's Engraved Illustrations of the Principal Antiquities of Oxfordshire, from original drawings by F. Mackenzie, accompanied with descriptive and historical notices.*

S95

1824. Newcastle upon Tyne. Bewick, Thomas. *A general history of quadrupeds, the figures engraved on wood by Thomas Bewick.* 8th ed.

S96

1824. London. Locker, Edward Hawke. *Views in Spain.*

S97

1825. Oxford. Bunyan, John. *Bunyan explained to a child.*

S98

1825. London. Walton, Izaac. *The lives of Dr. John Donne, Sir Henry Wotton, Mr. Richard Hooker, Mr. George Herbert, and Dr. Robert Sanderson.*

S99–9A

1827-8. London. Maund, B. *The botanic garden, consisting of highly finished representations of hardy ornamental flowering plants.* 2 volumes.

(Plates LXI & LXII)

S100–0A

1827. London, Dagley, Richard. *Death's Doings, consisting of numerous Original Compositions in Prose and Verse principally intended as illustrations of thirty plates Designed and Etched by R. Dagley.* 2nd ed. 2 volumes.

S101

1829. Chiswick. Northcote, James. *One hundred fables, original and selected.* 2nd ed.

S102

1829. London. Shepherd, Thomas H. *Modern Athens! displayed in a series of views, or, Edinburgh in the nineteenth century.*

S103

183–. London. Harrison, [W. H.]. *Christmas tales, historical and domestic.*

S104

183–. London. Parley, Peter. *Wonders of Art; ancient and modern.*

S105

1830. London. *Three courses and a Dessert.*

S106–6A

1832. Newcastle upon Tyne. Bewick, Thomas. *A history of British birds.* 2 volumes.

S107

1832. Guildford. Egan, Pierce. *Book of sports.*

S108–8A

?1834. London. Cunningham, Allan. *The gallery of pictures by the first masters of the English and foreign schools, with biographical and critical dissertations.* 2 volumes.

S109

1833. Brunswick. Campe, Joachim Heinrich. *Robinson der Jüngere, ein Lesebuch für Kinder.*

S110

1833. London. Jameson, A. *The beauties of the Court of King Charles the Second, a series of portraits illustrating the diaries of Pepys, Evelyn, Clarendon and other contemporary writers.*

S111

1833. Edinburgh. Jardine, Sir William. *The Naturalist's Library.* Vol. 1.

S112

1833. *Wood engravings,* drawn by Martin, Westall and Thurston, and engraved by Bewick, Nesbit and many others.

S113

1834. London. *Uncle Philip's conversations with children about the habits and mechanical employments of inferior animals.*

S114

1835. Edinburgh. Goldsmith, Oliver. *History of the earth, and, Animated nature.*

S115–5c

1835. London. Roscoe, Thomas. *The tourist in Spain and Morocco.* 4 volumes.

S116

1836. London. Gray, Thomas. *Elegy written in a country church-yard.*

(Plate LXIV)

S117

1836. Chiswick. Parley, Peter. *Tales about Great Britain and Ireland.*

S118

1836. Bungay. *A present for the young.* 5th ed.

S119

1837. London. 'Quiz.' *Sketches of young ladies. Sketches of young gentlemen. Sketches of young couples.* 3 volumes in 1.

S120–0A

[*c.* 1838.] London. Bartlett, W. H., illustrated by. *The scenery and antiquities of Ireland: the literary portion of the work by N. P. Willis and J. S. Coyne.* 2 volumes.

S121–1C

[*c.* 1838.] Edinburgh. Browne, James. *A history of the Highlands and of the Highland Clans.* 4 volumes.

S122–3

1838. London. Defoe, Daniel. *The life and surprising adventures of Robinson Crusoe.* 2 volumes.

S124–5

1838. London. Dibdin, Thomas Frognall. *A bibliographical tour in the northern counties of England and in Scotland.* 2 volumes.

S126

[1838.] London. Hall, S. C., edited by. *The Book of Gems from the poets and artists of Great Britain* (Chaucer to Dryden).

S127

1838. Chiswick. Parley, Peter. *Tales about Greece.* 2nd ed.

S128

[1838.] London. Peake, R. B. *Snobson's seasons, being annals of cockney sports.*

S129

1839. London. *The perilous adventures of Quintin Harewood and his brother Brian.*

S130

1839–40. Edinburgh. *Edinburgh Journal of Natural History and of the Physical Sciences.* Vols. 1–2 bound together.

S131

1839. Chiswick. Parley, Peter. *Tales about Rome and modern Italy.*

S132

1840. London. Ainsworth, William Harrison. *The Tower of London.*

S133

1840. London. Day, Thomas. *Sandford and Merton*; abridged and modernized by Rosina M. Zornlin.

S134

1840. London. Janin, Jules, *and others. Pictures of the French.*

S135

1841. London. Janin, Jules, *and others. Pictures of the French.*

S136

1841. London. '*The Moral of Flowers*, Author of.' *The Spirit of the Woods.*

S137

[1842.] London. Bartlett, W. H. *The scenery and antiquities of Ireland.*

S138–9

[1842.] London. Bartlett, W. H. *The scenery and antiquities of Ireland.* 2 volumes.

S140–0C

1842. Edinburgh. Kay, John. *A series of original portraits and caricature etchings, with biographical sketches and anecdotes.* 4 volumes.

S141

1842. London. [Templeton, Thomas.] *A book about pictures.*

S142

1843. London. *Entertaining Naturalist, The; being popular descriptions, tales, and anecdotes of more than five hundred animals*; revised by Mrs J. W. Loudon.

S143–5

1843. London. Yarrell, William. *A History of British Birds.* 3 volumes.

S146

1846. Stuttgart. Goethe, Wolfgang von. *Reineke Fuchs.*

S147

1846. London. Milner, Thomas. *The Gallery of Nature: a Pictorial and Descriptive tour through creation.*

S148–9

1847. London. A'Beckett, Gilbert Abbott. *The Comic History of England.* 2 volumes.

S150

1847. Paris. Grandville, J. J. *Les Fleurs animées.* 2 volumes in 1.

S151

1847. London. Hering, George E. *The Mountains and lakes of Switzerland, the Tyrol and Italy, from drawings by George E. Hering.*

S152

1847. Chiswick. Taylor, Jeremy. *The Rule and exercises of Holy Dying.*

S153

1848. London. Dickens, Charles. *Dombey and Son.*

S154

1849. London. Humphreys, Henry Noel. *A Record of the Black Prince; being a selection of such passages in his life as have been most quaintly and strikingly narrated by chroniclers of the period.*

(Plate LXV)

S155–5A

1849. London. Thackeray, William M. *The History of Pendennis.* 2 volumes.

S156

1850. London. Grant, James. *Sketches in London*; 3rd ed.

S157

1850. London. Roberts, Mary. *Voices from the woodlands, descriptive of forest trees, ferns, mosses, and lichens.*

(Plate LXVI)

S158

[1851.] Paris. Bégin, Émile. *Voyage pittoresque en Suisse, en Savoie et sur les Alpes.*

S159

1853. London. Longfellow, Henry W. *Hyperion: a romance.*

S160

1853. London. Stowe, Harriet Beecher. *Uncle Tom's Cabin.*

(Plate LXVII)

S161

1853. London. Wingfield, W., and Johnson, G. W. *The Poultry book.*

S162

1854. London. Tupper, Martin F. *Proverbial philosphy.*

S163

1854. London 'Young Naturalist, A.' *Stories about beasts.*

(Plate LXVIII)

S164

1855. London. Goldsmith, Oliver. *The Deserted Village.*

(Plate LXIX)

S165

1855. London. Milton, John. *L'Allegro and Il Penseroso.*

(Plate LXX)

S166–6A

1855. London. Thackeray, William M. *The Newcomes, memoirs of a most respectable family*; edited by Arthur Pendennis, Esqre. 2 volumes.

Plate LII (N53)

GREAT PRIMER, No 2.

Quousque tandem abutere, Catilina, patientia nostra? quamdiu nos etiam furor iste tuus eludet? quem ad finem sese effrenata jactabit audacia? nihilne te nocturnum præsidium palatii, nihil urbis vigiliæ, nihil timor populi, nihil consensus bonorum omnium, nihil hic munitissimus habendi senatus locus, nihil horum ora vultusque moverunt? patere tua consilia non sentis? constrictam jam omnium horum conscientia teneri conjura-

ABCDEFGHIJKLMNOPQRS
TUVWXYZ

ABCDEFGHIJKLMNOPQRSTUVWXYZ

£1234567890

Quousque tandem abutere, Catilina, patientia nostra? quamdiu nos etiam furor iste tuus eludet? quem ad finem sese effrenata jactabit audacia? nihilne te nocturnum præsidium palatii, nihil urbis vigiliæ, nihil timor populi, nihil consensus bonorum omnium, nihil hic munitissimus habendi senatus locus, nihil horum ora vultusque moverunt? patere tua consilia non sentis? constrictam jam om-

*ABCDEFGHIJKLMNOPQRS
TUVWXYZÆ*

W. MILLER & CO.

1841. Edinburgh. Miller, William, and Co.
Specimen of printing types by William Miller & Co. 285 x 217 mm.

Plate LIII (S73–3A)

1812. London. Ackermann, R.

The History of the Abbey Church of St. Peter's Westminster, its antiquities and monuments. 350 x 290 mm.

Plate LIV (S73–3A)

HISTORY

OF THE

ABBEY CHURCH

OF

ST. PETER'S, WESTMINSTER.

CHAPTER THE FIRST.

THE FOUNDATION OF THE CHURCH.

THE history of those monasteries which were founded at periods subsequent to the Conquest, may, in general, be readily traced from the existing charters of their respective founders, or the authentic accounts of contemporary writers: but the origin of such as were established in earlier times, is involved in great obscurity; and is not only subject to the varying conjectures of ingenious and fanciful men, but to the idle dreams of credulous superstition. Several of the more ancient monastic institutions have their histories, such as they are; and the charters of others, which are said to have survived the long lapse of time and the accidents of the world, are produced to establish their remote antiquity. But as these histories appear to have been written at

VOL. I.   B

Plate LV (S65–5A)

REMARKS
on
Local Scenery & Manners
in
SCOTLAND
during the Years 1799 and 1800,
by
John Stoddart L.L.B.
Vol. I.

St BERNARD'S WELL. Engraved by W. Poole.

London Publish'd by William Miller. Old Bond Street, 1801.

1801. London. Stoddart, John.
Remarks on Local Scenery and Manners in Scotland during the Years 1799 and 1800.
230 X 156 mm.

Plate LVI (S71)

the neck are of a dingy brownish ash colour, in some specimens narrowly streaked with white: the throat is white: fore part of the neck mottled or streaked with brown spots, on a white or pale ash-coloured ground. The whole upper parts of the plumage are of a glossy bronze, or olive brown, elegantly marked on the edge of each feather with small roundish white spots: the quills are without spots, and are of a darker brown: the secondaries and tertials are very long; the insides of the wings are dusky, edged with white grey; and the inside coverts next the body are curiously barred, from the shaft of each feather to the edge, with narrow white lines, formed nearly of the shape of two sides of a triangle. The belly, vent, tail coverts, and tail, are white; the last broadly barred with black, the middle feathers having four bars, and those next to them decreasing in the number of bars towards the outside feathers, which are quite plain: the legs are green.

This bird is not any where numerous, and is of a solitary disposition, seldom more than a pair being seen together, and that chiefly in the breeding season. It is a scarce bird in England, but is said to be more common in the northern parts of the globe, even as far as Iceland. It is reported that they never frequent the sea-shores, but their places of abode are commonly on the margins of the lakes in the interior and mountainous parts of the country.

white: the shaft of the first quill is white; as in the Green Sandpiper; and the secondaries have white tips.* the legs are brown." Brunnich mentions a further variety, wherein the first quill has a black shaft, and the spots on the back and wings are less; and observes, that they differ in age and sex. †

THE GREEN SANDPIPER.

(*Tringa Ochropus*, Lin.—*Le Becasseau, ou Cul-blanc*, Buff.)

THIS bird measures about ten inches in length, to the end of the toes nearly twelve, and weighs about three ounces and a half. The bill is black, and an inch and a half long: a pale streak extends from it over each eye, between which and the corners of the mouth, there is a dusky patch. The crown of the head and hinder part of

* These are marks so common to many of this genus, that they cannot be considered as a feature sufficient to distinguish any particular species.

† Buffon's figure in use *Plancbes Enluminees* differs from this description.

1809. Newcastle upon Tyne. [Bewick, Thomas.]
A History of British birds. 210 x 128 mm.

Plate LVII (S75–6)

coining. For the apparatus, the government is indebted to Mr. Bolton of Soho. Several of his people are now here engaged in completing the necessary works.

In the walls and bastions which bulwark this castellated island are cells, or rather state prisons, where many a wretched being has lingered out an anxious life. In one of these places died the son of Peter the First after his condemnation. And here the unhappy and beautiful Princess Tarrakanoff met her fate. In 1771 the Neva rose to a tremendous height, and inundating part of the city, entirely overflowed the fortress. All who were in the dungeons perished under the waters; and amongst the number, *it is said*, was her whose tale so darkly shadows the brilliant career of the Great Empress.

Take the whole of this fortified island together, with its embattled towers and pinnacles; and when under a setting-sun you view it from the long perspective of the opposite street, no object can be finer. The burnished spire burning in brightness, and casting its stream of light over the turrets of the fortress; the Neva flowing in shining waves at its base, and bearing on its bosom myriads of boats passing and repassing, some filled with the treasures of merchandise, and others in which the happy navigators chant their national strains as they float along. No scene can possess more of the picturesque and beautiful. And when we contrast the gay court air of these northern gondolas with the savage barks from more distant quarters, and take in the variously attired groupes busy on the shore, a wilderness is mingled with the polished features of the view, which makes the whole appear the effect of enchantment.

Having led you through this fatal, romantic island, I shall re-conduct you across the waves, and bring you before the walls of the marble palace and church. The ideas suggested by the names of those two

1813. London. Porter, Robert Ker.
Travelling Sketches in Russia and Sweden during the years 1805, 1806, 1807, 1808.
295 x 236 mm.

Plate LVIII (S75–6)

Plate LIX (S92c)

THE

BOUQUET OF MELODY,

A

MUSICAL ANNUAL,

FOR

MDCCCXLVIII.

COMPRISING A CHOICE COLLECTION OF

SONGS, WALTZES, &C.,

AND

TEN BEAUTIFULLY EXECUTED LITHOGRAPHIC EMBELLISHMENTS;

THE MUSIC, BY RESIDENT

AMERICAN COMPOSERS.

NEW-YORK;
FIRTH & HALL, No. 1 Franklin Square, & FIRTH, HALL & POND, No. 239 Broadway.

1848. Annual.
The Bouquet of Melody. 335 x 260 mm.

Plate LX (S92c)

Plate LXI (S99–9A)

THE

BOTANIC GARDEN;

CONSISTING OF

HIGHLY FINISHED REPRESENTATIONS

OF HARDY

ORNAMENTAL FLOWERING PLANTS,

CULTIVATED

IN GREAT BRITAIN;

WITH

THEIR NAMES, CLASSES, ORDERS, HISTORY, QUALITIES, CULTURE,
AND PHYSIOLOGICAL OBSERVATIONS.

BY

B. MAUND, F.L.S.

VOL. II.

" Not a tree,
A plant, a leaf, a blossom, but contains
A folio volume. We may read and read,
And read again, and still find something new,
Something to please, and something to instruct."
HURDIS.

London:

PUBLISHED BY BALDWIN AND CRADOCK, PATERNOSTER ROW.

1827—8.

1827–8. London. Maund, B.
*The botanic garden, consisting of highly finished representations of hardy ornamental
flowering plants.* 190 x 145 mm.

Plate LXII (S99–9A)

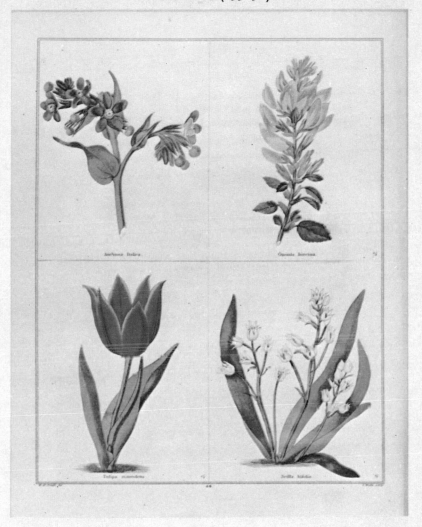

Plate LXIII (S89–9B)

DIEPPE. 25

England. Forgive this *new* reading : but I cannot help, in spite of all the marvels by which I am surrounded, putting in a good word now and then for my own country. So God bless you.

————

P. S. Mr. Lewis has just brought me another spirited drawing, of what may be considered equally characte-ristic of the MARKET WOMEN, look at it attentively; for I can assure you that the fidelity is equal to the spirit, of the performance.

1821. London. Dibdin, Thomas F.
A bibliographical, Antiquarian and picturesque tour in France and Germany.
249 x 160 mm.

Plate LXIV (S116)

ELEGY

WRITTEN IN

A COUNTRY CHURCH-YARD.

LONDON:

JOHN VAN VOORST, 3, PATERNOSTER ROW.

MDCCCXXXVI.

1836. London. Gray, Thomas.
Elegy written in a country churchyard. 195 x 122 mm.

Plate LXV (S154)

1849. London. Humphreys, Henry Noel.
*A Record of the Black Prince; being a selection of such passages in his life as have been
most quaintly and strikingly narrated by chroniclers of the period.* 197 x 134 mm.
Contemporary binding. Black morocco spine, titled in gold, with the addition of
pierced boards in high relief, imitative of carved ebony. Gilt edges.

Plate LXVI (S157)

CHAPTER IX.

ALDER OR OWLER.

Alnus glutinosa.

Light quivering on some river brink,
Where stoops the panting hart to drink,
On rocky bank, in glade, or dale,
The alder tells her simple tale.

MORALISTS have said that all trees have characters analogous to those of men. Behold in me, said a widely spreading alder, a vegetable type of one whose facility of disposition enables him to dwell contentedly wherever he sojourns. Such am I, an alder, growing either beside a highland stream, or in quiet hedgerows, in woods, or shading public

1850. London. Roberts, Mary.
Voices from the woodlands, descriptive of forest trees, ferns, mosses, and lichens.
246 x 159 mm.

Plate LXVII (S160)

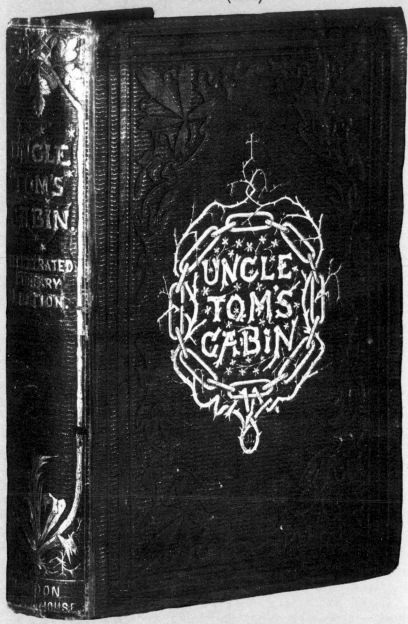

1853. London. Stowe, Harriet Beecher.
Uncle Tom's Cabin. 230 x 150 mm. Case binding in blue grained bookcloth with
blind blocking on both boards. Spine and centre of front board stamped in
gold with allegorical designs and lettering by J. Leighton. Gilt edges.

Plate LXVIII (S163)

1854. London. 'Young Naturalist, A.'
Stories about beasts. 200 x 160 mm.

Plate LXIX (S164)

THE DESERTED VILLAGE.

Sweet Auburn! loveliest village of the plain,
Where health and plenty cheer'd the labouring swain,
Where smiling spring its earliest visit paid,
And parting summer's lingering blooms delay'd.

1855. London. Goldsmith, Oliver.
The Deserted Village. 197 x 130 mm.

Plate LXX (S165)

L'ALLEGRO.

Then to come, in spite of sorrow,
And at my window bid good-morrow,
Through the sweet-brier or the vine,
Or the twisted eglantine :
While the cock, with lively din,
Scatters the rear of darkness thin,
And to the stack, or the barn-door,
Stoutly struts his dames before :
Oft listening how the hounds and horn
Cheerly rouse the slumbering morn,
From the side of some hoar hill,
Through the high wood echoing shrill ;

1855. London. Milton, John.
L'Allegro and Il Penseroso. 270 x 180 mm.

Plate LXXI (S168–8A)

1856. Edinburgh. Burns, Robert.
Life and works of Robert Burns; edited by R. Chambers. 217 x 134 mm.

Plate LXXII (S181)

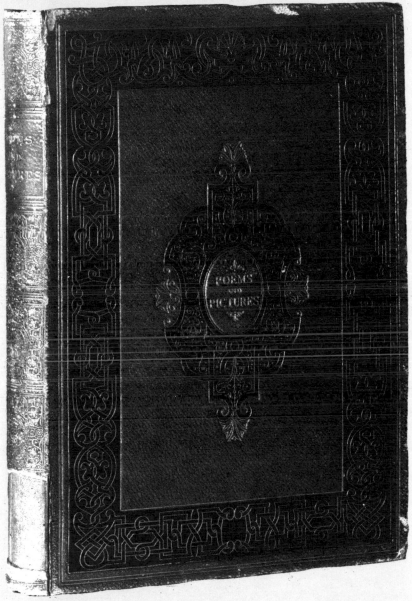

1860. London.
*Poems and Pictures, a collection of Ballads, Songs and other Poems, illustrated by
English artists.* 240 x 170 mm. Case binding of red morocco with full gilt spine.
Both boards stamped in gold, with panel and central motif onlayed in dark
green smooth skiver. Gilt edges.

Plate LXXIII (S183)

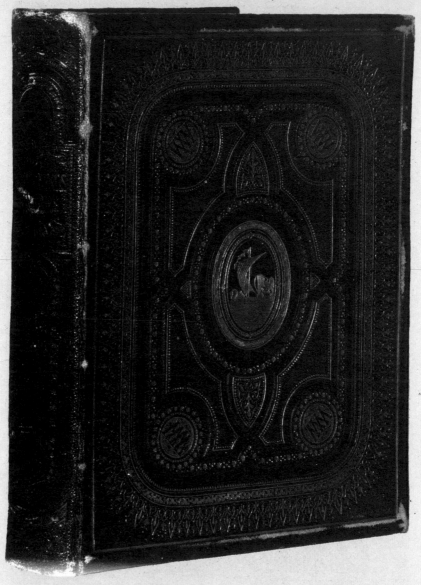

1864. London. Wordsworth, William.
Our English Lakes, mountains and waterfalls, as seen by William Wordsworth.
205 x 165 mm. Contemporary binding in dark green morocco with bevelled
boards. Heavily blocked in gold and blind on spine and both boards, with
tooled panels and turn-ins. Gilt edges.

Plate LXXIV (S185–5A)

1865. London. Dickens, Charles.
Our Mutual Friend; with illustrations by Marcus Stone. 213 x 135 mm.

S167

1856. London. Andersson, Charles J. *Lake Ngami; or, Explorations and discoveries, during four years' wanderings in the wilds of S.W. Africa*; 2nd ed.

S167A

1856. London. Jones, Owen. *The Grammar of Ornament. One hundred folio plates drawn on stone by F. Bedford and printed in colours by Day and Son.*

S168–8A

1856. Edinburgh. Burns, Robert. *Life and works of Robert Burns*; edited by R. Chambers. 4 volumes in 2.

(Plate LXXI)

S169

1856. London. Moore, Thomas. *Irish melodies.*

S170

—— Another copy. New edition.

S171–1A

1857. London. Dickens, Charles. *Little Dorrit.* 2 volumes.

S172

1857. London. Humphreys, H. Noel. *River Gardens.*

S173

1857. Edinburgh. Pollok, Robert. *The Course of Time.*

S174

1857. Glasgow. Rhind, William. *A History of the vegetable kingdom.*

S175

1858. London. Lawson, John P. *Scotland delineated, a series of views . . . from drawings made expressly by Sir William Allan, Clarkson Stanfield, George Cattermole and others.*

S176

1858. London. Longfellow, Henry W. *Kavanagh, a tale.*

S177

1859. London. Goldsmith, Oliver. *The Poems of Oliver Goldsmith*; edited by Robert Aris Willmott.

S178

1859. London. Kingsley, Charles. *Glaucus; or, The Wonders of the Shore*; 4th ed.

S179

1860. London. *Book of Favourite Modern Ballads.*

S180

[*c.* 1860.] London. Foster, Birket. *A Series of seventeen steel engravings after Birket Foster*; by A. Willmore and others.

S181

1860. London. *Poems and Pictures, a collection of Ballads, Songs and other Poems, illustrated by English artists.*

(Plate LXXII)

S182

1860. London. Surtees, Roberts. *"Plain or Ringlets?"*

S183

1864. London. Wordsworth, William. *Our English Lakes, mountains and waterfalls, as seen by William Wordsworth.*

(Plate LXXIII)

S184

1865. London. Archer, Thomas C. *Profitable plants.*

S185–5A

1865. London. Dickens, Charles. *Our Mutual Friend*; with illustrations by Marcus Stone. 2 volumes.

(Plate LXXIV)

S186

1865. London. Goldsmith, Oliver. *Dalziel's Illustrated Goldsmith.*

S187

1865. London. *Good Words for 1865.*

S188

1866. London. Buchanan, Robert. *Ballad stories of the affections from the Scandinavian.*

S189

1867. London. Lose, Federigo. *The Terra cotta architecture of North Italy (XIIth–XV centuries), descriptive text by V. Ottoline and F. Lose; edited by Lewis Gruner.*

S190

1867–8. Various printers. (Christmas stories, taken from the annuals.)

S191

1867. London. Ingelow, Jean. *Poems.*

S192

1867. London. *Quiver, The.* Vol. II.

S193

1868. London. Buchanan, Robert. *North Coast and other Poems.*

S194

[1868.] London. Tennyson, Alfred, Lord. *Idylls of the King, the Doré gift book.*

S195

[1870.] London. Blakston, W. A. and others. *The Illustrated book of Canaries and Cage Birds, British and Foreign.*

S196

1870. London. Hood, Thomas. *Miss Kilmansegg and her Precious Leg, a golden legend.*

S197

1870. London. Jackson, Thomas. *Our Feathered Companions.*

S198

1871. London. Hood, Thomas. *Poems.*

S199

1871. London. Mercier, Jerome J. *Mountains and Lakes of Switzerland and Italy*; with descriptive notes by J. J. Mercier.

S200

1871. Edinburgh. Whymper, Edward. *Scrambles amongst the Alps in the years 1860–69.*

S201

[1874.] London. *Beauty in Common Things.*

S202

1874. London. Surtees, Robert S. *Jorrocks' Jaunts and Jollities*; 4th ed.

S203

1874. London. Walton, Elijah. *The Bernese Oberland, twelve scenes among its peaks and lakes*; with descriptive text by T. G. Bonney.

S204

1875. London. Reynardson, C. T. S. Birch. *'Down the Road'; or, Reminiscences of a gentleman coachman*; 2nd ed.

S205

1878. Edinburgh. Bewick, Thomas. *Bewick's Select Fables of Æsop and others.*

S206

1879. London. Mitford, Mary Russell. *Our Village.*

S207

[c. 1880.] London. Grey, Sydney. *Story-Land.*

S208

1880. Edinburgh. Ramsay, Allan. *The Gentle Shepherd: a pastoral comedy.*

S209

1882. London. Cook, James. *Three voyages round the world, with a sketch of his life*; edited by Charles R. Low.

S210

1882. Edinburgh. Irving, Washington. *Bracebridge Hall.*

S211

1882. New York. *St. Nicholas: an Illustrated Magazine For Young Folks.*

S212

1883. London. *English Illustrated Magazine, 1883–4.*

S213

1883. London. *Old tayles newlye relayted enryched with all ye ancyente embellyshmentes.*

S214

1883. Khayyám, Omar. *Rubáiyát*; rendered into English verse by E. Fitzgerald.

S215

[1884.] London. *Language of flowers.*

S216–7

1884. New York. Mayer, Alfred M. *Sport with gun and rod in American woods and waters.* 2 volumes.

S218

1885. Edinburgh. Cameron, Verney Lovett. *Across Africa*; new ed.

S219

1885. London. Mavor, William. *The English Spelling Book.*

S220

1886. London. [Addison, Joseph.] *Days with Sir Roger de Coverley*. Reprint from 'The Spectator'.

S221

1886. Edinburgh. Kingsley, Charles. *The Water-Babies, A Fairy Tale for a Land-Baby*.

S222

1888. London. Caldecott, Randolph. *The Complete collection of Randolph Caldecott's contributions to the 'Graphic'*, with a preface by Arthur Locker.

S223

1888. Edinburgh. 'Petrel.' *In Southern Seas, A Trip to the Antipodes*.

S224

1888. London. Tristram, William Outram. *Coaching days and coaching ways*.

S225

1888–9. London. De la Rue & Co. *Playing cards*.

S226

[*c.*1890.] London. *Babes in the Wood*.

S227

[*c.* 1890.] London. Crane, Walter. *The Baby's Bouquet*.

S228

[*c.* 1890.] London. D., A.Y. *The Owls of Olynn Belfry: a Tale for Children*.

S229

1890. Edinburgh. Darwin, Charles. *Journal of researches into the natural history and geology of the countries visited during the voyage round the world of H.M.S. 'Beagle'*.

S230

1890. Edinburgh. Gibb, William. *The Royal House of Stuart,* illustrated by a series of forty plates in colours, drawn from relics of the Stuarts; introduction by J. Skelton; descriptive notes by W. H. St. J. Hope.

S231

[*c.* 1890.] London. Goldsmith, Oliver. *The Mad Dog.*

S232

[*c.* 1890.] London. Greenaway, Kate. *Marigold Garden—pictures and rhymes.*

S233

[*c.* 1890.] London. Harte, Francis Bret. *The Queen of the Pirate Isle.*

S234

1890. London. *The Old farm gate.*

S235

1890. Edinburgh. Paton, James, edited by. *Scottish National Memorials.*

S236

1890. London. Walter, James. *Shakespeare's true life.*

S237

[*c.* 1890.] London. Watts, Isaac. *Divine and Moral songs for children.*

S238

1891. London. Hibberd, Shirley. *New and rare beautiful-leaved plants*; 2nd ed.

S239

1891. Vienna. Strohl, Hugo G. *Die Wappen der Buchgewerbe.*

S240

1891. London. Wilde, Oscar. *A House of Pomegranates.*

547

S241

1891. New York. Wordsworth, William. *A Selection from the Sonnets of William Wordsworth.*

S242

1892. New York. Coppée, François. *Ten tales*; translated by Walter Learned.

S243

1892. Edinburgh. Whymper, Edward. *Travels amongst the Great Andes of the Equator*; 2nd ed.

S244

1893. Edinburgh. Whymper, Edward. *Scrambles amongst the Alps in the years 1860–69*; 4th ed.

S245

1894. London. *Coridon's Song, and other Verses from various sources.*

S246

1894. London. *Art Pictures from the Old Testament, Sunday Readings for the Young:* a series of ninety illustrations from original drawings by Sir F. Leighton and others.

S247

1894. London. Austen, Jane. *Pride and Prejudice.*

S248

1894. Edinburgh. Wilde, Oscar. *Salome: a tragedy in one act.*

S249–9E

1894–6. London. *Yellow Book, The: an illustrated quarterly.* Vols. 1, 2, 4, 6, 8, 9: Apr. 1894–Apr. 1896.

S250

1897. London. *Book of Nursery Rhymes.*

S251

1898. Edinburgh. Young, Archibald. *Summer sailings by an old yachtsman.*

S252

[1899.] London, Crane, Walter. *The Baby's Opera.*

S253

1899. London, Crane, Walter. *A Floral Fantasy.*

S254

[c. 1900.] Limoges. Feval, Paul. *La Fée des grèves, légende bretonne.*

S255

1901. Edinburgh. Allen, James Lane. *A Kentucky Cardinal, and Aftermath*; with illustrations by Hugh Thomson.

S256

1901. London. Lamb, Charles. *A Masque of Days: from the Last essays of Elia; newly dressed and decorated by Walter Crane.*

S257

1904. Edinburgh. Gaskell, Elizabeth Cleghorn. *Cranford.*

S258

1904. Edinburgh. Mitford, Mary Russell. *Our Village.*

S259

1904. London. Norway, Arthur H. *Highways and Byways in Devon and Cornwall.*

S260

1909. London. Ashbee, C. R. *Modern English Silverwork, an essay, together with a series of designs by the author drawn upon a hundred separate lithograph plates and coloured by hand.*

S261

1909. Edinburgh. Malory, Sir Thomas. *Le morte d'Arthur.*

S262

1925. Stratford-upon-Avon. *Of Aucassin and Nicolette, a translation in prose and verse from the old French, together with Amabel and Amoris,* by Laurence Housman; with drawings by Paul Woodroffe engraved on wood by Clemence Housman.

S263–4A

1926. London. Russell, Charles E. *English mezzotint portraits and their states from the invention of mezzotinting until the early part of the 19th century.* 2 volumes.

S265

1927. Edinburgh. Malory, Sir Thomas. *The birth, life and acts of King Arthur . . . ,* the text as written by Sir Thomas Malory and imprinted by William Caxton the year MCCCCLXXXV and now spelled in modern style, embellished with many original designs by Aubrey Beardsley. With a foreword by Aymer Vallance.

S266

1927. Edinburgh. Malory, Sir Thomas. *Reproductions of eleven designs omitted from the first edition of Le morte d'Arthur,* illustrated by Aubrey Beardsley and published in MDCCCXCIII, with a foreword by Aymer Vallance and a note on the omitted designs by Rainforth Armitage Walker.

S267

1928. Oxford. McDowall, Arthur. *Peaks and frescoes, a study of the Dolomites.*

S268

1928. Edinburgh. Malory, Sir Thomas. *The death of King Arthur, being the twenty-first book of Sir Thomas Malory's Book of King Arthur and of his noble knights of the round table.*

S269

1928. Plaistow. Ovid. *The heroycall epistles*; translated into English verse by George Turberville.

S270

1929. Farquhar, George. *The Beaux Stratagem, a comedy*; with seven engravings on copper by J. E. Laboureur.

S271

1929. Pilcher, Velona. *The searcher, a war play*; with nine wood-engravings by Blair Hughes-Stanton.

S272

1931. Edinburgh. Moore, Clement C. *The Night before Christmas.*

S273

1931. Guernsey. Gerard, John. *Leaves from Gerard's herball*; arranged for Garden Lovers by Marcus Woodward.

S274

1935. Edinburgh. Gilmour, Margaret. *Ameliaranne at the seaside.*

S275

1936. London. Bates, H. E. *Through the Woods: the English woodland—April to April*; with engravings by Agnes Miller-Parker.

S276

1936. London. Bone, Stephen, and Adshead, Mary. *The Little Boy and His House.*

S277

1937. U.S.A. Artzybasheff, Boris. *Seven Simeons.*

S278

1937. London. Bates, H. E. *Down the river.*

S279–9E

1938. Pope, Arthur U., and Ackerman, Phyllis, edited by. *A survey of Persian art from prehistoric times to the present.* 6 volumes.

S280

1939. Bristol. Henry, O. *The Gift of the Magi.*

S281

1939. London. Woodruff, Douglas. *The story of the British Colonial Empire.*

S282

194?. London. *Arts, The.* No. 1.

S283

194?. *Cathedral and figured rolled glass.*

S284

194?. *Insulight glass bricks.*

S285

194?. *Vitrolite specifications.*

S286

1940. Hagen, Victor W. von, and Hawkins, Quail. *Quetzal Quest, the story of the capture of the quetzal, the sacred bird of the Aztecs and the Maya.*

S287

1940. Birmingham. Imperial Chemical Industries Ltd. *Auxiliary Products for the textile and allied industries.*

S288

1941. Chapman, D. H. *The Seasons and the Woodman, A Book for Children.*

S289

1941. Darling, F. Fraser. *The Seasons and the Fisherman, A Book for Children.*

S290

[1941.] Ipswich. Gardner, James. *On the Farm*; a Puffin picture book.

S291

[1941.] Ipswich. Garnett, David and Gardner, James. *The Battle of Britain*; a Puffin picture book.

S292

1941. Perth. Lewitt-Him. *Polish Panorama*.

S293

1941. London. War Office. *Destruction of an Army: The First Campaign in Libya: Sept. 1940–Feb. 1941.*

S294

?1942. London. Ross, Diana. *The little red engine gets a name*; pictures by Lewitt-Him.

S295

1942. London. Smith, E. Cadwallader. *Kodru, the Monkey*.

S296

1942. London. Sperry, Armstrong. *The Boy Who Was Afraid*.

S297

1942. New York. Thackeray, William M. *The Rose and the Ring*.

S298

1942. Wisbech. Tunnicliffe, C. F. *My country book*.

S299

1943. Plaistow. Beerbohm, Sir Max. *The poet's corner*.

S300

1943. London. Bulatov, M. *The wild geese, and other Russian fables*; translated by V. de S. Pinto.

S301

1943. Glasgow. De la Mare, Walter. *Love*

S302

1943. Ipswich. Hale, Kathleen. *Orlando, the Marmalade Cat: A Trip Abroad.*

S303

1943. London. Hastings, Barbara. *Lobby Lobster, a story for children.*

S304

1943. London. Nelson, C. *Jungle-town tales.*

S305

1943. London. Ramal, Elizabeth. *Timothy.*

S306

1943. London. Ramsbottom, John. *Edible fungi.*

S307

1943. Edinburgh. Stephens, Lucian. *Family rhymes for children, parents and all those who find it easier to grow old than to grow up.*

S308

1943. London. Wolo. *Amanda.*

S308A

1943. Edinburgh. Duncan, F. Martin. *British shells.* (King Penguin Books.)

S309

1943. Edinburgh. Laver, James. *Fashions and Fashion Plates, 1800–1900.* (King Penguin Books.)

S310

1943. Edinburgh. Norman, J. R. *Fishes of Britain's rivers and lakes.* (King Penguin Books.)

S311

1943. Edinburgh. Rowlandson, Thomas, and Pugin, Charles A. *The microcosm of London*; text by John Summerson. (King Penguin Books.)

S312

1943. Edinburgh. Stoker, Fred. *A Book of Lilies.* (King Penguin Books.)

S313

1943. Edinburgh. Winter, Carl. *Elizabethan miniatures.* (King Penguin Books.)

S314

[1944.] Ipswich. Æsop. *Fables from Æsop and others.*

S315

1944. London. Arkell, Ruby L. *The Applejohns up the river.*

S316

[1944.] Leicester. Bell, Vera L. *Susan and the sailor boy.*

S317

[1944.] Chiang Yee. *The story of Ming*, a Puffin picture book.

S318

1944. New York. Dmitri, Ivan. *Flight to Everywhere.*

S319

1944. Andover. Fyleman, Rose. *Hob and Bob, A Tale of Two Goblins.*

S320

1944. Ipswich. Hale, Kathleen. *Orlando (the Marmalade Cat); His Silver Wedding.*

S321

1944. Edinburgh. Hill, Oliver, and Tisdall, Hans. *Balbus: a picture book of building.*

S322
1944. London. Laski, Marghanita. *Love on the supertax.*

S323
1944. London. Pardoe, M. *Bunkle butts in.*

S324
1944. Ipswich. Piper, Myfanwy, chosen by. *Sea Poems.*

S325
1944. London. Salten, Felix. *Bambi: a life in the woods.*

S326
1944. Plaistow. Stebbing, Hilary. *Monty's new house.*

S327
1944. Plaistow. Stephenson, T. A. *Seashore life and pattern.*

S328
[1944.] Glasgow. Townend, Jack. *Ben.*

S329
[1944.] London. Townend, Jack. *Jenny the Jeep.*

S330
1944. London. Tomlinson, R. R. *Children as artists.*

S331–1A
1944. London. Tozer, Katherine. *The Wanderings of Mumfie.* 2 copies.

S332
1944. London. Ward-Jackson, C. H. *No bombs at all, Some Short Stories of the Royal Air Force.*

S333
1944. London. Watson, E. L. Grant. *Walking with fancy.*

S334

1945. Birmingham. Adams, George A. *A New A B C in colour-photography*.

S335

?1945. Birmingham. *Story of Aladdin and his wonderful lamp*.

S336

1945. Ipswich. Brunhoff, Jean de. *Babar's Travels*.

S337

1945. Edinburgh. Carrington, Noel. *Popular art in Britain*. (King Penguin Books.)

S338

1945. London. Cross, John Keir. *Jack Robinson*; with pictures by John R. Parsons.

S339

1945. Edinburgh. Darling, Frank Fraser. *Crofting agriculture, its practice in the West Highlands and Islands*.

S340

?1945. Edinburgh. Freedman, Claudia. *My toy cupboard*. (Bantam Picture Book.)

S341

[1945.] Norwich. Glass, Douglas. *The Bread we eat, shown in colour photography*; described by Margaret Fisher.

S342

1945. Edinburgh. Jacobs, Robert L., and others. *Puccini's 'Madame Butterfly'*.

S343

1945. Leicester. Lingstrom, Freda, and others, edited by. *Junior*.

S344

1945. Edinburgh. Lockley, R. M. *Birds of the sea*. (King Penguin Books).

S345
1945. Buenos Aires. Lydis, Mariette. *Œuvres de Mariette Lydis figurant dans des collections privées en Argentine.*

S346
1945. Letchworth. Massingham, H. J., edited by. *The Natural Order, Essays in the return to husbandry.*

S347
1945. Ipswich. Pulling, Norah. *Mary Belinda and the ten aunts.*

S348
1945. London. Rattenbury, Harold B. *Face to face with China.*

S349
[1945.] Ipswich. 'Trix.' *Make your own farm*, part 1. (Puffin Cut-out Picture Books.)

S350
[1945.] Ipswich. 'Trix.' *Make your own zoo*, part 1. (Puffin Cut-out Picture Books.)

S351
1945. Norwich. Tubbs, Ralph. *The Englishman builds.*

S352
1945. Norwich. Beaton, Cecil. *Chinese album.*

S353
1946. Norwich. Beaton, Cecil. *Indian album.*

S354
1946. Plymouth. De la Mare, Walter. *Peacock Pie, a book of rhymes.*

S355
[1946.] Ipswich. Gabler, Grace. *A Child's alphabet.* (Puffin Picture Books.)

S356

1946. Ipswich. Hutton, Clarke. *A Picture history of Britain*.

S357

?1946. Perry, Powell. *A B C book*.

S358

1946. London. Ross, Diana. *Whoo, whoo, the wind blew*; pictures by Leslie Wood.

S359

1946. London. Slater, Humphrey, edited by. *Polemic, 2*.

S360

1946. Haarlem. Spreekmeester, I. *Chipo and Jumbo, how they became Friends*.

S361

1946. Haarlem. Spreckmeester, I. *Why the Snail carried his House on his back*.

S362

[1946.] Ipswich. Stebbing, Hilary. *Extinct animals*. (Puffin Picture Books.)

S363

1946. London. Thomas, M. G. Lloyd, chosen by. *Travellers' verse*.

S364

1946. London. Thompson, Flora. *Lark Rise to Candleford: a trilogy*.

S365

1947. London. Nicholson, Phyllis. *Country bouquet*.

S366

1947. London. Rogerson, Sydney, and Tunnicliffe, Charles F. *Our Bird Book*.

S367

1948. Athens. Benaki, Antony E., edited by. *Hellenic national costumes, Benaki Museum*; text by Mrs Angeliki Hadzimichali, plates by Nicholas Sperling. Vol. 1.

S368

1950. Kingswood [Surrey]. Galsworthy, John. *The Forsyte saga.*

S369

1951. Blake, William. *Jerusalem*; foreword by Geoffrey Keynes.

S370

1952. Ipswich. Wilson, Sir John. *The Royal philatelic collection*; edited by Clarence Winchester.

S371–2

n.d. London. *Future books.* Vols. 1, 3.

XIV

T. *Drawings and Prints*

T1

T. J. Cobden-Sanderson, 1915. Portrait in crayon by Sir William Rothenstein.

T2

Eric Gill. Portrait in crayon by Sir William Rothenstein.

T3

Count Harry von Kessler, 1933. Portrait in conté by Sir William Rothenstein.

T4

Edward Johnston. Portrait in conté by Sir William Rothenstein.

T5

Etching by W. H. Lizars: *State of the Parliament Square, Edinburgh at daybreak on Wednesday 17 November 1824.*

T6–7

—— *Preparations for pulling down the Great Gable, Friday evening 19 November 1824.* Plus 1 print.

T8–9

—— *Appearance of the ruins on the eastern side of Parliament Square, the instant after the mines were sprung at noon on Saturday 20 November 1824.* Plus 1 print.

T10–1

Etching by W. H. Lizars: *General view of the ruins, Friday 19 November 1824.* Plus 1 print.

T12–3

—— *View from the Old Fish Market Close.* Plus 1 print.

T14–5

—— *Remnant of the Great Gable, the highest in Edinburgh, from the Cowgate at 1 o'clock on Saturday 20 November 1824.* Plus 1 print.

T16–17

Print of *Cow's Close 17 November 1824 (spot where three men were crushed to death).* 2 copies.

T18–19

Print of *the Old Assembly Close 17 November 1824.* 2 copies.

T20

Lithographic print by W. Turner: *View of the great fire of Edinburgh taken on the 16 November 1824.*

T21

—— *View of the great fire in Parliament Square, Edinburgh.*

T22–4

Aquatints *Latest Paris Fashions* from 'The Queen', by Falconer, Paris.

T25–37

Prints from paintings by F. Wheatley, R.A., 1747–1801. *Cries of London.*
Two bunches a penny, primroses. D'après Schiavonetti.
Milk below maids. D'après Schiavonetti.
Sweet China oranges. D'après Schiavonetti.
Do you want any matches? D'après Cardon.
New mackerel. D'après Schiavonetti, jun.

Knives, scissors and razors. D'après Vendramini.
Fresh gathered peas. D'après Vendramini.
Round and sound five pence a pound. D'après Cardon.
Strawberries, scarlet strawberries. D'après Vendramini.
Old chairs to mend. D'après Vendramini.
A new love song. D'après Cardon.
Hot spice ginger bread. D'après Vendramini.
Turnips and carrots. D'après Gaugain.

T38

Aquatint. *The Gairloch, Ross-shire.* 1819. Drawn and engraved by William Daniell.

T39

—— *The storming of the Lesser Stockade at Kemmendine near Rangoon 10 June 1824.* Drawn by J. Moore and engraved by G. Hunt, 1826.

T40

—— *View of the lake and part of the Eastern Road near Rangoon taken from the advance of the 7th Madras native infantry.* Drawn by J. Moore and engraved by H. Pyall, 1826.

T41

—— *The attack of the stockade at Pagoda Point 8th July 1824.* Drawn by J. Moore and engraved by Reeve, jun.

T42

Print. *Laurens Coster.* Engraved by L'Armessin after Campen.

T43–4

Woodcut prints in colour by H. & R. Knofler, Vienna.
Johann Rudolph Kutschker.
Ecce agnus Dei, after B. Pinturicchio.

T45–51

Baxter Prints.
Four Scenes: The Ascent of Mont Blanc.

Winter Scene with Farmhouse.
The Swan Inn.
The Bridesmaid.
The Pompeian Court of the Crystal Palace.
The Great Exhibition. 1851. Interior.
The Great Exhibition. 1851. Exterior.

T52

Portrait of Fray Feliz Hortensio Palaviciano. Engraved on wood by Timothy Cole after the portrait by El Greco in the Boston Art Museum. 1930.

T53–4

Type Pictures.
1820. By John Johnson. *The Printers' Address to the Queen.*
1826. By John Johnson, said to contain more than 60,000 moveable pieces of metal.

XV

U. *Additions*

UI

Aldis, H. G. *List of books printed in Scotland before 1700.* 1970.
See also LI.

UIA

Alphabet and Image, 2–8.

U2–3

Alt, Robert. *Bilderatlas zur Schul und Erziehung Geschichte.* 1966.
2 volumes.

U4–7

Argelati. *Bibliotheca scriptorum mediolanensium.* 4 volumes
1965–6.

U8

Arnold, X. *Sammlung von Initialen.* n.d.

U9

Avis, F. C. *Early printers' chapel in England.* 1971.

U10

Barber, G. G. *Bookmaking in Diderot's Encyclopédie.* 1973.

U11

Barker, N. and Cleverdon, D. *Stanley Morison.* 1969.

U12

Batey, C. *The printing and making of books.* 1954.

U13

Berry, Duc de. *Les très riches heures du Duc de Berry.* 1969.

U14

Bett, W. R. *Preparation and writing of medical papers for publishing.* n.d.

U14A

Thomas Bewick. Glasgow School of Printing, 1949.

U15

Biblia Pauperum. 1967. Facsimile of the Esztergom Block Book.

U16

Bibliothèque Nationale. *Les plus beaux manuscrits français à peintures du moyen âge de la Bibliothèque Nationale.* 1937.

U17

Birrell and Garnett. *Catalogue of typefounders' specimens etc.* 1928.

U18

Blackwell. *Catalogue 929, Kelmscott Press books.* 1971.

U19

Blake, William. *Songs of innocence and experience.* 1967.

U20

Boece, H. *History and chronology of Scotland.* 1540 (facsimile *c.* 1816).

U21–6

Book Design and Production, Vols. 1–5, 7. 1959–64.

U26A

Bookplates.

U27–8

Bories and Bonassies. *Dictionnaire pratique de la presse*, Vols. 1 & 2. 1971.

U29

Bremner, Marjorie. *ABC Read about reading.* 1960.

U30

Brewer, R. *Eric Gill: The man who loved letters.* 1973.

U31

British Federation of Master Printers. *Approach to print* (Handbook 1). 1971.

U32

—— *Hand and mechanical composition* (Handbook 2). 1971.

U33

—— *Graphic reproduction* (Handbook 3). 1971.

U34

—— *Paper* (Handbook 4). 1971.

U35

—— *Paper samples* (Handbook 4 supplement). 1971.

U36

—— *Lithography gravure* (Handbook 5). 1971.

U37

—— *Print finishing* (Handbook 6). 1971.

U38

British Museum. *Stanley Morison.* Catalogue of an Exhibition. 1969.

U39

—— *Stanley Morison: A portrait.* 1971.

U40

Care of matrices, spacebands and magazines. n.d.

U41

Carey, G. V. *Making an index*. 1951.

U41A

Carter, H. *A History of the Oxford University Press*. Vol. I to 1780. Oxford. 1974.

U42

Caslon, H. W., & Co. *Caslon Old Face Roman and Italic*. 1923.

U43–54

Cave, R. and Others, editors. *Private Press Books 1959–1972*. 15 volumes. 1960–72.

U55

Chubb, Thomas. *Printed maps and atlases of Great Britain and Ireland: A bibliography 1579–1870*. n.d.

U56

Churton, E. *The Authors' Handbook: A complete guide to the art and system of publishing on commission*. 1844.

U57

Coates, G. *Roman alphabet and Albrecht Dürer*. 1969.

U58

Collins, F. H. *Authors' and printers' dictionary*, 6th edition. 1928.

U59

Cowell, W. S., Ltd. *A book of typefaces*. 1952.

U60

Craig, E. G. *Nothing, or the book plate*. 1924.

U60A

Cranach, Dürer, Rembrandt. 4 parts. Woodcut illustrations. B. H. Newdigate.

U61

Curwen Press: a short history. 1970.

U62

Darton, F. J. H. *Modern book illustration in Great Britain and America.* 1931.

U63

De Bury, Richard. *Philobiblon: Text and illustrations of E. C. Thomas.* 1970.

U64

Delacolonge, The type specimen of, with introduction and notes by Harry Carter. 1969.

U65

De La Mare, Richard. *A publisher on book production.* 1936.

U65A

Design and Industry. Proposal to form an Association.   JOII.

U65B

Design and Industries Association Year Book. 1922.

U65C

Wynkyn De Worde and his contemporaries. Henry R. Plomer. Grafton & Co., 1925.

U65D

Wynkyn De Worde. 1512. *The Golden Legend.* 35 leaves. STC. 24879.

U65E

Double Crown Club Menus.

U66

Drabble, M. *The millstone.* 1965.

U66A

Early Colour Printing and George Baxter. Cordingley, James. N.W. Polytechnic, London. 1948–9.

U67
Edinburgh Royal Observatory. Catalogue of the Crawford Library of the Royal Observatory. 1930.

U68
English printers' marks of the 15th Century 1964. F. C. Avis.

U69
English printers' marks of the 16th Century 1965. F. C. Avis.

U70
Enschedé en Zonen, Joh. *A selection of types.* 1930.

U71
Farnsworth, S. *Illumination.* 1922.

U71A
Fell Types. Broadsides of these types and other material presented by Dr Fell to Oxford University, *c.* 1672.

U72
The first English Copyright Act 1709. 1965. F. C. Avis.

U73
Folio Society. *Folio 21: A bibliography of the Folio Society 1947–1967.* 1967.

U74
Forman, Maurice B. *Meredithiana.* 1924.

U74A
Robert and Andrew Foulis, and the Glasgow Press and the Academy of Fine Arts. MacLehose, 1913.

U75–8
Fowkes, J. E. Reeve. *Print in Britain 1953–57.* 4 volumes. 1953–7.

Additions

U79

French, George. *Printing in relation to graphic art.* 1903.

U80

Gill, Eric. *The Monotype Recorder.* 1958. Vol. 41, No. 5. Monotype Corporation Ltd.

U81

Gossop, R. P. *Book illustration.* 1937.

U82

Goudy, F. W. *Elements of Lettering.* 1922

U83

—— *The Trajan capitals.* 1936.

U84

Hart, H. *Notes on a Century of Typography at the University Press, Oxford, 1693–1794.* A facsimile reprint with additional Notes. 1970.

U85

Hellwig, Wilhelm. *Wörterbuch der Fachausdrucke des Buch und Papiergewerbes.* 1926.

U86

Holloway, Owen E. *French rococo book illustration.* 1969.

U87

Hutt, A. *Fournier.* 1973.

U88

Huyghe, R. *Art treasures of the Louvre.* 1951.

U89

John Johnson Collection. *Catalogue of an exhibition.* 1971.

U90

Johnston, E. *Formal penmanship.* 1971.

U91

Jones, Brian. *A family album*. 1968.

U91A

K'ang Hsi, Blue and White. Specimen of 16 pt Estienne.

U92

Kelly, Rob Roy. *American wood type 1828–1900*. 1969.

U93

Leach, Mac Edward. *Paris et Vienne: Translated from the French by William Caxton*. 1970.

U94

Lewis, John. *Anatomy of printing*. 1970.

U95

Linkenbach, H. L. *The miracle of John Gutenberg*. 1932.

U95A

Loquendo Mirabilis. Latin Press 1936.

U96

Lydenberg and Archer. *The care and repair of books*. 1931.

U97

McKenzie, D. F., and Ross. *A ledger of Charles Ackers*. 1968.

U98

McLean, Ruari. *Reminiscences of Edmund Evans*. 1968.

U99

—— *Victorian book design*. 2nd ed. 1972.

Additions

U100

MacRobert, T. M. *Fine illustrations in Western European books.* 1969.

U101–1B

Manchester Public Library's Reference Library Subject Catalogue Section 094: *Private press books.* 1960. Section 655: *Printing*: Parts 1, 2. 1961, 1963.

U102

Masse, H. J. L. J. *The Art Workers' Guild 1884–1934.* 1935.

U103

Moran, J. *Printing presses.* 1973.

U104

—— *Stanley Morison his typographic achievement.* 1971.

U105

Morison, Stanley. *The English newspaper.* 1932.

U106

—— *First principles of typography.* 1951.

U107

—— *The Roman, Italic and Black Letter bequeathed by Dr Fell to the University of Oxford.* 1950.

U108

——*A tally of types*, with additions by several hands. Edited by Brooke Crutchley. 1973.

U109

Mosley and Chambers. *Charles Holtzapffel's printing apparatus for the use of amateurs.* 1971.

U109A

Motif. 7 parts.

U110

Musper, H. T. *Die Haarlemer Blockbucher und der Costerfrage.* 1939.

U111

Napier, Mark. *Memoirs of John Napier of Merchiston; His life, lineage and times with a history of the invention of logarithms.* 1934.

U112

National Library of Scotland. *Treasures from Scottish libraries.* 1964.

U112A

Newspaper with Stamp Tax.

U113

O'Dwyer, E. S. *Thomas Frognall Dibdin.* 1967.

U113A

Oxford Lectern Bible, An account of the making of The.

U114

Orcutt, W. D. *The book in Italy.* 1928.

U115

Osborne, N. H. *Eric Gill Memorial Collection: A Catalogue.* 1967.

U116

Oxford Bibliographical Society. *Proceedings and papers Vol. IV Part 2 1935.* 1936.

U117

Palmer, Edward. *Glyphography.* 1844.

U117A

Penrose Annual, The. 1898 to 1965. 59 volumes.

U117B

Philobiblon. 20 parts 1934–38.

U117C

The Pitt Press. E. A. Crutchley. 1938. Cambridge University Press.

U118

Plenderleith, H. J. *Preservation of leather book bindings.* 1967.

U118A

Plomer, Henry R. *English Printers' Ornaments.* 1924.

U118B

Potter, Beatrix. The Tailor of Gloucester. London. 1900.

U118C

Print Design and Production. 16 parts.

U118D–8Q

The Printers International Specimen Exchange. 14 volumes. 1880 onwards.

U119

Printers of Fleet Street & St Paul's Churchyard in the 16th Century 1964.

U119A

Printing and the Mind of Man. Catalogue of the Exhibitions at the British Museum and at Earls Court, London. 1963.

These exhibitions were intended to be 'a display of printing mechanisms and printing materials arranged to illustrate the History of Western Civilization and the means of the multiplication of Literary Texts since the XV Century'.

U119B

Printing Review. 66 parts (some duplicated).

U120

Reed, T. B. *History of old English letter foundries.* New edition revised and enlarged by A. F. Johnson. 1952.

U121

Reid, Anthony. *Checklist of book illustrations of John Buckland Wright.* 1968.

U122

Rosart, J. F., *The type specimen, Brussels 1768. Facsimile by F. Baudin & N. Hoeflake.* 1973.

U123

Rostonberg, Leona. *Literary, political, scientific, religious and legal publishing, printing and bookselling in England,* Vols. 1 & 2. 1965.

U124

Scholderer, Victor. *Johann Gutenberg.* 1970.

U125

Shakespeare, William. *The complete Pelican Shakespeare.* 1969.

U126

Shepard, Leslie. *John Pitts: Ballad printer of Seven Dials, London, 1765–1844.* 1969.

U127

Simon, H. *Songs and words: A history of the Curwen Press.* 1973.

U127A–7B

Simon, Oliver. *Printer and Playground.* Autobiography. Faber & Faber, 1956. (2 copies.)

U127C

Simon, Oliver and Rodenberg, Julius. *Printing of Today.* Peter Davies, 1925. Curwen Press.

U128

Simpson, Percy. *Proof reading in the 16th, 17th & 18th Centuries.* 1970.

U129

Slythe, R. *The art of illustration 1750–1900.* 1969.

U130

Smail, J. Cameron. *Scottish enterprise printing.* 1923.

U131

Smith, P. *Lettering (A plea).* 1932.

U132–42

Spread of printing. 11 volumes. 1969, 1972.

U143

Stannard, W. J. *Anaglyphography.* 1967.

U144–5

Taubert, S. *Bibliopola.* Vols. 1 & 2. 1966.

U146

Thomas, David. *Type for print.* 1936.

U147–8

Thomas, Isaiah. *History of printing in America*, Vols. 1 & 2. n.d.

U149

Tronnier, A. *Von Gutenberg, dem Mainzer Psalter und einem Schelmenstreich.* 1936.

U150

Twyman, Michael. *Lithography 1800–1850.* 1970.

U151

Twyman, Michael. *Printing 1770–1970.* 1969.

U152–2A

Type Specimen Facsimiles. General Editor John Dreyfus. Vol. I *Reproductions of Fifteen Type Specimens issued between the Sixteenth and Eighteenth Centuries,* with notes by various hands and an Introductory Essay by Stanley Morison. 1963. Vol. II The *Index characterum of Plantin and the Le Bé-Moretus Specimen,* annotated by H. D. L. Vervliet and H. Carter. 1972.

U153

Typographical Association, The. 1954.

U154

Upton, P., and Banks. *Production of electrotype from wax moulds without the use of graphite.* 1947.

U155

—— and Soundy. *Electrotyping by the Patra method.* 1950.

U156

Vervliet, H. D. L. *16th Century printing types of the Low Countries.* 1968.

U157

—— *Type specimens of the Vatican Press 1628.* 1967.

U158

Walpole, H. *Journal of the printing office at Strawberry Hill.* 1923.

U159–63

Werdet, Edmond. *Histoire du livre en France.* 5 volumes. 1971.

U164

Wolpe, Berthold. *Vincent Figgins' type specimens 1801 and 1815.* 1967.

Items printed under the direction of Leonard Jay at the Birmingham School of Printing.

U165

1926. Ought art to be taught in schools?

U166

1926. Let us now praise famous men and our fathers that begat us, and other passages from the Holy Bible.

U167

1927. The Odes of John Keats.

U168

1927. Christ's Sermon on the Mount.

U169

1927. Four parables from the Holy Bible.

U170

1927. Sutton Chase.

U171

1928. About Beauty.

U172

1928. Art and the Community.

U173-4

1928. The Creation of Heaven and Earth. 2 copies.

U175

1928. An essay on life by Percy Bysshe Shelley.

U176

1928. A fairy's song, and other verses for children.

U177

1928. Rubáiyat of Omar Khayyám.

U178

1929. An early Spanish printer, Arnald Guillen de Brocar.

U179

1929. Eight sonnets. John Keats.

U180

1929. An elegy written in a country churchyard. Thomas Gray.

U181

1929. The giving of the law.

U182

1929. On decoration in printing.

U183

1929. A selection of Shakespeare's sonnets.

U184

1930. Art and workmanship. W. R. Lethaby.

U185

1930. Auguries of innocence. William Blake.

U186–7

1930. The book of Ruth. (2 copies.)

U188

1930. Birmingham School of Printing Booklet No. 9.

U189

1930. Elizabethan lyrics, selected and arranged by Leonard Jay.

U190

1930. An essay of gardens. Francis Bacon.

U191

1930. The Eve of St Mark. John Keats.

U192

1930. Four speeches by Abraham Lincoln.

U193

1930. Modern printed books. Oliver Simon.

U194

1930. Modern typography. Leonard Jay.

U195

1930. Preface to Milton's 'Paradise Lost'.

U196

1930. Rabbi Ben Ezra. Robert Browning.

U197

1930. The song of the three holy children.

U198

1930. Ten Sonnets. William Wordsworth.

U199

1931. Four tracts relative to the Battle of Birmingham.

U200

1931. A garland of poems by various authors.

U201

1931. The sunken garden and other verses. Walter de la Mare.

U202

1932. Crossing the bar. Alfred, Lord Tennyson.

U203

1932. Birmingham School of Printing. Booklet No. 11.

U204

1932. Hero and Leander. Christopher Marlowe.

U205

1932. The hymn of the morning of Christ's Nativity. John Milton.

U206

1932. Letters of John Baskerville of Birmingham.

U207

1932. Lucian's The Dreame.

U208

1932. Ode by John Masefield.

U209

1932. Modern typography in Monotype Gill Sans-Serif.

U210

1932. Elizabethan Sonnets selected and arranged by Leonard
Jay.

U211

1933. Catalogue of books issued . . . from March 1925 to July
1933.

U212

1933. The deserted village. Oliver Goldsmith.

U213

1933. Famous passages in prose and poetry selected by Leonard
Jay.

U214

1933. Exempli Gratia. Book pages composed and cast on the
Linotype.

U215

1933. The makers of the summer. Richard Jefferies.

U216

1933. Ten precepts. William Cecil, Lord Burghleigh.

U217

1933. Verses grave and gay. Bernard Sleigh.

U218

1934. Ancient charters of Birmingham.

U219

1934. The Bible in Type.

U220

1934. Choruses to Abraham Lincoln. John Drinkwater.

U221

1934. Mostly moonshine. Madeline Nightingale.

U222

1934. The Sensitive Plant. P. B. Shelley.

U223

1934. Ten Sonnets. E. M. Rudland.

U224

1935. England, an address by the Rt. Hon. Stanley Baldwin.

U225

1935. Poems. T. Green.

U226

1935. Saint Philip's Church Birmingham and its Groom-Porter Architect, Benjamin Walker.

U227

1935. Sir Christopher Wren.

U228

1935. William Caslon 1692–1766.

U229

1935. The Home of Lovely Players. Sidney Charteris.

U230

1936. Georgius V. Orationes in Vicesimo Quinto anno regni dictas.

U231

1936. John Baskerville the printer 1706–1775.

U232

1937. Exempli Gratia. A few examples of general commercial work.

U233

1937. Sculpture on machine-made building.

U234–5

1939. The immortal hour. Fiona McLeod (William Sharp). 2 copies.

U236

1940. Tragedy of Hamlet.

U237

1941. Life . . . of Brother Giles.

XVI

V. *Bernard Newdigate Books*

V1

Extracts from *The London Mercury*. 1921–37.

The main importance of the books contained in the Collection of Bernard H. Newdigate, is that so many of them were reviewed by him in *The London Mercury*.

Between the years 1921 and 1939 this magazine contained reviews of books, not for their literary content, but for their typographical style.

These reviews were written by Bernard Newdigate and there is a complete set of newspaper cuttings, pasted into scrapbooks. This enables the review to be compared with the actual volume reviewed.

V2

ADAMS BROS. & SHARDLOW. Armfield, Maxwell. *Stencil Printing*. Dryad Handicrafts. 1927.

V3

ALCUIN PRESS. Taylor, G. S., edited by. *The book of the knight of la tour Landry*. Verona Society. 1930.

V3A

—— *Marriage of H. P. R. Finberg and Miss J. H. P. Payne*. 1933.

V4

—— Musaeus. *Hero and Leander* . . . translated . . . by E. H. Blakeney. Basil Blackwell. 1935.

V5

AQUILA PRESS. Marlowe, Christopher. *Edward the Second*. 1929.

V6

ARDEN PRESS. Bridgett, J. E. *A History of the Holy Eucharist in Great Britain.* Unwin, Burns & Oates. 1908.

V7

—— THORP, Joseph. *A Knight's Heart and Other Verses.* Elkin Mathews. 1909.

V8

—— Morris, W. *The Life and Death of Jason.* (Collected Works Vol. II). Longmans Green & Co. 1910.

V9

ASHENDENE PRESS. *A Descriptive Bibliography of the Books Printed at the Ashendene Press MDCCCXCV-MCMXXXV.*

V10

——*The Children's Garden, A Memory of the Old Porch House.* E. H. Christmas. 1913.

V11

—— *Vita di Santa Chiara Vergine composta per Ugolino Verino cittadino Florentino.* 1921.

V12

—— *I fioretti del glorioso poverello di Cristo S. Francesco di Assisi.* 1901.

V13

BALLANTYNE PRESS. Campion, Thomas. *Fifty Songs.* 1896.

V14

BALLANTYNE, HANSON & Co. Jack, George. *Wood carving: Design and workmanship.* John Hogg. 1903.

V14A

—— Hope, W. H. St. J. *Heraldry for Craftsmen and Designers.* John Hogg. 1913.

V15

BOAR'S HEAD PRESS. *The Magic Forest:* A Story told, printed and illustrated by Christopher and Lettice Sandford. 1931.

V16

—— Sappho. *Translations and Introduction* by E. M. Cox. 1932.

V17

—— Spenser, Edmund. *Thalamus, or the Brydall Boure.* 1932.

V18

—— Sandford, Christopher. *Primeval Gods.* 1934.

V19

BUTLER AND TANNER. Baker, C. H. Collins. *Design in Modern Industry.* Benn Bros. 1922.

V20

CAMBRIDGE UNIVERSITY PRESS. Milton, John. *Paradise Regained.* The Fleuron. 1924.

V21

—— *Cambridge University Press.* Cambridge University Press. 1925.

V22

—— Milton, John. *Comus, a Mask.* Julian Editions. 1926.

V23

—— W.L. [Walter Lewis]. *The Forty Third Dinner of the Double Crown Club.* 1934.

V24

—— Herodotus. *The History of Herodotus of Halicarnassus.* Nonesuch Press. 1935.

V25

—— *Ten Minutes Advice to Freshmen.* J. Deighton. 1935.

V26

CAMBRIDGE UNIVERSITY PRESS. Meynell, Francis, *et al. The Nonesuch Century.* Nonesuch Press. 1936.

V27

—— Austin, Richard. *Cambridge University Press.* 1937.

V28

—— *The Form and Order . . . Coronation . . . King George VI and Queen Elizabeth . . .* Cambridge University Press, 1937.

V29

—— CRUTCHLEY, E. A. *A History and Description of the Pitt Press.* Cambridge University Press. 1938.

V30

—— Morison, Stanley. *Latin Script since the Renaissance.* 1938.

V31

CAMELOT PRESS. Blunden, Edmund. *Votive Tablets.* Cobden-Sanderson. 1931.

V32

CAYME PRESS. Campion, Thomas. *The Maske.* 1924.

V33

CENTRAL SCHOOL OF ARTS AND CRAFTS. Coleridge, Samuel Taylor. *The Rime of the Ancient Mariner.* 1937.

V34

CHISWICK PRESS. Drayton, Michael. *The Battaile of Agincourt.* 1893.

V35

—— Crane, Walter. *Of the Decorative Illustration of Books Old and New.* 1896.

V36

CHISWICK PRESS. Morris, William. *Some Hints on Pattern Designing*. 1899.

V37

—— Cobden-Sanderson, T. J. *Ecce Mundus. Industrial Ideals and the Book Beautiful*. Hammersmith Publishing Society. 1902.

V38

—— *Arts and Crafts Essays*. William Morris and others. 1903.

V39

—— *The Hollow Land, and Other Contributions to the Oxford and Cambridge Magazine*. Longmans. 1903.

V40

—— Pope, Alexander. *The Rape of the Lock*. 1925.

V41

R. & R. CLARK. Housman, Laurence. *Bethlehem: A Nativity Play*. Macmillan & Co. 1902.

V42

—— *The Monotype Recorder*. Fournier le jeune. 1926.

V43

—— Walton, Izaak. *The Compleat Angler, The Lives of Donne, Wotton, Hooker, Herbert and Sanderson*. Nonesuch Press. 1929.

V44

—— Jackson, Holbrook. *The Early History of the Double Crown Club*. 1935.

V45

RICHARD CLAY AND SONS. Gay, John. *Polly*. 1923.

V46

RICHARD CLAY AND SONS. Dryden, John. *Of Dramatick Poesie.* Etchells & Macdonald. 1928.

V47

CLOISTER PRESS. Theocritus. *Six Idillia.* Duckworth & Co. 1922.

V48

—— Flaubert, Gustave. *Three Tales.* 1923.

V49

COCK ROBIN PRESS. Byron, John. *Careless Content.* 1932.

V50

CURWEN PRESS. Gidvani, M. M. *Shah Abdul Latif.* 1922.

V51

—— Scott, Geoffrey. *A Box of Paints* . . . With Drawings by Arthur Rutherston. 1923.

V52

—— Fine Ornament and Decorative Material Available to "Monotype" Users. Lanston Monotype Corporation. 1924.

V53

—— *Bible. First Chapter of Genesis.* Nonesuch Press. 1924. Woodcuts by Paul Nash.

V54

—— Hardy, T. *Yuletide in a Younger World.* Faber & Gwyer Ltd, n.d.

V55

—— Seaby, Allen W. *Colour Printing with Linoleum and Wood Blocks.* Dryad Handicrafts. 1925.

V56

—— HORACE. *Horatii Carminum Libri IV.* Peter Davies. 1926.

V57

Curwen Press. Anacreon. 29 *Odes*. Gerald Howe. 1926.

V58

—— Greenwood, J. F. *Twenty-Four Woodcuts of Cambridge.* Bodley Head. 1926.

V59

—— Balston, Thomas. *Sitwelliana.* Duckworth. 1928.

V60

—— Blackwell, Basil. *Bernard Newdigate, Typographer.* 1945.

V61

—— *Sunday Times.* n.d. *c.* 1954.

V62

De La More Press. Dekker, Thomas. *The Gull's Hornbook.* 1904.

V63

—— Newdigate, C. A. Notes on the 17th Century Printing Press at St. Omers. 1920.

V64

Eragny Press. Ronsard, Pierre de. *Choix de sonnets de P. de Ronsard.* 1902.

V65

—— Jonson, Ben. *Songs by Ben Jonson.* 1906.

V66

—— Gautier, Judith. *Album de Poèmes Tirés du Livre de Jade.* 1911.

V67

Essex House Press. Ashbee, C. R. *An Endeavour Towards the Teaching of John Ruskin and William Morris.* 1931.

V68

FANFARE PRESS. Butler, Samuel. *Butleriana,* edited by A. T. Bartholomew. Nonesuch Press. 1932.

V69

—— Tennyson, Alfred. *In Memoriam.* Nonesuch Press. 1933.

V70

—— Coleridge, S. T. *Selected Poems of Coleridge.* 1935.

V71

VINCENT FIGGINS. Caxton, William. *The Game of Chesse.* 1855 (facsimile).

V72

FLORENCE PRESS. Chaucer, Geoffrey, translated by. *The Romaunt of the Rose.* 1908.

V73

FOREST PRESS. Hubbard, Hesketh. *Simple Colour Block Print Making.* 1930.

V74

GOLDEN COCKEREL PRESS. Clay, Enid. *Sonnets and Verses.* 1925. Awarded the Crown for the year 1925 by the Double Crown Club.

V75

—— Sterne, Laurence. *A Sentimental Journey Through France and Italy.* 1928.

V76

—— Tellier, Jules. *Abd-er-Rahman in Paradise.* 1928.

V77

—— *Consequences;* in nine chapters, each by a different author. 1932.

V78

GOLDEN COCKEREL PRESS. Coppard, A. E. and Gibbings, Robert. *Rummy, That Noble Game Expounded.* 1932.

V79

—— Davies, Rhys. *Daisy Matthews and Three Other Tales.* 1932.

V80

—— Lord Dunsany. *Lord Adrian.* 1935.

V81

—— *Cupid and Psyches.* Translated from The Golden Asse of Apuleius by W. Adlington. 1934.

V82

—— Gill, Eric. *The Lord's Song,* A Sermon. 1934.

V83

—— Nash, Paul, *et al. Sermons by Artists.* 1934.

V84

—— Bates, H. E. *Flowers and Faces.* 1935.

V85

—— Jonson, Ben. *A Croppe of Kisses: Selected Lyrics.* 1937.

V86

—— *Per Ardua Ad Victoriam:* Programme of the Golden Cockerel Press. 1944.

V87

E. B. GORDON. Fox, Adam. *Ten Poems.* 1923. Lancing.

V88

GREGYNOG PRESS. Herbert, George. *Poems.* 1923.

V89

GREGYNOG PRESS. Vaughan, Henry. *Poems.* 1924.

V90

—— Thomas, Edward. *Chosen Essays.* 1928.

V91

—— Thomas, Edward. *Selected Poems of,* with introduction by Edward Garnett. 1927.

V92

—— Bible. *Llyfer y Pregeth- wr.* (Book of Ecclesiastes). 1927.

V93

—— Davies, W. H. *Selected Poems.* 1928.

V94

—— Herbert, Lord. *The Autobiography of Edward, Lord Herbert of Cherbury;* with an Introduction by C. A. Herford. 1928.

V95

—— Peacock, Thomas Love. *The Misfortunes of Elphin.* 1928.

V96

—— Rossetti, Christina. *Poems.* Chosen by Walter de la Mare. 1930.

V97

—— Caxton, William. *The Fables of Esope.* 1931.

V98-9

—— Euripides. *The Plays of Euripides,* translated in to English rhyming verse by Gilbert Murray. Vols. 1 & 2. 1931.

V100

—— Milton, John. *Comus.* 1931.

V101

Gregynog Press. Bible. *Revelation of St John the Divine.* 1932.

V102

—— Butler, Samuel. *Erewhon.* 1932.

V103

—— Vansittart, Robert. *The Singing Caravan.* A Sufi Tale. 1932.

V104

—— Davies, W. H. *The Lover's Song-Book.* 1933.

V105

—— Milton, John. *Four Poems: L'Allegro, Il Penseroso, Arcades, Lycidas.* 1933.

V106

—— Bible. *The Lamentations of Jeremiah.* 1934.

V107

—— Madariaga, Salvador de. *Don Quixote* : An Introductory Essay in Psychology. 1934.

V108

—— Bridges, Robert. *Eros and Psyche*: A Poem in XII Measures. 1935.

V109

—— Waddell, Helen. *New York City.* To bring greetings and best wishes for 1936 from Gregynog. 1935.

V110

—— Greville, Fulke, Lord Brooke. *Caelica,* Edited with Introduction by Una Ellis Fermor. 1936.

VIII

GREGYNOG PRESS. Xenophon. *Cyrupædia*: The Institution and Life of Cyrus. 1936.

VII2

—— Joinville, John, Lord of. *The History of Saint Louis*, translated by Joan Evans. 1937.

VII3

—— Hartzenbusch, Juan E. *The Lovers of Teruel*. 1938.

VII4

STUART GUTHRIE. *The Death and Burial of Cock Robin*. 1932.

VII5

HAGUE AND GILL. Shewring, Walter. *Greek and Latin Versions*. 1933.

VII6

HAMPDEN PRESS. Binyon, Laurence. *Three Poems*. 1934.

VII7

HAZELL, WATSON AND VINEY. Tennyson, Alfred. *Songs from 'The Princess'*. Duckworth. 1924.

VII8

HIGH HOUSE PRESS. Farjeon, Eleanor, *Young Folk and Old*. 1925.

VII9

—— *The Shepheards Holy Day*. 1925.

VI20

——Suckling, Sir John. *A Ballade Upon a Wedding*. 1925.

VI21

—— *Poems*. 1925.

V122-3

HIGH HOUSE PRESS. Townsend, Lewis W. *The Gossips*. 1926. (2 copies).

V124-7

—— *A List of Booklets*. Printed and Published by James E. Masters. 1926, 1926, 1927, 1928.

V128-9

—— Petrarca, M. Francesco. *Some Sonnets and Songs of the Divine Poet*. 1926. (2 copies).

V130

—— Shenstone, William. *Twenty Songs of William Shenstone*. 1926.

V131

—— Waller, Edmund. *Songs and Verses*. 1926.

V132

—— Anacreon. *The First Three Odes of Anacreon*, done into English. 1927.

V133

—— *Rymes of the Minstrels*. 1927.

V134

—— Parnell, Thomas. *The Vigil of Venus* : A Rendering of the Pervigilium Veneris into English Verse. 1927.

V135-6

—— White, Eric Walter. *The Room*. 1972 (2 copies).

V137

—— *Good Wine*. A Song. 1928.

V138

HIGH HOUSE PRESS. White, Eric Walter. *The Harmony of Birds*. 1928.

V139

—— Martin, E. M. *The Reckoning and Other Poems*. 1928.

V140

—— Shenstone, William. *A Pastoral Ballad in Four Parts*. 1928.

V141

—— Donne, John. *An Anatomie of the World*. 1929.

V142

—— Petrarca, M. Francesco. *Some 26 Sonnets and Songs of M. Francesco Petrarca*. 1929.

V143

—— Theocritus. *Hylas*. 1929.

V144

—— *Twelve Songs from the Plays of John Lyly*. 1930.

V145

—— Milton, John. *Arcades*. 1930.

V146

—— *The Poem of Amriolkais*. 1930.

V147

—— Goethe, J. W. von. *Prologue in Heaven from Faust*. 1932.

V148

—— Ibbett, W. J. *A Medley*. 1932.

V149

HIGH HOUSE PRESS. Masters, James E. *Shaftesbury.* 1932.

V150

—— Masters, James E. *How a Merchant did his Wife Betray.* 1933.

V151

—— Horace. *365 Short Quotations from Horace.* 1935.

V152

—— *Hero and Leander.* Translated by George Chapman. 1936.

V153

—— Heywood, Thomas. *A Marriage Triumphe.* 1936.

V154

—— *Old English Wines and Cordials.* 1938.

V155

—— *The Pleasant and Sweet History of Patient Grissell.* 1939.

V156

—— *The Old Village.* Alys Fane Trotter. n.d.

V157–8

HIS MAJESTY'S STATIONERY OFFICE. Committee on Type Faces. *Report of the committee appointed to select the best faces of type and modes of display for government printing.* HMSO. 1922. 2 copies.

V159

G. W. JONES. AT THE SIGN OF THE DOLPHIN. *Pearl: An English Poem of the Fourteenth Century.* 1918.

V160

—— Vergil. *The Georgics.* 1931.

V161

HOWARD JONES, ROBERTS AND LEETE. Lyell, J. P. R. *Mrs Piozzi and Isaac Watts*. Grafton & Co. 1934.

V162

KYNOCH PRESS. Fairbank, A. J. *A Handwriting Manual*. The Dryad Press. 1932.

V163

—— Jonson, Ben. *English Grammar*. Lanston Monotype Corp. 1928.

V164

—— Judson, Muriel. *Lettering for Schools*. Dryad Handicrafts. n.d.

V165

LANSTON MONOTYPE CORPORATION. Almanack 1929.

V166

LATIN PRESS. Blackett, Basil Philpott. *Translations*. 1937.

V167

LONDON SCHOOL OF PRINTING. Jarrold, W. T. F. *Christopher Plantin*. 1922.

V168

LUND, HUMPHRIES AND CO. Thorley, W. *The Londoner's Chariot*. Cape. n.d.

V169

ROBERT MACLEHOSE. Willoughby, Edwin Elliott. *A Printer of Shakespeare*. Philip Allan & Co. 1934.

V170

—— Bliss, Douglas Percy, edited by. *The Devil in Scotland*, Alexander Maclehose, 1934.

V171

NEILL AND CO., EDINBURGH. Q., R. *Reflections in Verse.* Scholartis Press. 1928.

V172–3

B. H. NEWDIGATE. *Quem Vidistis Pastores.* 1949. 2 copies.

V174

NORTH WEST POLYTECHNIC PRINTING SCHOOL. Goldsmith, Oliver. *The Deserted Village.* 1930.

V175

OXFORD UNIVERSITY PRESS. Farquhar, George. *The Recruiting Officer.* Peter Davies. 1926.

V176

—— Howells, Herbert. *Lambert's Clavichord.* Double Crown Club. 1928.

V177

—— Beaumont and Fletcher. *Songs and Lyrics from the Plays.* Etchells and Macdonald. 1928.

V178

—— Hewitt, Graily. *The Pen and Type-Design.* First Edition Club. 1928.

V178A

—— Horne, R. H. *Orion.* Scholartis Press. 1928. First published book set in Treyford type.

V179

—— Gardiner, Alan H. *Catalogue of the Egyptian Hieroglyphic Printing Type*, Oxford University Press. 1928.

V180

—— Coleridge, Samuel Taylor. *The Ancient Mariner.* 1930. Designed by Bruce Rogers.

V181

OXFORD UNIVERSITY PRESS. *The Four Gospels in the Original Greek* (Clarendon Press, Oxford, using the Proctor Types). 1932. The third book in which these types were used, the others being the *Oresteia* of Aeschylus, 1904, and the *Odyssey* of Homer, 1909.

V182

—— Percy, Thomas. *Ancient Songs Chiefly on Moorish Subjects.* Oxford University Press. 1932.

V183–4

—— Milton, John. *The Mask of Comus.* Nonesuch Press. 1937. 2 copies.

V185

—— Shaw, Thomas. *Barbary and the Levant*, Oxford, 1738.

V186

PEAR TREE PRESS. *A Little Anthology of Hitherto Uncollected Poems by Modern Writers.* Edited, printed by hand and published by Stuart Guthrie. 1922.

V187

—— Guthrie, James. *To the Memory of Edward Thomas.* 1937.

V188

—— Shakespeare, William. *The Phoenix and Turtle.* Edited with an Introduction by Gerald Bullett. 1938.

V189

PELICAN PRESS. Trevelyan, R. C. *The Pterodamozels.* 1916.

V190

—— *The Craft of Printing.* 1921.

V191

PELICAN PRESS. Marlowe, Christopher. *Hero and Leander*. Etchells and Macdonald. 1924.

V191A

—— *Bible. Book of Ruth*. Nonesuch Press. 1923. Only 250 copies printed.

V192

PILLANS AND WILSON. *The Kalendar and Compost of Shepherds*. Peter Davies. 1931.

V193

P., K Henryson, Robert. *The Testament of Cresseid*. The Porpoise Press. 1925.

V194

PRIORY PRESS, TYNEMOUTH. *Old Tyneside Street Cries*: Collected by Robert King. 1924.

V195

—— *Seven Poems* by Joseph Skipsey. 1924.

V196

—— *Alps of Gold*: Poems by Gwen Grant. 1927.

V197

—— *The North Shields Lighthouses* by Madeleine Hope Dodds. 1928.

V198

—— *Barnabe Barnes*. Ten Poems from 'Parthenophil and Parthenophe'. 1929.

V199

PRIDE, JOHN. Pride, John. *A quair of Sonnets and Ballads*. Written, etched and printed by hand by John Pride. 1929.

V200

PURNELL AND SONS. Buckton, A. M. *Eager Heart*. Elkin, Mathews & Marrot. 1931.

V201

RAVEN PRESS. Holy Bible. *The Book of Tobit From the Apocrypha.* 1931.

V202

—— Milton, John. *Samson Agonistes.* 1931.

V203

—— Shakespeare, William. *Venus and Adonis.* 1931.

V204

—— Southey, Robert. *A Vision of Judgement.* (Containing Lord Byron's The Vision of Judgment.) 1932.

V205

RICCARDI PRESS (CHARLES T. JACOBI). Malory, Sir Thomas. *Le Morte d'Arthur.* Medici Society. 4 volumes. 1932. Volume 2 only.

V206

—— Morison, Stanley. *On Type Faces.* Medici Society and The Fleuron. 1923.

V207

SAINT DOMINIC'S PRESS. McNabb, Vincent. *Geoffrey Chaucer, A Study in Genius and Ethics.* 1934.

V208

FRANK E. SEARY. Edwards, Cyril. *Seven Sonnets.* 1934.

V209

SEVEN ACRES PRESS (LOYD HABERLY). *Verses on Man's Mortalitie.* 1925.

V210

SHAKESPEARE HEAD PRESS. Shakespeare, William. *Shakespeare's Sonnets.* 1905.

V211

SHAKESPEARE HEAD PRESS. Shakespeare, William. *A Lover's Complaint & The Phoenix and Turtle.* 1906.

V212

—— Tatius, Achilles. *The Loves of Clitophon and Leucippe.* 1923.

V213

—— Hemminge, W. *William Hemminge's Elegy on Randolph's Finger.* 1923.

V214

—— Shakespeare, William. *The Merchant of Venice*; printed from the folio of 1623. 1923.

V215

—— Chidgey, H. T. *Black Square Memories.* 1924.

V216

—— Drayton, Michael. *Nimphidia, The Court of Faerie.* 1924.

V217

——Ovid. *Ovyde Hys Booke of Methamorphose.* 1924.

V218–19

—— Drayton, Michael. *Endimion & Phœbe.* 1925. 2 copies, one on handmade paper.

V220

—— Drayton, Michael. *England's Helicon.* 1925.

V221

—— Sleigh, H. *The Initials and Other Poems.* 1925.

V222

—— Martindale, C. C. *Catholics in Oxford.* 1925.

V223

SHAKESPEARE HEAD PRESS. Drayton, Michael, *The Ballad of Agincourt*. 1926.

V223A

—— Drayton, Michael, *The Hundreth Sundrie Flowres*. Etchells and Macdonald. 1926.

V224–33

—— Fielding, Henry. *Works*, in 10 volumes, 1926: *Amelia* (3 volumes); *Jonathan Wild*; *Joseph Andrews* (2 volumes); *Tom Jones* (4 volumes).

V234–44

—— Smollett, Tobias. *Works*, in 11 volumes, 1926: *Ferdinand, Count Fathom* (2 volumes); *Humphrey Clinker* (2 volumes); *Peregrine Pickle* (4 volumes); *Roderick Random* (2 volumes); *Sir Lancelot Greaves, the History of an Atom*.

V245–51

—— Sterne, Laurence. *Works*, in 7 volumes 1926–7: *Letters*; *A Sentimental Journey*; *The Sermons of Mr Yorick* (2 volumes); *Tristram Shandy* (3 volumes).

V251A

—— Alexander, Russell George. *The Engraved Work of F. L. Griggs*—Catalogue. 1928.

V252–5

—— Bourchier, Sir John, Lord Berners. *Froissart's Cronycles* (set of 4 parts), volume 1. 1927.

V256–9

—— Bourchier, Sir John, Lord Berners. *Froissart's Cronycles* (set of 4 parts), volume 2. 1928.

V260–1

—— Pindar. *Odes of Victory*. 2 volumes. 1928–30.

V262

SHAKESPEARE HEAD PRESS. Bacon, Francis. *The Essayes or Counsels Civill and Morall of Francis Lord Verulam Viscount St Alban* [published] at The Cresset Press. 1928.

V263–70

—— Chaucer, Geoffrey. *Works*, in 8 volumes, 1928–9: *Boece de Consolac: Philosophie*; *The Canterbury Tales* (3 volumes); *The House of Fame & Minor Poems*; *The Parson's Tale & Minor Poems*; *The Romaunt of the Rose*; *Troilus and Criseyde*.

V271

—— Bierce, Ambrose. *Battle Sketches*. 1930.

V272

—— Bede. *The History of the Church of Englande*, compiled by Venerable Bede, Englishman. 1930.

V273

——Newdigate, B. H. *A Note on the S H P, Stratford-upon-Avon, MCMIV–MCMXXX*. 1930.

V274

—— DE QUINCEY, Thomas. *Confessions of an English Opium Eater*. 1930.

V275

—— Sheridan, R. *School for Scandal*. 1930.

V276–83

—— Spenser, Edmund. *Works*, in 8 volumes, 1930: *Colin Clout & Shorter Poems*; *The Faerie Queen*, Books 1–6 (5 volumes); *The Shepheardes Calendar and Complaints*; *A Vewe of Ireland, Letters*.

V284

—— *Exhibition of Books Printed at the S H P. 1930*.

V285-7

S<small>HAKESPEARE</small> H<small>EAD</small> P<small>RESS</small>. Bronte, Anne. *Works*, in 3 volumes, 1931: *Agnes Grey*; *Wildfell Hall* (2 volumes).

V288-94

—— Bronte, Charlotte. *Works*, in 7 volumes, 1931: *Jane Eyre* (2 volumes); *The Professor*; *Shirley* (2 volumes); *Villette* (2 volumes).

V295

—— Bronte, Emily. *Wuthering Heights*. 1931.

V296-300

—— Homer. *Works*, in 5 volumes (translated by George Chapman). 1931: *Batrachomyomachia*; *Iliads* (2 volumes); *Odysses* (2 volumes).

V301

—— Jaggard, Capt. W. *Shakespeare, Once a Printer and Bookman*. 1933.

V302-3

—— Malory, Thomas. *Le Morte d'Arthur* (2 volumes). 1933.

V304-5

—— Boccaccio. *The Decameron* (2 volumes). 1934.

V306

—— Newdigate, Bernard H., editor, *The Poems of Ben Jonson* 1936.

V307

—— Haberly, Loyd. *Mediæval English Pavingtiles*. 1937.

V308

—— Newdigate, B. H., editor, *The Phœnix and Turtle*. 1937.

V309

SHAKESPEARE HEAD PRESS. Ferrall, Rose Nolan. *The D X V Prophecy, Dante and the Sabbatum Fidelium.* 1938.

V310

—— Sitwell, Sir George. *Idle Fancies.* 1938.

V311

—— Griggs, F. L. *Campden.* 1940.

V312

SIGN OF THE THREE CANDLES. Trench, W. F. *Tom Moore.* 1934.

V313

OLIVER AND HERBERT SIMON. Clare, John. *Autumn.* 1921.

V314

W. H. SMITH AND SON. Cockcrell, Douglas. *A Note on Bookbinding.* 1904.

V315

—— Hornby, St J. *Jubilee Celebration.* 1943.

V316

SPOTTISWOODE, BALLANTYNE AND CO. Ovid. *Ovid's Elegies,* translated by Christopher Marlowe. Etchells and Macdonald. 1925.

V317

JAMES STANLEY. *Memorials of Stonyhurst College.* Burns and Oates. 1881.

V318

ROBERT STOCKWELL. Thorn-Drury, G. *A Little Ark.* P. J. & A. E. Dobell. 1921.

V319

STANTON PRESS. Vida, M. *The Game of Chess.* 1921.

V320
STOURTON PRESS. Dryden, John. *All for Love*. 1931–2.

V321
—— Marloe, Christopher. *Hero and Leander*. 1934.

V322
SYLVAN PRESS. Williams, Charles, *Heroes and Kings*. 1930.

V323
TEMPLE PRESS. Johnson, John. *The Printer, His Customers and His Men*. J. M. Dent & Sons. 1933.

V324
TINTERN PRESS. Chubb, Ralph. *Songs Pastoral and Paradisal*. 1935.

V325
A. P. TROTTER. Trotter, Alys Fane. *The Old Village*. 1929.

V325A
UNIVERSITY COLLEGE LONDON. DEPARTMENT OF ENGLISH. Duke, Arthur. *The Larke*, A Seventeenth Century Poem. 1935.

V325B
H. D. AND H. G. WEBB, CHISWICK. *The Old Ballad of the Boy and the Mantle*. 1900.

V326
WESTMINSTER PRESS. Bacon, Francis. *Essayes*. Etchells and Macdonald. 1924.

V327
—— Voltaire. *The Princess of Babylon*. Nonesuch Press. 1927.

V328

WESTMINSTER PRESS. *Bodkin Permitting*, Being the Prospectus and Retrospectus for 1929 of the Nonesuch Press. Nonesuch Press. 1929.

V329

—— *Everyman*. Thomas Derrick. 1930.

V329A

JOHN WRIGHT AND SONS, BRISTOL. De Villiers, Jean-Marie Matthias Phillipe Auguste, Comte de L'Isle-Adam. *Axel*. Jarrolds. 1925.

V330

NO PRINTER'S IMPRINT
Wornum, Ralph N. *Hans Holbein and The Meier Madonna*. 1871.

V331

Aston, John. *Sketches of Christ Church, Oxford*. Methuen. n.d.

V332

Aquinas, St Thomas. *Of God and His Creatures*. Burns & Oates. 1905.

V333

Richard Beauchamp, Earl of Warwick, K.G., 1389–1439. Longmans Green & Co. 1914.

V334

Peckham, John. *Philomena*. Burns, Oates & Washbourne. 1924.

V335

Double Crown Club. Typographic frivolities. n.d.

V336

Whitehouse, J. H. *Craftsmanship and Books*. George Allen & Unwin. 1929.

V337

1930 Prospectus and Retrospectus of the Nonesuch Press. 1930.

V338

Shakespeare, William. *King Lear.* Shakespeare Association. 1939.

EUROPE AND ASIA

Austria

V339

HERBERT REICHNER. *Die Druckerkunst in den Vereinigten Staaten von Nordamerika.* 1927.

Czechoslovakia

V340

METHOD KALÁB. Rosenback, A. S. W. *Neuverejnitelné Memoáry* 1925.

France

V341

L'ART CATHOLIQUE. François d'Assise, St. *Les Petites Fleurs.* 1919.

V342

COULOUMA PRESS. Pushkin, Alexander. *Queen of Spades.* Blacka-more Press. 1928.

V343

—— Green, Julian. *The Pilgrim on the Earth.* 1929.

Germany

V344

BRAUN & SCHNEIDER. *Munchener Kalender.* 1903.

V345

DEUTSCHEN BUCHGEWERBEVEREINS. Bammes, Reinhold. *Der Titelsatz, seine Entwicklung und seine Grundsätz*. 1911.

V346

—— Wolff, Hans. *Die Buchornamentik*. 1913.

V347

GUTENBERG GESELLSCHAFT. Ruppel, A. *Die Errichtung des Mainzer Gutenberg-Denkmals*. 1937.

V348

—— *Peter Schöffer aus Gernsheim*. 1937.

V349

INSEL-VERLAG. Koch, R. *Das kleine Blumenbuch*. n.d.

V350

KLINGSPOR. *Kalender*. 1939.

V351

POESCHEL & TREPTE. Reichner, H. *Jean Grolier, der König der Bibliophilen*. 1925.

Italy

V352

OFFICINA BODONI. *San Zena Vescovo*. 1937.

Japan

V353

ELKIN MATHEWS. Yone Noguchi. *Hiroshige*. 1921.

V354

—— Yone Noguchi. *Hokusai*. 1925.

V355
ELKIN MATHEWS. Yone Noguchi. *Utamaro.* 1925.

The Netherlands

V356
HALCYON PRESS. Blake, W. *The Marriage of Heaven and Hell.* 1928.

V357
—— Keats, J. *The Collected Sonnets of John Keats.* 1930.

V358
JOH. ENSCHEDÉ EN ZONEN (HAARLEM). De Musset, A. *Fantasio.* 1929.

V359
—— Crashaw, R. *Three Poems from Carmen Deo Nostro.* 1930.

V360
—— Irving, W. *The Christmas Dinner.* 1931.

V361
—— Mary, Queen of Scots. *The Poems of Mary, Queen of Scots.* 1932.

V362
—— *The Greek Portrait,* An Anthology of English Verse Translations from the Greek Poets. 1934.

V363
—— Thomas à Kempis. *Sermo in Nocte Nativitatis Christi.* 1934.

V364
—— *L'Adoration des Trois Rois Mages.* 1935.

V365

JOH. ENSCHEDÉ EN ZONEN (HAARLEM). Thomas à Kempis. *Hymnus in Nativitate Christi.* 1937.

V366

—— Boutens, P. C. *Three Poems.* Translated by Sir Herbert Grierson. 1938.

Sweden

V367

ALMQVIST & WIKSELLS. *Almanack.* 1931.

Switzerland

V368

OFFICINA BODONI. Plato. *Crito.* 1926.

V369

—— Moyllus, D. *Classic Letter Design.* 1927.

UNITED STATES

V370

AMERICAN MAGAZINE OF ART. Gallatin, A. E. *Modern Fine Printing in America.* 1921.

V371

BARTLETT. Wither, G. *A Christmas Carrol.* 1913.

V372

CROSBY GAIGE, Tomlinson, H. M. *Thomas Hardy.* 1929.

V373

DODD, MEAD & CO. Hildeburn, C. R. *Sketches of Printers and Printing.* 1895.

V374

DOUBLEDAY. *Homes of Doubleday Doran and Company.* 1930.

V375

ELKIN, MATHEWS & MARROT. Reid, J. *The Life of Christ.* 1930.

V376

THE FOUNTAIN PRESS. Hardy, Thomas. *The Three Wayfarers.* 1930.

V377

—— Milne, A. A. *When I Was Very Young.* 1930.

V378

THE HARBOR PRESS. *Extracts from the Diary of Roger Payne.* New York. 1928.

V379–80

HARVARD UNIVERSITY PRESS. *Stephen Daye and his Successors 1639–1921.* Cambridge, Mass. 1921. 2 copies.

V381

—— Updike, Daniel Berkeley. *In the Day's Work.* 1924.

V382

THE LABORATORY PRESS. Garnett, Porter, edited by. *The Fine Book—A Symposium.* 1934.

V383

LAUREL PRESS. Adlington, W. *Cupid and Psyches.* 1924.

V384

LEBANON PENNSYLVANIA. Conrad, J. *Preface to The Nigger of the Narcissus.* 1927.

V385

LIMITED EDITIONS CLUB. *Ten Years and William Shakespeare.* 1940.

V386

LIMITED EDITIONS CLUB. The Limited Editions Club. *Quarto-Millenary*. 1959.

V387

—— Shakespeare, William. *Poems*, Vols. I & II. 1941.

V388

McMURTRIE. McMurtrie, D. C. *Benjamin Franklin, Type-founder*. 1925.

V389

W. G. MATHER. Murdock, Kenneth B. *The Portraits of Increase Mather*. 1924.

V390

MERRYMOUNT PRESS. Condivi, A. *Life of Michelagnolo*. 1904.

V391

—— Della Casa, Giovanni. *Galateo of Manners & Behaviours, A Renaissance Courtesy-Book*. 1914.

V392

——MIRANDOLA, PICO DELLA. *A Platonick Discourse Upon Love*. 1914.

V393

—— SARGENT, MARIA DE ACOSTA. *Pierrot's Verses*. 1917.

V394-5

—— Amory, Martha Babcock. *Mrs Amory's Letters*, 2 volumes. 1922.

V395A

METROPOLITAN MUSEUM OF ART. Ivins, W. M. *A Guide to an Exhibition of the Arts of the Book*. New York, 1924.

V396

OSWALD PUBLISHING COMPANY. Gress, Edmund G. *A Dash Through Europe*. New York, 1923.

V397

PETER PAUPER PRESS. Tory, Geofroy. *Champ Rosé*. 1933.

V398

—— Haas, Irvin. *Bruce Rogers: A Bibliography*, Hitherto Unrecorded Work 1899–1925. Complete Work 1925–36. 1936.

V399

PYNSON PRINTERS. Zweig, Stefan. *The Invisible Collection*. 1926.

V400

—— Voltaire. *Candide*. Random House, New York. 1928.

V401

THE REED PALE PRESS. Holy Bible. *The Book of Ruth*. 1934.

V402

RUDGE. Field, Eugene. *The Symbol and the Saint*. 1921.

V403

—— Barrie, J. M. *George Meredith*. 1924.

V404

—— Dürer, A. *Construction of Roman Letters*. 1924.

V405

—— Lamb, C. *New Year's Eve*. 1924.

V406
RUDGE. Spicer-Simson, Theodore. *Men of Letters.* 1924.

V407
—— Adams, E. L. *Joseph Conrad: The Man.* 1925.

V408
—— Moore, T. Sturge. *Roderigo of Bivar.* 1925.

V409
—— Symons, Arthur. *Studies on Modern Painters.* 1925.

V410
—— Morley, Christopher. *Good Theatre*—A Fancy in One Scene. 1926.

V411
—— Waldman, Milton. *America Conquers Death.* 1928.

V412
—— *Modern Book-Illustration.* 1931.

V413
THE SPIRAL PRESS. Wigglesworth, M. *The Day of Doom.* New York, 1929.

V414
TROVILLION. Rae, G. *In Country Places.* 1937.

CATALOGUES

V415
Catalogue of an exhibition of Mediaeval manuscripts and jewelled book covers.
1912. The John Rylands Library, Manchester.

V416

Description of an extraordinary volume of Shakespeareana, the property of Richard Francis Burton, Esq. of Longner Hall, near Shrewsbury, where it is believed to have been preserved for at least 200 years.
1920. Sotheby, Wilkinson & Hodge.

V417

A short memoir of The Reverend Doctor Adrian Fortescue with a catalogue of the Memorial exhibition.
1923. The Book Club, Letchworth.

V418

In Commemoration of the First Folio Tercentenary. A re-setting of the preliminary matter of the First Folio, with a catalogue of Shakespeareana exhibited in the Hall of The Worshipful Company of Stationers, illustrative facsimiles, and Introduction by Sir Israel Gollancz, Litt.D., F.B.A., Chairman of the Shakespeare Association.
1923. The Worshipful Company of Stationers.

V419

A guide to an exhibition of the Arts of the Book. By W. M. Ivins, Jr., Curator of Prints.
1924. The Metropolitan Museum of Art, New York.

V420

The earliest catalogues of the Bodleian Library. Described by G. W. Wheeler.
1928. The University Press, Oxford. The first use of Graily Hewitt's Treyford type.

V421

Catalogue of an exhibition of books illustrating British and foreign printing, 1919–1929.
1929. British Museum.

V422

A catalogue of books, newspapers &c. printed by John Bell and John Browne Bell.
1931. The First Edition Club, London.

V423

Exhibition of printed books from world-wide sources.
1933. Heriot-Watt College, Edinburgh.

V424

Catalogue of an exhibition of contemporary book-typography.
1933. Heriot-Watt College, Edinburgh.

V425

Exhibition of printed books from world-wide sources.
1935. Stow College School of Printing and Kindred Trades, Glasgow.

V426

An exhibition of printing at the Fitzwilliam Museum, Cambridge.
1940. Cambridge University Press.

V427

Exhibition of the fifty books (1945) chosen for the National Book League from those published during 1944.
1945. National Book League, London.

V428

The English at school. An exhibition arranged by Arnold Muirhead.
1949. National Book League, London.

V429

Catalogue of the Romany Collection, presented to the University of Leeds.
1962. Brotherton Collection, and Thomas Nelson and Sons, Ltd., Edinburgh.

PERIODICAL PARTS

V430

Bodleian Quarterly Record. Vol. VIII, No. 90. February 1936. Supplement. Some proclamations of Charles I, being addenda to *Bibliotheca Lindesiana*, by E. J. S. Parsons, B.A., B.Litt.

V431

Bodleian Quarterly Record. Vol. VIII, No. 94. Summer 1937.

V432

Bulletin of the John Rylands Library Manchester. Vol. 27, No. 2. June 1943.

V433

Classical Philology. Vol. XXVI, No. 2. April 1931. *Reprint of*: Materials for the history of a popular classical theme, by Joseph G. Fucilla.

V433A

Colophon. Parts: 9, 10, 11, 14, 15.

V434

The Dome—a quarterly containing examples of all the Arts. Nos. 1 and 2. 1897.

V435

Graphic Arts Education. Spring 1953.

V436

The Library. October 1901. (New Series, Vol. II.)

V437

London Mercury. *20* No. 120 Oct. 1929. *25* No. 145, Nov. 1931.

V438

PM. *3*. June 1964.

V439

Publications of the Modern Language Association of America. Vol. LVI, No. 1. March 1941. *Reprint of*: Donne's *Letters to several persons of honour*, by R. E. Bennett.

V439A

Print VII. 5. November 1952.

V440

The Quest. No. 4. November 1895.

V441

Signature. New Series, No. 1. July 1946.

V442–61

Signature. Parts 1–18 (2 copies of 7 and 9).

V462–93

Typographica, 1–16. New Series, 1–16.

V494–501

Typography. 1–8

w. *Books Presented to The Collection*

WI

ABERDEEN MASTER PRINTERS GUILD. *Record of the celebration of the tercentenary of the introduction of the art of printing into Aberdeen by Edward Raban in the year 1622.* 16th and 17th June 1922. Aberdeen: Master Printers Guild, 1922.

W2

ACREMANT, GERMAINE. *Les dames aux chapeaux verts.* Illustrations de Jacques Touchet. Bruxelles: Parmentier, 1943.

W3

AIRD, ANDREW. *Reminiscences of editors, reporters, and printers, during the last sixty years.* Glasgow: Aird & Coghill, 1890.

W4

ALLEN LITHOGRAPHIC COMPANY. *50 years of service: a short history of the Company and review of the organisation.* Kirkcaldy: Allen Lithographic Company Limited, 1950.

W5

BAKER, C. H. COLLINS. *Design in modern industry.* The year-book of the Design and Industries Association 1922. With an introduction by C. H. COLLINS Baker. London: Benn, 1922.

W6

BAYNARD PRESS. *Types.* 1936.

W7

BAYNARD PRESS. *Borders.* 1936.

W8

Bemrose, The House of. 1826–1926.

W9

BOUCHOT, HENRI. *The printed book: its history, illustration, and adornment, from the days of Gutenberg to the present time.* Translated and enlarged by Edward C. Bigmore. London: Grevil, 1887.

W10

BRITISH FEDERATION OF MASTER PRINTERS. *Programme of the annual meeting and congress at Llandudno, June 11th–14th, 1932, on the invitation of the Midland Master Printers' Alliance.*

W11

British Printer, The. 12 volumes.

W12

BULL, A. J. *Photoengraving.* London: Arnold, 1934.

W13

CARLTON STUDIO THE. *Finishing Touches of the Printer's Handwork.* n.d. London: The Carlton Studio.

W13A

Carter, H. *A View of Early Typography, up to about 1600.* Oxford. 1969.

W14

CLULOW, F. W. *The new applied Science Syllabuses of the City and Guilds of London Institute.* An address given at a conference in London for Heads of Printing Departments, March 8th, 1957.

W15

T. & A. CONSTABLE LTD. *Book founts.* Edinburgh: University Press n.d. c. 1933.

W16

COUNCIL OF INDUSTRIAL DESIGN. *Enterprise Scotland 1947.* Exhibition organised by the Scottish Committee of the Council of Industrial Design at the Royal Scottish Museum, Edinburgh. August 25–September 30. Edinburgh: H.M.S.O. (Exhibition Catalogue.)

W17

COUNCIL OF INDUSTRIAL DESIGN. Scottish Committee. *Report of the Conference on Printing held in the North British Hotel, Edinburgh on Friday 18th April, 1947.*

W18

ALEX COWAN & SONS. *The Craft of Papermaking.* Penicuik, Alex Cowan & Sons n.d.

W19

DESIGN AND INDUSTRIES ASSOCIATION. *Year book and membership list, 1967–68.* Hull: A. Brown & Sons, 1967.

W20

Dryden, John. Works. Scott, Sir Walter edited by George Saintsbury. William Paterson. Printed by T. & A. Constable. 11 volumes Large Paper edition, 9 volumes Small Paper edition. 1882–5.

The type was originally cut by Millar & Richard in 1808, but the sales had been slight. T. & A. Constable obtained the exclusive use of this type for a number of years. It was first used in this work and was therefore known in the firm as Dryden. At a later date the Dryden type was cut by the Lanston Monotype Corporation under the name of Scotch Roman (Old Face) in the series No. 46 and, later, more successfully in the series No. 137.

W21

EDINBURGH COLLEGE OF ART. *Prospectus for 1964–65.*

W22

Edinburgh *Evening News,* of 24th February 1940. *A Stronghold of Printing.*

W23

EDINBURGH PRESS, THE. *Specimen Book Types.* n.d. Edinburgh: The Edinburgh Press.

W24

ENGLISH MASTERS OF BLACK AND WHITE. McLean, Ruari. *George Cruikshank.* 1948. London: Art & Technics.

W25

—— Hambourg, Daria. *Richard Doyle.* 1948. London: Art & Technics.

W26

—— Mayne, Jonathan. *Barnett Freedman.* 1948. London: Art & Technics.

W27

—— Thorpe, James. *Phil May.* 1948. London: Art & Technics.

W28

—— Thorpe, James. *E. J. Sullivan.* 1948. London: Art & Technics.

W29

—— Sarzano, Frances. *Sir John Tenniel.* 1948. London: Art & Technics.

W30

Esparto Papers. c. 1935. T. & A. Constable Ltd., for Esparto Papermakers Association.

W31

EVANS, I. O. *The World of tomorrow: A junior book of forecasts.* 1933. London: Denis Archer.

W32

FEDERATION OF MASTER PRINTERS AND ALLIED TRADES OF THE UNITED KINGDOM OF GREAT BRITAIN AND IRELAND. *Souvenir of the fifth annual meeting, held in London, May 23rd to 26th, 1905.* London: Chiswick Press, 1905.

W33

FEDERATION OF MASTER PRINTERS & ALLIED TRADES. *30th Annual Meeting 1930: Edinburgh 31st May–4th June.* 1930. London: Fedcration of Master Printers.

W34

FEDERATIONS OF MASTER PRINTERS. *Proceedings at the fourth international congress, Utrecht, 25th & 26th October 1934.* International Bureau of the Federations of Master Printers. 1935.

W35

GLASGOW PRINTERS, THE EARLY.

W36

GRIFFITH, W. P., & SONS LTD. *Type Fashions:* (3 *Supplements*) *1. Specimens of types & Borders 2. Typographical treatments of Caslon Old Face & Nicholas Cochin type faces 3. Further specimens of types & borders.* n.d. London: Old Bailey Press.

W37

HARLING, ROBERT, edited by. *Image: A Quarterly of the Visual Arts.* Nos. 1, 2, 3, 5, 6, 7. Summer 1949–Spring 1952. London: Art & Technics.

W38

HARRISON & SONS LTD. *A Catalogue of Type Faces.* 1954. London. Harrison & Sons Ltd.

W39

HAZELL, WATSON & VINEY LTD. *Hazell's: being Some account of the Provident and Social institutions connected with Hazell, Watson & Viney Ltd.* London: Hazell, 1923?

W40

HILDEBURN, CHARLES R. *Sketches of printers and printing in Colonial New York.* New York: Dodd, Mead, 1895. (Limited edition. No. 345.)

W41

JACKSON, HOLBROOK. *Typophily*. An essay forming an introduction to a catalogue for typophiles, issued originally by the antiquarian booksellers Messrs. Durham & Co. Ltd. London W.1. London: North-Western Polytechnic Printing Department, 1955.

W42

JOINT INDUSTRIAL COUNCIL OF PRINTING & ALLIED TRADES. *Workshop Training of Apprentices*. 1947. London. Joint Industrial Council of Printing & Allied Trades.

W43

KLINGSPOR. *Wissenswerter für den Besteller von Schriften*. Zierat: Ausschluss und Messinglinien. Offenbach.

W44

LANSTON MONOTYPE CORPORATION LTD. *The Monotype Book of Information*. 1929. London: Lanston Monotype Corporation Ltd.

W45

LEWIS, WYNDHAM. *The Childermass*. Section 1. (All published.) 1928. London: Chatto & Windus.

W46

—— *The art of being ruled*. London: Chatto and Windus, 1926.

W47

—— edited by. *Blast: Review of the Great English Vortex. No.* 1. June 20th 1914. London: John Lane, The Bodley Head.

W48

—— *The Enemy: A Review of Art and Literature*. Vol. 1. January 1927. London: The Arthur Press.

W49

LEWIS, WYNDHAM. *The Enemy No. 2: A Review of Art and Literature*. 1927. London: The Arthur Press.

W50

—— *The Enemy No. 3: A Review of Art and Literature*. 1st Quarter 1929. London: The Arthur Press.

W51

LINKLATER, ERIC. *Private Angelo*. Privately printed for Sir Allen Lane and for Richard Lane by McCorquodale & Co. Ltd. 1957. On a Christmas Card enclosed with this book the following wording appears:

'Of this edition of *Private Angelo* which accompanies this card two thousand copies were privately printed for Sir Allen Lane and Richard Lane. The endpaper decorations are by David Gentleman. It is believed to be the first book produced in England without the use of metal type. Text and display were composed on the Intertype Fotosetter. In this new method photo-matrices are assembled into lines on a normal keyboard. They are then automatically photographed, one by one, on a film positive which advances horizontally by the correct width of each letter and, when the line is completed, moves vertically into position ready to receive the next line.

'The book was printed in offset-lithography by McCorquodale & Co. Ltd., deep-etched plates having been made from the film positives described above.

'The text of this card, too, was composed photographically, but it was printed in letterpress from a Dow-etched magnesium plate. For help in its production we are indebted to Intertype Limited.'
See also F326A.

W52

LINOTYPE AND MACHINERY LTD. *A Baker's Dozen of Emblems*: Drawings by DWIGGINS, W. A. and Verses by BENET, WILLIAM ROSE. Collected from various numbers of the *Saturday Review of Literature* issued in 1927 and 1928 and 'Electra': a new Linotype face from the hand of the Said W.A.D. 1937. London: Linotype and Machinery Ltd.

W53

LUND HUMPHRIES. *A Selection of Types from the Country Press.* 1929. Bradford: Lund Humphries.

W54

MCLEAN, RUARI, edited by. *Motif: A Journal of the Visual Arts.* Vols. 1, 2, 3, 4, 6, 8, 9, 10, 11. November 1958–Winter 1963–64. London: Shenval Press Ltd

W55

MARR TYPE-FOUNDING COMPANY LTD. *Specimens of Ancient & Modern Printing Types, Rules & Borders.* n.d. Edinburgh: Marr Type-Founding Company Ltd.

W56

MASON, JOHN. *Twelve by eight: some adventures in papermaking: A talk to the Double Crown Club, 11th December 1957.* 1958. Leicester: College of Art.

W57

MAXWELL, WILLIAM. *An address delivered to the Edinburgh Typographia, Wednesday 30th October, 1935.* Edinburgh: Heriot-Watt College, 1936. (4 copies.)

W58

Meredith, The Works of George. 37 volumes. T. & A. Constable. Meredith Type. 1896–1911.

This type, which might be described as an Old Style Antique, was a private type used by T. & A. Constable. It was a style popular at that time but which now looks heavy and coarse. This type was obtained under conditions of great secrecy from Italy. In order that its origin should not be traced it was shipped to Holland, Germany and then to France before being despatched to Edinburgh. The arrangements were so complex that, when a further supply was required, it was found to be impossible to trace the original typefounder from whom it had been ordered. Many years later the original invoice was found, revealing its Italian origin.

W 59

MINISTRY OF LABOUR AND NATIONAL SERVICE. *Report of a Court of Inquiry into the nature and circumstances of a dispute between the British Federation of Master Printers and The Printing and Kindred Trades Federation.* (Cmd. 6912.) London: H.M.S.O., 1946.

W 60

MORAN, JAMES. *Wynkyn de Worde: Father of Fleet Street.* 1960. London: Wynkyn de Worde Society.

W 61

NATIONAL BOOK LEAGUE. *Children's books of yesterday.* With a foreword by the Poet Laureate John Masefield. London: National Book League, 194?.

W 62

PAPYRUS 1895–1945 PÅ TRADITIONSRIK GRUND. *Minnesskrift till Aktiebolaget Papyrus fementioarsyubiteum pa uppdrag utarbetad av Torsten Althin* Mölndal: 1945.

W 63

PUNCH. *Its history its humour, its people.* London: *Punch*, 1963.

W 64

RAVILIOUS, ERIC. *Almanack 1929.* With twelve designs engraved on wood by Eric Ravilious, and a specimen of the Roman and Italic of Fournier-le-Jeune. Composed on the 'Monotype'. London: Lanston Monotype Corporation, 1929?

W 65

SCHLEINITZ, OTTO VON. *Walter Crane.* Bielefeld: Velhagen & Klasing, 1902.

W66

Signet Library. *Catalogue of an exhibition of 18th Century Scottish books at the Signet Library Edinburgh.* Cambridge: University Press for the Scottish Committee of the Festival of Britain 1951 and the National Book League, 1951.

W67

Smail, J. Cameron. *James Watt and the Heriot-Watt College.* An address delivered to the Watt Club at Edinburgh on 29th January 1949. Edinburgh: Heriot-Watt College, 1949.

W68

Stone, Reynolds & Lewis, Walter, selected by. *British Book Design, 1947:* One Hundred Books Published during 1947 selected for the National Book League for exhibition. 1948. Cambridge: C.U.P.

W69

Type Specimen Books:—
Wilsons & Sinclair, 1833
Alex. Wilson & Son, 1834
Duncan Sinclair & Sons, 1847
Sir Charles Reed & Sons, after 1850
Reed & Fox, *c.* 1865
Metzger & Wittig, after 1870
Stephenson & Blake, Brass Rules, *c.* 1880
Bruce's, New York, 1881
Marr & Co., between 1857 & 1901
Caslon, 1887
P. M. Shanks, 1893
P. M. Shanks, 1902
T. & A. Constable, 1907
American Type Founders, 1923
Catalogue of type Founders Specimens, 1928
Stephenson Blake 'Verona', after 1939
Nebiolo, Turin. n.d.

W70

Virginia Historical Index. *Two reviews.* Roanoke, Virginia: Stone Printing and Manufacturing Co., 1936.

W71

Walker, Sir Emery. Obituary Notices from *The Times* and other Papers on his death on 22nd July 1933. Privately Printed by Emery Walker Ltd.

W72

Whistler, Laurence. *Rex Whistler: his Life and drawings, 1905–44.* 1948. London: Art & Technics.

W73

Willmer, Wrayford. *Family Business: The Story of Willmer Brothers & Haram Ltd.* 1961.

W74

Wyndham, George. *The springs of romance in the literature of Europe.* An address delivered to the Students of the University of Edinburgh, October 1910. London: Macmillan, 1910.

INDEX

This Index is essentially an index of the names of authors, printers, publishers, editors, illustrators, designers of type and type-founders. There are a number of cases where the name of the author is not given in the text of the catalogue. When this occurs, the title of the book is included in the index. This leads to some rather peculiar anomalies. For instance *The Golden Legend* normally will be found under 'Voragine, Jacobus de' but in two cases the name of the author is not given in the text. In these cases the book appears under its title.

The use of a superior figure after a page number indicates the number of times that the name appears on that page. Therefore 123^4 shows that the name appears four times on page 123.